Hike

PENNSYLVANIA

Contact

Dear Readers:

Every effort was made to make this the most accurate, informative, and easy-to-use guidebook on the planet. Any comments, suggestions, and corrections regarding this guide are welcome and should be sent to:

The Globe Pequot Press
Reader Response/Editorial Dept.
P.O. Box 480
Guilford, CT 06437
editorial@GlobePequot.com

We'd love to hear from you so we can make future editions and future guides even better.

Thanks and happy trails!

Hike AMERICA™

PENNSYLVANIA

An Atlas of Pennsylvania's
Greatest Hiking Adventures

John Young

The Globe Pequot Press

GUILFORD, CONNECTICUT

Produced by
Beachway Press Publishing, Inc.
300 West Main St., Ste A
Charlottesville, VA 22903
www.beachway.com

Cover Design   Beachway Press

Photographer   John Young

Maps designed and produced by Beachway Press © Morris
Book Publishing, LLC.

Cover photo: Index Stock Imagery

Library of Congress Cataloging-in-Publication Data
is available

ISBN-13: 978-0-7627-0924-3
ISBN-10: 0-7627-0924-3

Printed in the United States of America
First Edition/Fifth Printing

To buy books in quantity for corporate use
or incentives, call **(800) 962–0973, ext. 4551,**
or e-mail **premiums@GlobePequot.com.**

Acknowledgments

I would like to thank my wife, Debra, for her support and encouragement during the writing of this book. Besides her duties as co-pilot, navigator, and camp cook, she turned out to be a darn good hike-mate as well. I'd also like to thank my brother, Jim Young, and his wife, Billie, for the room and board in Centre County.

Kudos to the staff at Beachway Press, starting with editor Chris Crehan, who played a large role in making this book what it turned out to be. Thanks also to editor Ryan Croxton for keeping it all together, cartographer Brandon Ray for drawing a fine line, and thanks to the resident Fearless Leader, the man of many hats, Scott Adams.

I would like to thank the State Park, State Forest, State Game Lands, Department of Conservation & Natural Resources, U.S. Wildlife Service, and National Park Service employees who answered many questions, returned my telephone calls, and mailed me materials. I honestly don't know of any other agencies where a person can get so much help for free.

And finally, this book is dedicated to all the hiking clubs and volunteers who go out week after week, year after year, and, sometimes, decade after decade to maintain the trails of Pennsylvania.

John Young

Table of

Contents

HIKES AT A GLANCE

1. John Heinz Ntl Wildlife Refuge/Impoundment Loop

Length: 3.5-mile loop
Difficulty Rating: Easy
Time: 1–2 hours
Nearby: Philadelphia, PA

2. Wissahickon Gorge North Loop

Length: 5.5-mile loop
Difficulty Rating: Moderate
Time: 3 hours
Nearby: Chestnut Hill, PA

3. Valley Forge National Historical Park

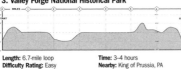

Length: 6.7-mile loop
Difficulty Rating: Easy
Time: 3–4 hours
Nearby: King of Prussia, PA

4. The Pinnacle

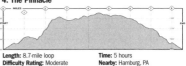

Length: 8.7-mile loop
Difficulty Rating: Moderate
Time: 5 hours
Nearby: Hamburg, PA

5. Swatara State Park

Length: 3.9-mile loop
Difficulty Rating: Easy
Time: 2 hours
Nearby: Pine Grove, PA

6. Dingmans Falls

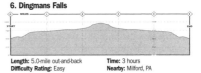

Length: 5.0-mile out-and-back
Difficulty Rating: Easy
Time: 3 hours
Nearby: Milford, PA

7. Mount Minsi

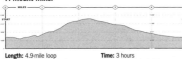

Length: 4.9-mile loop
Difficulty Rating: Moderate
Time: 3 hours
Nearby: Stroudsburg, PA

8. Hawk Falls

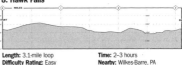

Length: 3.1-mile loop
Difficulty Rating: Easy
Time: 2–3 hours
Nearby: Wilkes-Barre, PA

9. Hickory Run Boulder Field

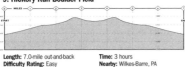

Length: 7.0-mile out-and-back
Difficulty Rating: Easy
Time: 3 hours
Nearby: Wilkes-Barre, PA

10. Ricketts Glen

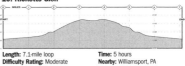

Length: 7.1-mile loop
Difficulty Rating: Moderate
Time: 5 hours
Nearby: Williamsport, PA

11. Canyon Vista

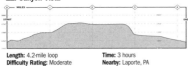

Length: 4.2-mile loop
Difficulty Rating: Moderate
Time: 3 hours
Nearby: Laporte, PA

12. Worlds End State Park

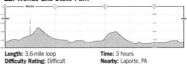

Length: 3.6-mile loop
Difficulty Rating: Difficult
Time: 3 hours
Nearby: Laporte, PA

13. Haystacks

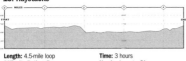

Length: 4.5-mile loop
Difficulty Rating: Easy
Time: 3 hours
Nearby: Laporte, PA

14. Mount Pisgah State Park

Length: 7.9-mile loop
Difficulty Rating: Moderate
Time: 4 hours
Nearby: Troy, PA

15. R.B. Winter State Park

Length: 7.5-mile loop
Difficulty Rating: Moderate
Time: 4 hours
Nearby: Lewisburg, PA

16. Loyalsock Trail

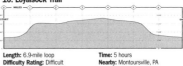

Length: 6.9-mile loop
Difficulty Rating: Difficult
Time: 5 hours
Nearby: Montoursville, PA

17. Gillespie Point

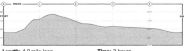

Length: 4.9-mile loop
Difficulty Rating: Moderate
Time: 3 hours
Nearby: Wellsboro, PA

18. Bohen Run Falls & West Rim Trail

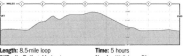

Length: 8.5-mile loop
Difficulty Rating: Moderate
Time: 5 hours
Nearby: Wellsboro, PA

19. Pine Trail & Hemlock Mountain

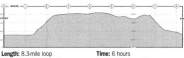

Length: 8.3-mile loop
Difficulty Rating: Difficult
Time: 6 hours
Nearby: Wellsboro, PA

20. Splash Dam Hollow

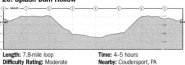

Length: 7.8-mile loop
Difficulty Rating: Moderate
Time: 4–5 hours
Nearby: Coudersport, PA

21. Wykoff Run Natural Area

Length: 4.8-mile loop
Difficulty Rating: Easy
Time: 2–3 hours
Nearby: Clearfield, PA

22. Black Moshannon State Park

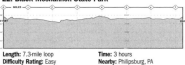

Length: 7.3-mile loop
Difficulty Rating: Easy
Time: 3 hours
Nearby: Philipsburg, PA

23. Gettysburg

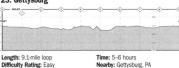

Length: 9.1-mile loop
Difficulty Rating: Easy
Time: 5–6 hours
Nearby: Gettysburg, PA

24. Sunset Rocks

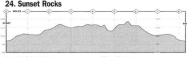

Length: 8.3-mile loop
Difficulty Rating: Moderate
Time: 5 hours
Nearby: Shippensburg, PA

25. Pole Steeple

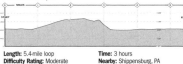

Length: 5.4-mile loop
Difficulty Rating: Moderate
Time: 3 hours
Nearby: Shippensburg, PA

26. Flat Rock

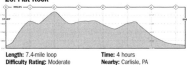

Length: 7.4-mile loop
Difficulty Rating: Moderate
Time: 4 hours
Nearby: Carlisle, PA

27. Little Buffalo State Park

Length: 6.2-mile loop
Difficulty Rating: Moderate
Time: 3–4 hours
Nearby: Newport, PA

28. Trough Creek State Park

Length: 8.2-mile loop
Difficulty Rating: Moderate
Time: 5 hours
Nearby: Huntingdon, PA

29. Canoe Creek State Park

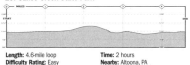

Length: 4.6-mile loop
Difficulty Rating: Easy
Time: 2 hours
Nearby: Altoona, PA

30. Greenwood Furnace State Park

Length: 5.5-mile loop
Difficulty Rating: Moderate
Time: 3 hours
Nearby: State College, PA

31. Indian Steps

Length: 4.1-mile loop
Difficulty Rating: Moderate
Time: 3 hours
Nearby: State College, PA

32. Alan Seeger Natural Area to Greenwood Fire Tower

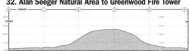

Length: 5.1-mile loop
Difficulty Rating: Moderate
Time: 4 hours
Nearby: State College, PA

HIKES AT A GLANCE

33. Conemaugh Gorge

Length: 7.2-mile loop
Difficulty Rating: Moderate
Time: 4 hours
Nearby: Johnstown, PA

34. Linn Run State Park

Length: 4.2-mile loop
Difficulty Rating: Moderate
Time: 3 hours
Nearby: Ligonier, PA

35. Wolf Rocks Trail

Length: 4.5-mile circuit
Difficulty Rating: Moderate
Time: 2–3 hours
Nearby: Ligonier, PA

36. Bear Run Nature Reserve

Length: 8.0-mile loop
Difficulty Rating: Moderate
Time: 5 hours
Nearby: Ohiopyle, PA

37. Mount Davis Natural Area

Length: 3.4-mile loop
Difficulty Rating: Easy
Time: 2–3 hours
Nearby: Somerset, PA

38. Ferncliff Peninsula Natural Area

Length: 2.4-mile loop
Difficulty Rating: Easy
Time: 2 hours
Nearby: Ohiopyle, PA

39. Youghiogheny River Trail to Jonathan Run Falls

Length: 6.4-mile out-and-back
Difficulty Rating: Easy
Time: 2 hours
Nearby: Ohiopyle, PA

40. Ryerson Station State Park

Length: 5.4-mile circuit
Difficulty Rating: Moderate
Time: 3 hours
Nearby: Waynesburg, PA

41. Presque Isle

Length: 5.0-mile loop
Difficulty Rating: Easy
Time: 2 hours
Nearby: Erie, PA

42. Hemlock Run

Length: 6.8-mile point-to-point
Difficulty Rating: Moderate
Time: 4 hours
Nearby: Warren, PA

43. Tom's Run

Length: 4.0-mile loop
Difficulty Rating: Easy
Time: 1–2 hours
Nearby: Sheffield, PA

44. Minister Creek

Length: 8.0-mile loop
Difficulty Rating: Moderate
Time: 3–4 hours
Nearby: Sheffield, PA

45. Cook Forest State Park

Length: 6.6-mile loop
Difficulty Rating: Moderate
Time: 4 hours
Nearby: Cooksburg, PA

46. Oil Creek State Park

Length: 5.9-mile loop
Difficulty Rating: Moderate
Time: 2–3 hours
Nearby: Titusville, PA

47. Allegheny Gorge

Length: 8.0-mile loop
Difficulty Rating: Difficult
Time: 4 hours
Nearby: Franklin, PA

48. Schollard's Wetlands

Length: 5.8-mile out-and-back
Difficulty Rating: Easy
Time: 2–3 hours
Nearby: Grove City, PA

49. McConnell's Mill State Park

Length: 3.3-mile loop
Difficulty Rating: Moderate
Time: 2 hours
Nearby: New Castle, PA

50. Moraine State Park

Length: 10.5-mile circuit
Difficulty Rating: Difficult
Time: 6 hours
Nearby: Butler, PA

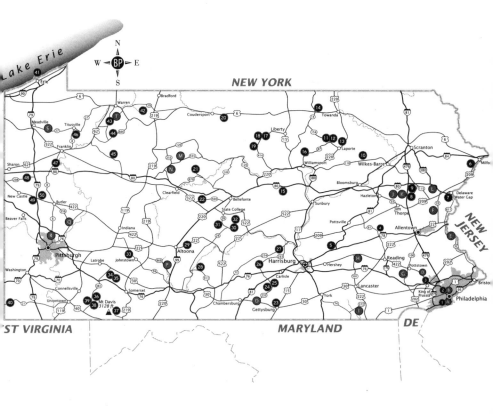

HOW TO USE THIS BOOK

Take a close enough look and you'll find that this little guide contains just about everything you'll ever need to choose, plan for, enjoy, and survive a hike in the state of Pennsylvania. We've done everything but load your pack and tie up your bootlaces. Stuffed with 364 pages of useful Pennsylvania-specific information, *Hike Pennsylvania* features 50 mapped and cued hikes and 20 honorable mentions, as well as everything from advice on getting into shape to tips on getting the most out of hiking with your children or your dog. And as you'd expect with any Outside America™ guide, you get the best maps man and technology can render. With so much information, the only question you may have is: How do I sift through it all? Well, we answer that, too.

We've designed our hiking guide series to be highly visual, for quick reference and ease-of-use. What this means is that the most pertinent information rises quickly to the top, so you don't have to waste time poring through bulky hike descriptions to get mileage cues or elevation stats. They're set aside for you. And yet, an Outside America™ guide doesn't read like a laundry list. Take the time to dive into a hike description and you'll realize that this guide is not just a good source of information; it's a good read. And so, in the end, you get the best of both worlds: a quick-reference guide and an engaging look at a region. Here's an outline of the guide's major components.

WHAT YOU'LL FIND IN THIS *HIKING* GUIDE. Let's start with the individual chapter. To aid in quick decision-making, we start each chapter with a **Hike Summary**. This short overview gives you a taste of the hiking adventure at hand. You'll learn about the trail terrain and what surprises the route has to offer. If your interest is peaked, you can read more. If not, skip to the next Hike Summary. The **Hike Specs** are fairly self-explanatory. Here you'll find the quick, nitty-gritty details of the hike: where the trailhead is located, the nearest town, hike length, approximate hiking time, difficulty rating, type of trail terrain, and what other trail users you may encounter. Our **Getting There** section gives you dependable directions from a nearby city right down to where you'll want to park. The **Hike Description** is the meat of the chapter. Detailed and honest, it's the author's carefully researched impression of the trail. While it's impossible to cover everything, you can rest assured that we won't miss what's important. In our **Miles/Directions** section we provide mileage cues to identify all turns and trail name changes, as well as points of interest. Between this and our Route Map, you simply can't get lost. The **Hike Information** box is a hodgepodge of information. In it you'll find trail hotlines (for updates on trail conditions), park schedules and fees, local outdoor retailers (for emergency trail supplies), and a list of maps available to the area. We'll also tell you where to stay, what to eat, and what else to see while you're hiking in the area. Lastly, the **Honorable Mentions** section details all of the hikes that didn't make the cut, for whatever reason—in many cases it's not because they aren't great hikes, instead it's because they're over-crowded or environmentally sensitive to heavy traffic. Be sure to read through these. A jewel might be lurking among them.

We don't want anyone, by any means, to feel restricted to just the routes and trails that are mapped here. We hope you will have an adventurous spirit and use this guide as a platform to dive into Pennsylvania's backcountry and discover new routes for yourself. One of the simplest ways to begin this is to just turn the map upside down and hike the course in reverse. The change in perspective is fantastic and the hike should feel quite different. With this in mind, it will be like getting two distinctly different hikes on each map.

For your own purposes, you may wish to copy the directions for the course onto a small sheet to help you while hiking, or photocopy the map and cue sheet to take with you. Otherwise, just slip the whole book in your backpack and take it all with you. Enjoy your time in the outdoors and remember to pack out what you pack in.

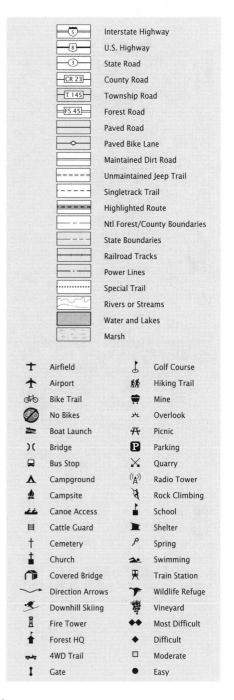

Interstate Highway	
U.S. Highway	
State Road	
County Road	
Township Road	
Forest Road	
Paved Road	
Paved Bike Lane	
Maintained Dirt Road	
Unmaintained Jeep Trail	
Singletrack Trail	
Highlighted Route	
Ntl Forest/County Boundaries	
State Boundaries	
Railroad Tracks	
Power Lines	
Special Trail	
Rivers or Streams	
Water and Lakes	
Marsh	

Airfield		Golf Course	
Airport		Hiking Trail	
Bike Trail		Mine	
No Bikes		Overlook	
Boat Launch		Picnic	
Bridge		Parking	
Bus Stop		Quarry	
Campground		Radio Tower	
Campsite		Rock Climbing	
Canoe Access		School	
Cattle Guard		Shelter	
Cemetery		Spring	
Church		Swimming	
Covered Bridge		Train Station	
Direction Arrows		Wildlife Refuge	
Downhill Skiing		Vineyard	
Fire Tower		Most Difficult	
Forest HQ		Difficult	
4WD Trail		Moderate	
Gate		Easy	

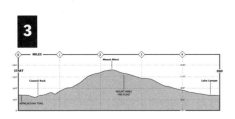

Area Locator Map

This thumbnail relief map at the beginning of each hike shows you where the hike is within the state. The hike area is indicated by the white star.

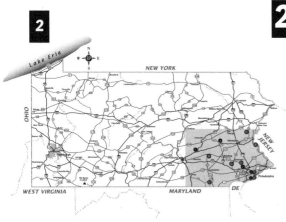

Regional Location Map

This map helps you find your way to the start of each hike from the nearest size-able town or city. Coupled with the detailed directions at the beginning of the cue, this map should visually lead you to where you need to be for each hike.

Profile Map

This helpful profile gives you a cross-sectional look at the hike's ups and downs. Elevation is labeled on the left, mileage is indicated on the top. Road and trail names are shown along the route with towns and points of interest labeled in bold.

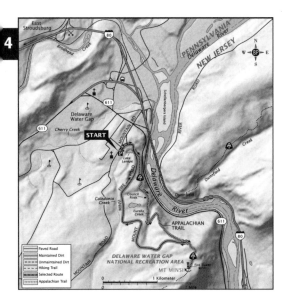

4 Route Map

This is your primary guide to each hike. It shows all of the accessible roads and trails, points of interest, water, towns, landmarks, and geographical features. It also distinguishes trails from roads, and paved roads from unpaved roads. The selected route is highlighted, and directional arrows point the way. Shaded topographic relief in the background gives you an accurate representation of the terrain and landscape in the hike area.

Hike Information (Included in each hike section)

☎ Trail Contacts:

This is the direct number for the local land managers in charge of all the trails within the selected hike. Use this hotline to call ahead for trail access information, or after your visit if you see problems with trail erosion, damage, or misuse.

⏱ Schedule:

This tells you at what times trails open and close, if on private or park land.

$ Fees/Permits:

What money, if any, you may need to carry with you for park entrance fees or tolls.

Ⓜ Maps:

This is a list of other maps to supplement the maps in this book. They are listed in order from most detailed to most general.

Any other important or useful information will also be listed here such as local attractions, outdoor shops, nearby accommodations, etc.

A note from the folks behind this endeavor...

We at Outside America look at guidebook publishing a little different-
ly. There's just no reason that a guidebook has to look like it was published
out of your Uncle Ernie's woodshed. We feel that guidebooks need to be
both easy to use and nice to look at, and that takes an innovative approach
to design. You see, we want you to spend less time fumbling through your
guidebook and more time enjoying the adventure at hand. We hope you
like what you see here and enjoy the places we lead you. And most of all,
we'd like to thank you for taking an adventure with us.

Happy Trails!

Introdu

Introduction

Hiking in Pennsylvania is an excellent example of the proverbial "best kept secret." There are over 3,000 miles of hiking trails, most on public lands. There are vast, remote areas where it's just you and Mother Nature. You can hike all day—sometimes for days—and not see another human being.

There are trails on abandoned railroad beds that are beautifully groomed and refreshingly level. And there are trails along ravines so steep that a water bottle dropped is a water bottle forever lost. Some trails are what I call SUC trails: Straight Uphill Climbs. As soon as you step out of your vehicle, you're climbing. Most other trails, those that are more civilized, allow you a warm-up period...*then* they make you climb.

Ultimately, Pennsylvania hiking is about climbing mountains. This is not to be confused with mountain climbing. Since the highest point in the state is less than 3,500 feet above sea level, there's little need for oxygen canisters, crampons, Sherpa guides, or other exotic (and expensive) equipment. All you'll need to hike the trails in this guide are a good pair of hiking boots, and maybe a walking stick you've picked up along the way.

When I started out across the state, I wanted to see sights I'd never seen before, so I chose hikes I felt had at least one interesting feature. I also chose hikes that I had done many times before, like Rickett's Glen, and wanted to share with readers.

What will you see on the hikes in this guide? How about a hike with over 22 waterfalls, one of which cascades 94 feet? Or a 1,200-year-old tree? Ever see a beaver dam larger than a football field? How about a "ghost town" state park? If you think you can handle it, you'll have the opportunity to sway in the breeze at the top of an 80-foot fire tower, or stand on a platform 300 feet above the Allegheny River. One of the hikes takes you past the first commercial oil well in the world. Another offers a glimpse of the catastrophic Johnstown Flood that wiped out a city. Walk the rims of Pennsylvania's Grand Canyon and watch an eagle as it swoops into the icy waters of Pine Creek and emerges with a fish in its talons.

You'll find that more than half the hikes are located in state parks. More people hike the trails, and consequently, this creates more resources that can be devoted to trail maintenance and other park features. Another reason state parks are a good place to hike is that many of them have preserved the history of their regions. Most of the remaining hikes are in state forests, national parks, and on state game lands; one is on land owned by the Western Pennsylvania Conservancy. These trails are cared for mostly by volunteers from regional and statewide trail clubs. If you want to get in shape, skip a Saturday at the gym and volunteer for trail maintenance. Carrying a chainsaw for five miles or so will give you all the workout you need.

There is much to explore in Pennsylvania's outdoors. With this guidebook you'll be able to set out on your own adventure.

1

Pennsylvania Weather

Pennsylvania's mountain ranges, proximity to the Great Lakes, and position on the East Coast contribute to a wide range of weather patterns across the state. The state averages a modest annual rainfall of anywhere from 32 to 48 inches, but in the mountainous regions it often exceeds 48 inches. And while most of the state can expect one to three feet of snow each winter, the annual snowfall along the New York border and in the Snow Belt near the West Virginia border is frequently 60 inches or more.

Weather on the Appalachian Mountains tends to be more severe than anywhere else in the state; the mountains serve as a barrier for storm systems coming off the Great Lakes and in from the Midwest. Basically, the folks on the mountain take the brunt of it. An exception to this, however, is in the northwest corner of the state. Here, the moist air picked up over the Great Lakes can create major snowstorms. Pennsylvania also has its share of thunderstorms.

There is an old saying among Pennsylvania deer hunters that my father passed on to me: "You can always take it off." I would offer the same advice to hikers: Overdress when you're out here in Pennsylvania; you can always remove a layer and be comfortable.

Flora and Fauna

When Europeans settled in Pennsylvania, the state was covered with trees. At the time, old-growth white pine and hemlocks accounted for about two-thirds of the forests. But in less than 100 years, the logging industry had clearcut the entire state. By the beginning of the twentieth century, the only hemlocks and white pines that remained were small pockets considered too difficult to log.

Today, the dominant forest types are hardwoods. The mixed hardwood forest is defined by a minimum forty percent composition of sugar maple, beech, and yellow birch; the mixed-oak forest is defined as anywhere oak is the dominant tree. The other notable forest—though comprising less than ten percent of the state's forests—is the hemlock stand. Generally found along streambeds and in moist ravine bottoms and slopes, its shallow root system allows it to cling to the edge of cliffs and other precarious locations. The Eastern hemlock is the state tree.

The state flower is the mountain laurel, which, for those who know, is far more like a bush or shrub than a flower (it grows from five to eight feet tall). But when it blooms in early June, it decorates the forest with white and pink cup-shaped flowers. Except for an area in the northwest tip, it can be found throughout the state. The rhododendron, a cousin to the mountain laurel, thrives in moister locales, although it can be found in dry areas. It's not uncommon for these shrubs to grow to heights of 20 feet. Its peak blossom time is the first week of July: look for large balls of either pink or white.

Wildflowers are abundant in the state. Some, like Black-eyed Susans, Queen Ann's Lace, wild bergamot, and common goldenrod are in bloom all summer. (That's because they exist in meadows, where the sunlight is never blocked.) Others, those that grow under the forest canopy, bloom in spring, before the trees sprout their leaves. One of these is the trillium, a member of the lily family. It has a single flower that may be white, pink, dark red, yellow, or green.

Over 60 species of mammals live in Pennsylvania. The most noticeable is the white-tailed deer—if you hike in this state, you will see deer. (In fact, one theory holds that in sparsely populated Potter County, there are more deer than people.) There are also black bears, some weighing in at over 500 pounds. But your chances of seeing one of these creatures in the wild are slim. You may never see a beaver either, but if you hike along streams and creeks, sooner or later, you will see evidence of their existence in the heavily gnawed trees. And, in the village of Benezette in Elk County, you can watch as elk from a herd of over 500 wander into civilization foraging for food.

There are two world-class birding sites in the state. Gull Point, situated on the eastern tip of Presque Isle in Lake Erie, has designated a special management area to protect shorebird habitat. Hawk Mountain Wildlife Sanctuary, on the Kittatinny Ridge between Reading and Pottsville, is considered the premier site in North America to view migrating raptors. The best time to be there is October.

As you hike along the lakeshores and mountain streams, you may never see a fish, but there are over 150 species here in Pennsylvania. You may never see the elusive wild turkey, either, but they're out there. More than likely you'll see a quail or a grouse or a ring-necked pheasant. If you're lucky, and know what to look for, you may see a northern river otter or a fisher, both of which had all but disappeared but have recently been successfully reintroduced.

Wilderness Restrictions/Regulations

There are no day-use or hiking fees in any of the 114 Pennsylvania state parks. (You should note that most day-use parks close at dusk, however.) Within the park system, there are over 22 natural areas—unique examples of natural history; there are no fees or restrictions associated with these areas. For more information call 1–888–PA–PARKS.

In all, 20 state forests cover over 2 million acres in 48 of Pennsylvania's 67 counties. Within this system, there are 61 natural areas set aside as examples of scenic beauty, or a place of historical, ecological, or geological importance. There are no restrictions. For more information call (717) 783–7941.

The Pennsylvania Game Commission owns land in almost every county. There are no hiking restrictions on state game lands. For more information call (717) 783–7507.

Thanks for purchasing *Hike America: Pennsylvania*. The role of the writer is to make old things new and new things familiar. I hope I've done that for you in this book. See you out there.

John L. Young

Getting around Pennsylvania

📞 AREA CODES

The **814** area code covers Erie in the northwest and extends east to Williamsport. It runs south to include the State College-Altoona area. The city of Pittsburgh's area code is **412**, with an **878** overlay. The area code for the Pittsburgh region is **724**. For the Williamsport-Hazelton-Wilkes-Barre region the area code is **570**. In Harrisburg and the Susquehanna Valley the area code is **717**. The area code for the Lehigh Valley is **610** and **484**. In Philadelphia the area code is **215** and the surrounding area is **267**.

🚗 ROADS

For driving conditions on interstate highways, call 1–888–783–6783. For driving conditions on the Pennsylvania Turnpike, call 1–800–331–3414 or visit *www.paturnpike.com*.

✈ BY AIR

Pennsylvania is served by two major airports **Philadelphia International Airport** (PHL) and **Pittsburgh International Airport** (PIT). A number of smaller airports throughout the state have connections through these airports. A travel agent can best advise you on the cheapest and/or most direct way to connect from wherever you're departing. They can also arrange transportation from the airport to your final destination.

To book reservations on-line, check out your favorite airline's website or search one of the following travel sites for the best price: *www.cheaptickets.com*, *www.expedia.com*, *www.previewtravel.com*, *www.priceline.com*, *http://travel.yahoo.com*, *www.travelocity.com*, *www.trip.com*—just to name a few. Many of these sites can connect you with a shuttle or rental service to get you from the airport to your destination.

🚌 BY BUS

Most major towns and a few trailheads in Pennsylvania are served by bus. The major carriers are **Greyhound, Capitol Trailways, Susquehanna Trailways**, and **Fullington Trailways**. These bus companies share ticketing and terminals. Fares, schedules, and tickets can be accessed online at Greyhound's website, *www.greyhound.com*. In addition, frequent commuter buses that go to New York's Port Authority Bus Terminal serve points in eastern Pennsylvania. These include **Martz Trailways**, which serves Delaware Water Gap (on the Appalachian Trail) and the Poconos, (570) 821–3800, *www.martztrailways.com*; **Beiber Tourways**, which serves Reading, (610) 375–0839, *www.beibertourways.com*; and **Trans-Bridge Lines**, which serves Allentown and Doylestown, (610) 868–6001, *www.transbridgebus.com*.

🚆 BY TRAIN

Philadelphia is the hub of Amtrak's **Acela** service, offering frequent trains between Washington, New York, and Boston. **Acela Regional** trains run up to 10 round trips daily between Philadelphia, Lancaster, and Harrisburg. Three long distance trains continue on to Johnstown, Pittsburgh, and Chicago. You can also connect to the buses at the Harrisburg Transportation Center. Erie is the lone Pennsylvania stop for the daily **Lake Shore Limited** between New York and Chicago. Amtrak information and reservations are available online at *www.amtrak.com* or by phone at 1–800–872–7245.

❷ VISITOR INFORMATION

For visitor information or a travel brochure, call the **Pennsylvania Visitors Guide** at 1–800–847–4872 or visit *www.experiencepa.com*.

The Hikes

Southeast
PENNSYLVANIA

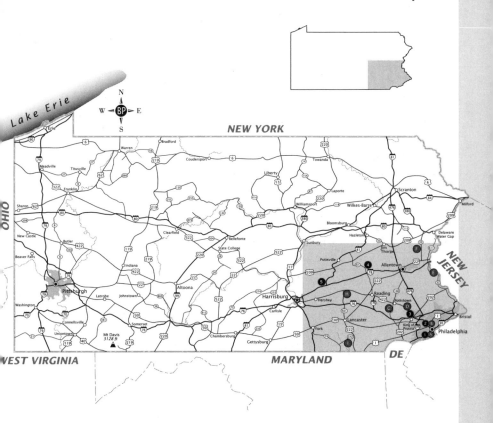

The Hikes

John Heinz Impoundment **1.**
Wissahickon Gorge **2.**
Valley Forge **3.**
The Pinnacle **4.**
Swatara State Park **5.**

Honorable Mentions

A. John Heinz National Wildlife
Refuge/Lagoon Loop
B. Wissahickon Gorge South Loop
C. Ridley Creek State Park
D. The Shippack Creek Trail
E. Delaware Canal State Park
F. Jacobsburg State Park
G. French Creek State Park: Red &
White Loop
H. Middle Creek Wildlife Area
I. Susquehannock State Park

Southeast Pennsylvania

PENNSYLVANIA: AMERICA STARTS HERE was the state slogan a few years back. But let's get specific: America really starts in Southeastern Pennsylvania. Even if the region were as flat as a Kansas wheat field and there were no old-growth forests or crystal-clear streams or tidal wetlands or wildlife refuges or natural areas boasting 300-year-old trees, it would still be well worth your while to hike this region—just to soak up the history.

For example, at Valley Forge, hikers can walk through the winter encampment of General George Washington and his Continental Army or they can step back in time to a year earlier and visit the site where Washington and his troops crossed the Delaware River. Hikers can visit the last remaining intact canal system of the great towpath building era or spend a day on a circa 1700 Quaker farm.

Tired of people? Desk stress got you down? Need to get away? Spend some time with Greater Snow Geese or migrating raptors. Really tired of people? Climb a rocky outcrop to one of the best views in the state or spend a day exploring a fossil pit in an undeveloped state park.

Geologically speaking, the southeast provides a landscape as diverse as its population. The Coastal Plain is a narrow strip along the Delaware border that encompasses Philadelphia. Just west of the Coastal Plain the Piedmont region begins. (A piedmont is a plateau near the foot of a mountain.) The Piedmont in southeastern Pennsylvania comprises the fertile farming region of the Lancaster Valley, from the Coastal Plain in the east, to the great Appalachian Mountain system in the west. Just west of the Piedmont, the Blue Mountains extend into Pennsylvania, where they are known as South Mountain.

The Reading Prong stretches across the Susquehanna Valley; it's sometimes considered an extension of the Blue Ridge Mountains. The Great Valley—which is 20 miles wide and extends from the Maryland border in the south to the Delaware River in the northeast—begins west of the Reading Prong and South Mountain and ends where the Valley and Ridge Province of central Pennsylvania begins. In Southeast Pennsylvania, it's known as the Cumberland Valley.

What does all this mean to hikers, eager to lace-up and get out there? It means that the same geological forces that created these mountains and land formations also created a lot of exciting features, like stunning waterfalls, water gaps, wind gaps, deep gorges, and on and on. Simply put, it means where there's a lot of geological diversity, there will also be a lot of great hiking.

Overview

John Heinz National Wildlife Refuge/Impoundment Loop

Want a hike where you can take your children *and* your parents? This is it. Along this easy, flat hike you're surrounded by nature's beauty and the excitement of spotting some of the 280 species of birds. In season, you can check out the migratory birds as they make their spring and fall journeys. On this 1,200-acre refuge you can bike, fish, or take a canoe and do your bird watching and amphibian and reptile tickling from the water. Once written off as a useless swamp, the refuge will surprise you with over 50 species of wildflowers, an abundance of deciduous trees, and wildlife from white-tailed deer to turtles. *(See page 12)*

Wissahickon Gorge North Loop

There are two major attractions on this hike that make this an absolute must for serious outdoor lovers. Hikers can investigate the history and the historical significance of Northwest Philadelphia while they're overwhelmed by the natural history and majestic beauty of Wissahickon Gorge. Be sure to bring your camera. Centered around Wissahickon Gorge and the wide-flowing Wissahickon Creek, which runs seven miles through Fairmount Park, this hike leads you through an historic stone arch to Indian Rock, where the Lenni-Lenape Indians held council until they disappeared from the valley in the mid 18th Century. Here you can take a photo of Tedyuscung, a stone statue called the Kneeling Warrior. Explore a 97-foot-long covered bridge built in 1737, or take a break near a small dam that sends water cascading five feet over its crest. And be sure to get a photo of the giant tulip poplars—with diameters up to four feet, these are some of the largest in the state. *(See page 16)*

10

Valley Forge National Historical Park

Visit one of the most important sites in American history. Walk through the encampment where General George Washington and 11,000 of his patriot soldiers spent the harsh winter of 1777–78, after suffering two crushing defeats in Philadelphia. Highlights are the reconstructed soldiers' huts, the Washington Memorial Chapel, the Memorial Arch, and the statue of Baron Frederic von Steuben, the Prussian military leader who volunteered to change Washington's army from a dissolute band of irregulars into a disciplined fighting machine. (*See page 22*)

The Pinnacle

Walk the Appalachian Trail for spectacular views of Hawk Mountain, the Lehigh Valley, and Blue Rocks. Many Appalachian Trail thru-hikers claim the views at the Pinnacle are the best views on the Pennsylvania stretch of the Appalachian Trail. On this hike, you'll get a vigorous workout climbing up the rocky path to the top (be sure to wear hiking boots). You then get a reprieve as you make a gentle descent on a wide dirt road. This is an extremely popular trail with hikers and mountain bikers. Mountain bikers are only allowed on the dirt road section of this hike, so you'll only have to watch for them there. (*See page 26*)

Swatara State Park

Set this hike aside to do after it rains and all your favorite trails are muddy. Except for a 0.1-mile stretch on a shale road, the trail surfaces here are paved. This hike is suitable for all ages. And, although it is almost a four-mile loop, you could walk, say, to the historic Waterville Bridge and never be farther than a mile or so from your vehicle. Other highlights include the stone ruins of a 19th century, flooded-out dam and the abandoned canal system that was connected to the dam. (*See page 32*)

John Heinz Ntl Wildlife Refuge/Impoundment Loop

Hike Specs

Start: From the parking area near the John Heinz Visitor Contact Station
Length: 3.5-mile loop
Approximate Hiking Time: 1–2 hours
Difficulty Rating: Easy, due to the level terrain
Terrain: Wide, level dirt and gravel roads that run through a 1,200-acre marsh
Elevation Gain: 28 feet
Land Status: National wildlife refuge
Nearest Town: Philadelphia, PA
Other Trail Users: Cyclists, joggers, and birdwatchers
Canine Compatibility: Leashed dogs permitted

Getting There

From Philadelphia: Drive south on I-95 to the Bartram Avenue Exit. Drive west on Bartram Avenue to 84th Street. Turn right onto 84th Street and drive to Lindbergh Boulevard. Turn left onto Lindbergh Avenue and follow the signs to the John Heinz Visitor Contact Station. Park in the lot just beyond the visitor center. *DeLorme: Pennsylvania Atlas & Gazetteer:* Page 82 D2 • **By Train:** From Market East Station, take the SEPTA R1 Airport Line to Eastwick Station. Now on foot, leave the station and turn left on 84th Street. Follow the driving directions to the Visitor Contact Station. *(It's about a three-quarter-mile walk to the trailhead from the train station.)* • **By Bus:** SEPTA bus routes 37 and 108 serve the corner of 84th Street and Lindbergh Boulevard. Follow the driving directions above from here. *(It's a couple of blocks to the trailhead from the bus stop.)*

The Tinicum National Environmental Center was established by an act of Congress in 1972 to protect the last 200 acres of freshwater tidal marsh in Pennsylvania. In 1991 the name was changed to the John Heinz National Wildlife Refuge to honor the late Senator who helped preserve Tinicum Marsh. The history of the marsh can be traced back to the mid 1600s when early settlers diked and drained part of the marsh for grazing. At that time, the marsh was over 5,700 acres, but with the rapid urbanization of the area that followed World War I, the marsh was reduced to a mere 200 acres.

In 1955, Gulf Oil donated 145 acres adjacent to the eastern end of the marsh and the area soon became a haven for wildlife. But in 1969, plans were on the table to route Interstate 95 right through the marsh. This started a series of injunctions and public hearings that ended in 1972 when Congress gave the Secretary of the Interior authorization to acquire the 1,200 acres that comprise the marsh today.

One of the popular ways to explore the refuge is by canoe, on the 4.5-mile section of Darby Creek that winds through the marsh. If you've got a canoe, bring it; there's a canoe launch, but there are no canoe rentals. Also,

keep in mind that the refuge waters are tidal and navigable only within two hours of high tide. If you plan to canoe, it's best to contact the Visitor Contact Station. They can provide you with a canoe map and 10 points of interest (or you can download the canoe map from the refuge's website listed below). Fishing is permitted, and you can use the same map for fishing.

From your canoe you'll see a diversity of waterfowl, wildlife, and amphibians. You may come upon the Eastern painted turtle or the state-endanger red-bellied turtle sunning himself on a log. Chances are you'll see one of these ducks: the hooded merganser, pintail, shovelers, or mallards. There are three nonpoisonous snakes that call the marsh home: the northern water snake, the eastern garter snake, and the northern brown snake. Eight species of toads, frogs, and turtles have been identified here.

In addition to the indigenous population, the refuge is along the Atlantic Flyway and serves as a stopover for migratory birds in the spring and fall. Sightings have included the great blue heron, Canadian geese, egrets, killdeer, and sandpipers. Over 280 species of birds have been sighted, with 80 of those species recorded as nesting in or near the marsh. Bring you binoculars and birdwatching book: you might just see a bird here you've never seen before, like a great-crested flycatcher, a Philadelphia Vireo, a hammons warbler, or a yellow-throated warbler.

There are a number of environmental education opportunities here for young and old. Educators and group leaders use the refuge as an outdoor classroom to enhance student learning. Field trips are free, but you need to reserve a place for your group in advance. Also, it's recommended that anyone planning on leading an educational field trip meet with the refuge staff for an introduction to the refuge.

There are ongoing, free programs with titles like Nature Photo Walk, Birding Basics, Waterfowl Wonderment, and Minnow Evolution. There are even free professional development workshops for educators offered throughout the year. Add to all this a resource library, located in the visitor center, with over 200 activity guides, videos, and other resources, and you have the perfect place to spend a day.

Hike Information

🌐 Trail Contacts:
John Heinz Visitor Contact Station, Tinicum, PA (215) 365–3118 or *www.heinz.fws.gov/recreate.htm*

🕐 Schedule:
Open year round

💲 Fees/Permits:
No fees or permits required

❓ Local Information:
The Philadelphia Convention & Visitors Bureau, Philadelphia, PA (215) 636–1666 or 1–800–537–7676 or *www.liberty net.org/phila-visitor/* or *www.pcvb.org*

📍 Local Events/Attractions:
Independence Mall, located between 4th and 8th streets, Philadelphia, PA – home of the Liberty Bell, Independence Hall, Congress Hall, and other points of interest • **The Italian Market,** 9th Street and Passyunk Avenue, Philadelphia, PA • **South Street,** between 3rd and 8th streets, Philadelphia, PA

🛏 Accommodations/Restaurants/Local Outdoor Retailers:
There are stores, hotels, and restaurants within five minutes of this hike. Contact the John Heinz Visitor Contact Station for directions to the nearest restaurants and hotels. The station is open from 9 A.M. to 4:30 P.M.

🏢 Organizations:
Friends of the Heinz Wildlife Refuge at Tinicum, FOHR Tinicum, Folcroft, PA (610) 521–0662

🅽 Maps:
USGS maps: Landsdowne, PA; Philadelphia, PA • **NWR maps:** John Heinz NWR – *available at the contact station*

MilesDirections

0.0 START from the parking area. Get on the Impoundment Trail toward the observation tower.

0.2 Pass a wooden footbridge on your left.

0.7 Arrive at the observation tower; continue straight.

1.3 Pass a spur trail to a viewing blind. Continue straight.

1.4 Turn left at a trail junction, still following the Impoundment Trail.

1.9 The trail turns left.

2.5 The trail bears left.

3.5 Arrive back at the parking area.

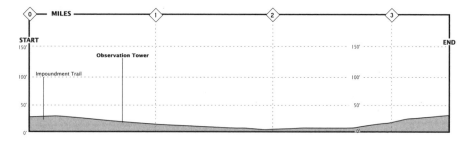

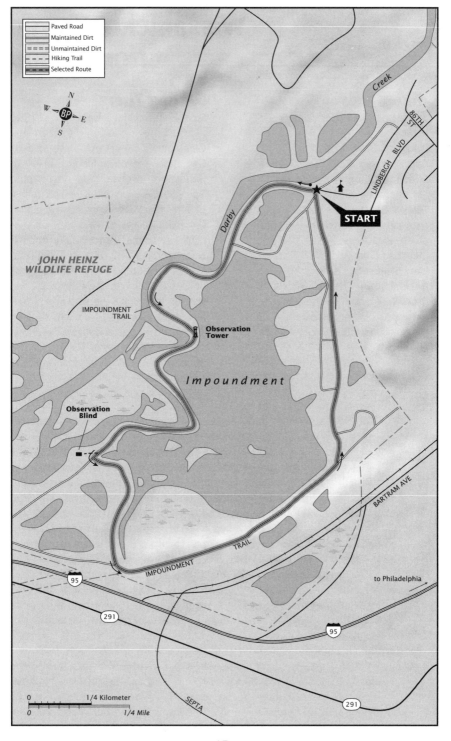

Wissahickon Gorge North Loop

Hike Specs

Start: From the Upper Valley Green parking area
Length: 5.5-mile loop
Approximate Hiking Time: 3 hours
Difficulty Rating: Moderate, due to a few strenuous sections
Terrain: Gravel paths, rocky footpaths, dirt roads, and paved roads navigate a steep-sided gorge.
Elevation Gain: 365 feet
Land Status: City park
Nearest Town: Chestnut Hill, PA
Other Trail Users: Cyclists, joggers, sightseers, and equestrians
Canine Compatibility: Leashed dogs permitted

Getting There

From Philadelphia: Drive west on I-76 to I-476. Drive north on I-476 to the Germantown Avenue exit. Drive east on Germantown Avenue for 6.1 miles to Springfield Avenue. Turn right onto Springfield Avenue and travel 0.7 miles. Bear right on Valley Green Road and drive 0.4 miles to the parking area on your right. *DeLorme: Pennsylvania Atlas & Gazetteer:* Page 82 D2 • **By Train:** From Market East Station, take the SEPTA R8 Chestnut Hill line to St. Martin's Station. Now on foot, leave the station and turn left on St. Martin's Lane. Turn right on Springfield Avenue and follow the driving directions to the Valley Green Inn. *(It's about a mile walk to the trailhead from the train station.)*

Fairmount Park stretches from the edge of downtown Philadelphia to the city's northwest corner, and at 4,500 acres, it's the largest urban park in any city in the world. Before the land for the park was acquired by the city of Philadelphia in 1812, it was an industrial area comprised mostly of mills—paper mills, sawmills, textile mills—run by waterwheels. The mill owners lived on top of the gorge and built roadways and paths so they could walk or take their buggies down to their factories. Many of those trails remain today. In fact, Forbidden Drive, the main thoroughfare that runs on the east side of Wissahockin Creek, was once a popular carriage road.

The world famous Philadelphia Museum of Art lies at the southern end of Fairmount Park atop the Faire Mount plateau. The mammoth structure, modeled after the ancient Greek temples, covers 10 acres and is home to 200 galleries, housing an amazing 300,000 works of art—including Van Gogh, Renoir, Picasso, and Rubens, to name but a few. If you visit Philadelphia, this museum is a *must-see*.

There's a pretty good chance, however, that you've already seen the museum. The 1976 film *Rocky*, written by and starring Sylvester Stallone, contains a now-famous scene where heavyweight contender Rocky Balboa runs up Benjamin Franklin Parkway to the front of the museum,

continuing up the museum's 99 steps to the terrace, where he raises both fists and exalts himself to "Gonna Fly Now," the highly recognizable *Rocky* theme song.

Meanwhile, back in the real world, you probably won't hear the *Rocky* theme as you continue your hike, but you may be enraptured by the tumbling waters of Wissahickon Creek as you make your way upstream, past outcrops and along the forested trails that rise up the gorge away from the creek. At the 2.6-mile mark, you have the option of crossing Bell's Mill Road at the crosswalk and walking north, a little over a half mile, to the Andorra Nature Center and Tree House Visitor Center.

The Andorra Natural Area is part of the old Andorra Nursery, once the largest nursery on the East Coast. The natural area, which is now a wooded plot that measures about a mile wide and a half-mile long, is included in the National Natural Landmark designation that includes the entire Wissahickon Valley. Follow the signs to the visitor center and get a trail

Wissahickon Creek.

17

map so you can explore the area on your own. If you visit here in spring, you'll see Solomon's seal, skunk cabbage, mayapples, wild ginger, spring beauties, and smooth yellow violets come to bloom.

Want to see a 250-year-old cucumber tree and some other enormous trees? Take the Central Loop to Cucumber Meadow. Here you'll find white-tailed deer and a bounty of birds, such as the northern cardinal, American redstart, red-bellied woodpecker, and scarlet tanager. On the way to Tulip Meadow, you'll walk under huge white birches, one over 100 years old. On the Azalea Loop, you'll pass enormous American beech trees and a white oak that is more than 300 years old.

MilesDirections

0.0 START from the Upper Valley Green parking area. Walk to a trail at the end of the parking area. Continue straight through the trail junction.

0.2 Turn right and begin a short uphill climb.

0.5 Turn right and head toward a trail junction.

0.7 The trail starts downhill as you pass over several waterbars.

1.1 The trail becomes rocky.

1.3 Cross a road and begin a steep climb to the Kneeling Warrior statue.

1.5 The Kneeling Warrior statue is on your left. Continue straight to steep steps that to a road.

1.9 The trail turns right.

2.0 Turn left and begin descent to Bell's Mill Road.

2.6 Turn left and cross over a bridge to Forbidden Drive. *[FYI. A right here will access the Andorra Natural Area.]*

2.7 Turn left and walk to a second trail on the right—the Red, Yellow, & Green Trail.

2.9 Turn left and head toward a trail junction.

3.1 Turn right toward a trail junction.

3.5 Turn right and begin an uphill climb to a trail junction.

3.7 Turn left to a trail junction.

4.1 Turn right again toward a bridge.

4.2 Cross the bridge to a trail junction.

4.6 Turn left and descend to Forbidden Drive.

5.2 Turn left, cross the bridge, and retrace your steps to the parking area.

5.5 Arrive back at your vehicle.

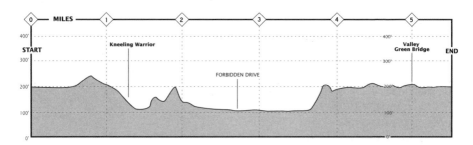

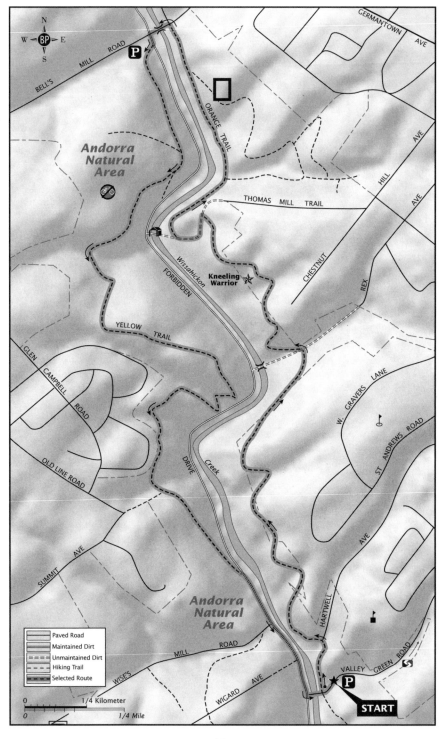

Cyclists are big fans of the trails along the Wissahickon.

There are over 230 species and 110 varieties of deciduous trees, evergreens, and shrubs left over from the nursery. Many of these, like the Japanese maple, are labeled. On the Big Tree Trail, you'll see some impressive trees—specifically, giant scarlet oaks, black oaks, and white oaks. And finally, when you get to the L.M.C. Smith Trail, you'll pass under *The Great Beech*.

After your visit to the Andorra Natural Area, retrace your steps to Bell's Mill Road and continue the North Loop Hike. Your mileage walked to and from the natural area isn't included in the directional cues.

Hike Information

🌕 Trail Contacts:
Fairmount Park Rangers, Philadelphia, PA (215) 685–2172 • **Fairmount Park Commission Visitors Center,** Philadelphia, PA (215) 685–2176

🕐 Schedule:
Open year round

💲 Fees/Permits:
No fees or permits required for hikers. Free permits are required for bicyclists and equestrians in certain sections of the park. Call for details.

❓ Local Information:
The Philadelphia Convention & Visitors Bureau, Philadelphia, PA (215) 636–1666 or 1–800–537–7676 or *www.libertynet.org/phila-visitor/* or *www.pcvb.org*

📍 Local Events/Attractions:
Andorra Natural Areas/Tree House Visitor Center, Philadelphia, PA (215) 685–9285 • **Morris Arboretum,** Chestnut Hill, PA (215) 247–5777 • **Woodmere Art Museum,** Philadelphia, PA (215) 247–0476

🛏 Accommodations:
General Lafayette Inn Bed & Breakfast, Lafayette Hill, PA (610) 941–0600 or 1–800–351–0181 or *www.generallafayetteinn.com* • **Beechwood Campground,** Coatesville, PA (610) 384–1457 or 1–800–226–7248

🍴 Restaurants:
Valley Green Inn, Philadelphia, PA (215) 247–1730 or *www.valleygreeninn.com* • **Bains Deli,** King of Prussia, PA (610) 265–6803

👥 Organizations:
Friends of Wissahickon, Philadelphia, PA (215) 247–0417 or *www.fow.org*

🏃 Local Outdoor Retailers:
Bryn Mawr Running Company, Bryn Mawr, PA (610) 527–5510

🗺 Maps:
USGS maps: Germantown, PA

Valley Forge National Historical Park

Hike Specs

Start: From the Washington Headquarters parking area

Length: 6.7-mile loop

Approximate Hiking Time: 3–4 hours

Difficulty Rating: Easy, due to the level terrain

Terrain: Asphalt path winding through rolling hills

Elevation Gain: 432 feet

Land Status: National park

Nearest Town: King of Prussia, PA

Other Trail Users: Tourists and cyclists

Canine Compatibility: Leashed dogs permitted

Getting There

From Philadelphia: Drive west on I-76 to King of Prussia and U.S. 202. Take U.S. 202 south to U.S. 422 and drive west for 1.6 miles to PA 23. Turn left onto PA 23 and pass the Valley Forge Visitor Center. Continue on PA 23 west for 2.4 miles to the Washington Headquarters parking area on the right. *DeLorme: Pennsylvania Atlas & Gazetteer:* Page 81 D7

The chain of events that led to the Revolutionary War actually began with the French and Indian War (1754–1763) between France and Great Britain, which was fought mostly throughout the Northern colonies. Although Britain won the war, it had accumulated a large debt in the process, which it hoped to pay off by imposing taxes on its American colonies. The first of these taxes came in 1765 with the Stamp Act, which set a levy on legal documents, pamphlets, newspapers, deeds, and even playing cards. The second tax was the Tea Act, which eliminated the customs duty on tea purchased from the East India Company, a British company, while maintaining the duty on teas imported from other countries. Frustrated to the point of revolt, the Tea Act motivated the colonists to hold the famous Boston Tea Party in December 1773.

It was nearly two years, however, before the revolution proper began: April 19, 1775. British troops were ordered to close the Massachusetts Assembly and capture a stockpile of colonial arms. The colonial militia opened fire on the Loyalists, first at Lexington, then at Concord, where the British had retreated. The skirmish was a strong American victory, with the British suffering nearly three times the American losses. Then, in June of 1775, the Continental Congress commissioned George Washington to organize and lead a Continental Army.

General Washington's Valley Forge encampment began when Sir William Howe loaded 20,000 British troops onto 250 ships and landed in

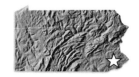

the upper end of the Chesapeake Bay. His objective was to capture Philadelphia, home of the Continental Congress. Although Congress had fled the city, Washington had little choice but to meet Howe and defend the city. Washington's 11,000 soldiers, outnumbered and poorly prepared, lost the Battle of Brandywine on September 11th and the Battle of Germantown on October 4th. Howe and his troops occupied Philadelphia.

With winter setting in, the prospects for more campaigning diminished. Washington withdrew his forces 18 miles northwest of Philadelphia to set up camp at Valley Forge, where one of their first tasks was to build 1,000 huts to fight off the bitter winds and snow. But the huts did little to stave off the hunger and disease the men faced with the onset of winter. The troops' shoes and garments were so tattered that at one point over 4,000 men were declared unfit for duty. More than 2,000 men died that winter from typhus, typhoid, dysentery, and pneumonia; about half of the surviving men deserted.

But as weeks wore on and supplies and equipment and fresh troops trickled in, morale began to lift. Skilled Prussian drillmaster Baron Frederic von Steuben volunteered to drill and train the troops in military tactics. Von Steuben's training resulted in better discipline among the ranks and a renewed sense of ability and confidence in the men.

With spring came the news that the French had signed an alliance with the colonists. Then word came that British troops had pulled out of Philadelphia and were heading to New York. But they would not make it in time. Because of Washington and his rag-tag troops' efforts to save Philadelphia, Howe could not move his men north quickly enough. This, in turn, led to the defeat of the British at Saratoga, New York, considered by many scholars as a turning point for the American Revolution.

Hiking this trail is much more than making a simple loop over rolling fields; it will take you back in time, where you can walk through the encampment and immerse yourself in the history and drama of an American landmark. If you were to walk this trail at a normal pace, it might take less than two hours. But it's more than likely you'll want to stop, read the educational plaques, and linger at the displays; you may even want to stop for lunch in the picnic area, or take a short break on the grass. For these reasons, it would be best to set aside three to four hours to complete this journey into American history.

MilesDirections

0.0 START by walking back to PA 23. Turn left onto the walking path and begin a gentle climb past several monuments and soldier huts on PA 23.

0.7 Cross PA 23. Veer left onto the path and pass the von Steuben statue.

1.2 Come to the Washington Memorial Chapel on your left.

1.3 Cross a paved road.

2.1 Cross a second road and make a short climb to the Visitor Center.

2.4 The trail veers left past the Visitor Center and enters an open field.

2.8 Arrive at a cluster of soldier cabins.

3.3 Pass the National Memorial Arch on your left. The trail turns right toward Wayne's Wood.

4.0 Arrive at Wayne's Woods and a picnic area.

4.8 Turn right at the fork in the trail.

5.9 Arrive back at the von Steuben statue. Retrace your steps back to the parking area.

6.7 Arrive back at your vehicle.

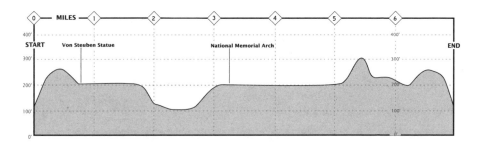

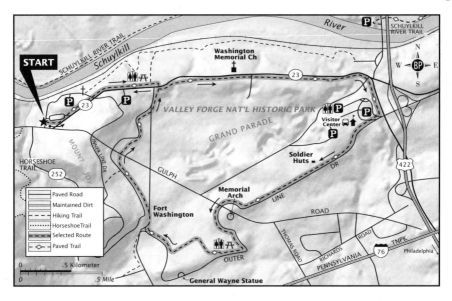

Hike Information

📞 Trail Contacts:
Valley Forge National Historical Park, Valley Forge, PA (610) 783–1077 or www.nps.gov/vafo

🕐 Schedule:
Open year round

💲 Fees/Permits:
No fees or permits required

❓ Local Information:
The Valley Forge Convention and Visitors Bureau, Plymouth Meeting, PA (610) 834–1550 or www.valley forge.org

💡 Local Events/Attractions:
Schuylkill Center for Environmental Education, Philadelphia, PA (215) 482–7300 or www.schuylkillcenter.org • Hopewell Furnace National Historical Site, Elverson, PA (610) 582–8773

🛏 Accommodations:
Valley Forge Bed & Breakfast, Phoenixville, PA (610) 933–6460 • Warwick Woods Campground, St. Peters, PA (610) 286–9655

🍴 Restaurants:
Michael's Deli, King of Prussia, PA (610) 265–3265

🏃 Local Outdoor Retailers:
Runner's Edge, Paoli, PA (610) 296–2868

🗺 Maps:
USGS maps: Valley Forge, PA

4

The Pinnacle

Hike Specs

Start: From the parking area at the Hamburg Reservoir
Length: 8.7-mile loop
Approximate Hiking Time: 5 hours
Difficulty Rating: Moderate, due to the steep, rocky climbs
Terrain: Rocky forest footpaths and abandoned roads follow forested mountain trails and mountain streams to a ridge-top boulder outcrop.
Elevation Gain: 868 feet
Land Status: Private and state game lands
Nearest Town: Hamburg, PA
Other Trail Users: Thru-hikers, cyclists, and hunters (in season)
Canine Compatibility: Leashed dogs permitted

Getting There

From Allentown: Drive west on I-78 for about 17 miles to Exit 11. Drive north on PA 143 for 0.9 miles to Mountain Road. Turn left onto Mountain Road and drive 2.4 miles to Reservoir Road. Turn right on Reservoir Road and drive to the parking area. *DeLorme: Pennsylvania Atlas & Gazetteer:* Page 66 D3

Many Appalachian Trail (AT) thru-hikers contend that Pennsylvania is one of the rockiest sections on the entire trail. Climbing up to the Pinnacle will give you an idea of just what they're talking about. It's also said that the deep forests of Pennsylvania make hikers feel as though they are out in the boonies, miles from the nearest town, when all along they're only a few miles from civilization. You'll get a taste of that here, as well. Actually, you're just a few miles from Interstate 78 and all the fast food, gasoline, and glory that comes with the average interstate outpost.

This trek along the AT affords some outstanding views of Hawk Mountain, the Lehigh Valley, and Blue Rocks, as well as opportunities to catch the hawks riding the wind currents along Kittatinny Ridge. The views from the Pinnacle are said to be among the best of those found along the Pennsylvania stretch of the AT. The climb up the rocky path to the top is strenuous, but the descent along the wide dirt road will give you time to recoup. Be mindful that mountain bikers are allowed on the dirt road section of the hike (the AT is hiker-only).

There's an optional side trip you can take before or after this hike that you'll not want to miss—even if you have to stay overnight. The Hawk

The Pinnacle.

Mountain Sanctuary, just a few miles north of the Pinnacle, is one of the most popular sites in the country for viewing raptor migration. And, as is often the case with other natural phenomena in Pennsylvania, the mountains play a major role.

Raptors (also known as birds-of-prey) are easy to spot because they don't flap their wings like smaller birds. They soar. And to do that, they need to catch rising air currents. In the Ridge and Valley Province of central Pennsylvania, the prevailing wind is from the northwest. When that wind hits the parallel ridges that run southwest to northeast, it's deflected upward, creating considerable updrafts. Hawk Mountain is located on Kittatinny Ridge, the southernmost ridge of the Ridge and Valley Province. The ridge is located just before the Great Valley, a broad flatland to the south. Raptors

MilesDirections

0.0 START at the Hamburg Reservoir parking area. Walk through the gate to the map board and pick up the blue blazes. Continue on the gravel road, which for a while is also the white-blazed Appalachian Trail.

0.4 Turn right and cross the bridge over Furnace Creek. On the other side, bear right, following the white blazes.

0.8 Come to a trail intersection and turn right onto an abandoned road.

1.9 Pass the blue-blazed side trail to the Blue Rocks Campground.

2.2 The trail turns right onto a rocky trail with stone steps.

2.4 Arrive at the Pulpit Rock.

4.2 Pass a yellow-blazed side trail.

4.5 Arrive at the blue-blazed trail to the right that leads about 150 yards to the Pinnacle Overlook. Retrace your steps back to the Appalachian Trail and keep to the right.

5.0 Pick up an abandoned road.

6.4 Arrive at the helicopter pad. Continue across the grassy area and turn left onto the dirt road, following the blue blazes.

7.8 Pass the Hamburg Reservoir on your right.

8.0 Pass a service road on your left.

8.3 Arrive at an intersection with the Appalachian Trail. Turn right, crossing Furnace Creek. Then retrace your steps on the gravel road.

8.7 Arrive back at your vehicle.

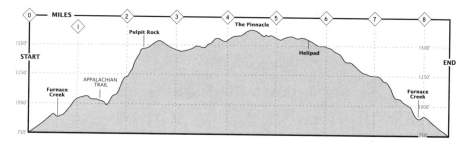

gather above Kittatinny Ridge to catch an updraft that will send them on their way, soaring south across the valley.

The sanctuary was founded in 1934 when Rosalie Edge, an environmental activist from New York, happened to see a photo of hundreds of dead raptors killed by hunters at Hawk Mountain. It became the first refuge in the world to protect birds-of-prey. In those days, raptors were not protected by federal law; in fact, many hunters who came to Hawk Mountain thought they were doing a worthy service to the area.

Since its inception, Hawk Mountain Sanctuary has kept a census of migrating raptors—the longest-running raptor census in the world. The sea-

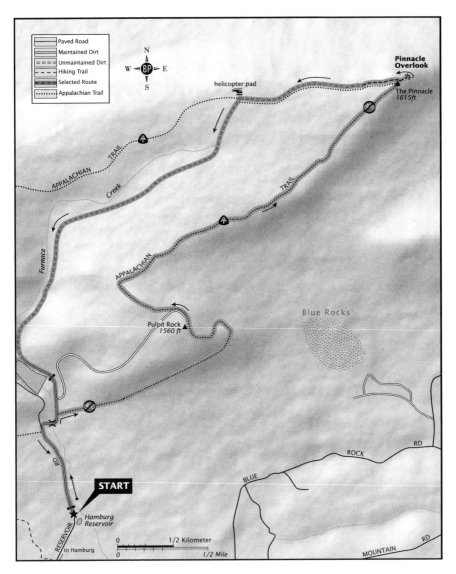

son begins August 15 and continues for four months, since migrating periods vary by species. Bald eagle and osprey migrate early, in August and September, while the golden eagle and goshawk cross the ridge in November. Visitors can spot an endless variety of hawks, including the northern goshawk, Cooper's hawk, the sharp-shinned hawk, the rough-legged hawk, and the red-shouldered hawk. There are also plenty of ospreys, peregrine falcons, merlins, and the American kestrel to be seen.

The official raptor migration count is conducted from the North Lookout, which is at an elevation of 1,521 feet. Aside from the birds, you'll discover a breathtaking view from North Lookout stretching 70 miles across the Ridge and Valley Province. During the peak migration season, the trail leading to North Lookout can be crowded. On the busiest days, it may be best to try the South Lookout—less popular and less crowded. Also, the trail to the South Lookout is only 300 yards long and is wheelchair accessible.

Hike Information

◑ Trail Contacts:
Southeast Pennsylvania Game Commission, Reading, PA (610) 926–1966 or *www.pgc.state.pa.us*

◔ Schedule:
Open year round

⑤ Fees/Permits:
No fees or permits required

❓ Local Information:
Berks County Visitors Bureau, Reading, PA (610) 375–4085 or 1–800–443–6610 or *www.reading-berkspa.com*

⑨ Local Events/Attractions:
Hawk Mountain Sanctuary, Kempton, PA (610) 756–6961 or *www.hawk mountain.org – one of the most active raptor migration centers and viewing areas in the world* • **Conrad Weiser Homestead,** Womelsdorf, PA (610) 589–2934 • **Yuengling Brewery,** Pottsville, PA (570) 628–4890 or *www.yuengling.com – oldest beer brewery in America; tours available*

⊟ Accommodations:
Hawk Mountain Bed & Breakfast, Kempton, PA (610) 756–4224 • **Serenity Farm & Milk House Bed & Breakfast,** Orwigsberg, PA (570) 943–2919 • **Blue Rocks Family Campground,** Lenhartsville, PA (610) 756–6366 • **Robin Hill Camping Resort,** Lenhartsville, PA (610) 756–6117 or 1–800–732–5267

⑪ Restaurants:
Indian Fort Inn, Reading, PA (610) 562–4315

⑪ Organizations:
Potomac Appalachian Trail Club, Vienna, VA (703) 242–0965 or www.patc.net

⑤ Local Outdoor Retailers:
Aardvark Sports Shop, Bethlehem, PA (610) 866–8300

Ⓝ Maps:
USGS maps: Hamburg, PA

Hawk Mountain Sanctuary receives 80,000 visitors a year from all over the world. Look for the impressive visitor center that contains a raptor museum, a gift shop with a variety of natural history books, and an art gallery. There is a network of hiking trails and paths that lead visitors to the same outcroppings where hunters once stood and slaughtered these birds as they floated by. Today, of course, these ledges are filled with birders, amateur naturalists, and professional ornithologists from all over the world. In fact, this gathering of raptor fans has earned the sanctuary the nickname the *Crossroads of Naturalists*.

How to get to Hawk Mountain Sanctuary

From the Pinnacle Trailhead, return to Interstate 78. Drive five miles west on Interstate 78 to Exit 9. Take Exit 9 and drive north four miles to the town of Molino. In Molino, turn right onto Pennsylvania 895 and drive east two miles to the village of Drehersville and the Hawk Mountain Sanctuary sign. Turn right onto Hawk Mountain Road and drive two miles up the mountain to the sanctuary parking lot on your right.

Swatara State Park

Hike Specs

Start: From the intersection of PA 443 and Moonshine Road

Length: 3.9-mile loop

Approximate Hiking Time: 2 hours

Difficulty Rating: Easy, due to the flat terrain

Terrain: This hike is centered around an historic iron bridge that crosses a sizable creek. You'll walk mostly paved roads and an abandoned railroad grade, pass a trout stream, and visit stone ruins.

Elevation Gain: 529 feet

Land Status: State park

Nearest Town: Pine Grove, PA

Other Trail Users: Backpackers and cyclists

Canine Compatibility: Leashed dogs permitted

Getting There

From Harrisburg: Take I-81 east for 19 miles to the junction with I-78. At the junction with I-78, take I-81 north for about nine miles to Exit 31. Drive west on PA 443 exactly 8.2 miles to the intersection with Moonshine Road and the abandoned section of Old State Road on your left. Park on your left by the access gate across abandoned Old State Road. **DeLorme: Pennsylvania Atlas & Gazetteer:** Page 79 A5

Note: There's an optional hike (described below), bicycle ride, or car ride to a popular fossil pit within the park.

The highlight of this hike is the historic, cast-iron Waterville Bridge. It was originally built across Little Pine Creek in Lycoming County in 1890. In the 1980s, the Pennsylvania Department of Transportation determined that the bridge was too narrow for safe automobile travel. It was dismantled, repaired, and reconstructed at its present site so that day-hikers and Appalachian Trail thru-hikers could cross Swatara Creek without having to use an automobile bridge.

The modern history of this region began in the early 1800s when anthracite coal was discovered. The coal needed to be exported, so the Union Canal was built to connect the Schuylkill and Susquehanna Rivers. (A branch of the Union Canal was built to run from Lebanon to Pine Grove, through what is now Swatara State Park.) In 1830, a dam and 672-acre reservoir were built where the Waterville Bridge stands today. The dam was washed away in the Flood of 1862 and has never been rebuilt; you can check out the remnants of the dam and canal locks on the bank of Swatara Creek. The stone ruins under I-81 are remains of the canal.

After the canal came the railroad, which ran through the park on the north side of Swatara Creek. After the railroad's heyday, the state acquired the land, created the park, and built the multi-use trail on the

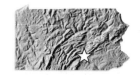

abandoned railroad bed. To complete the park, the Department of Conservation and Natural Resources (DCNR)—the agency that runs the state parks—has plans to build a dam in the park near the location of the original dam. However, the DCNR is getting pressure from environmental groups concerned that the land below the dam could flood, so the project is on hold. A compromise is expected, most likely in the form of a considerably smaller dam.

Swatara Creek from Waterville Bridge.

Despite the fact that Swatara State Park is classified as "undeveloped," there's still plenty to do here. Swatara Creek is a big, brawny creek with hemlocks and deciduous trees growing right up to its banks. There are a number of put-in spots along the way, making the creek an excellent spot to canoe through the picturesque setting. And, best of all, because the park is not well known, there's little chance of the creek being crowded. Canoeists can paddle in virtual solitude.

> **The Geologic Calendar**
> *There are four distinct intervals used to establish the earth's age. The longest intervals are eons, which are subdivided into eras. Each era can be divided into periods, and each period is divided into epochs.*

Anglers can fish Swatara Creek for warm water species like smallmouth bass and panfish. Trout Run is a (stocked) cold-water trout stream that empties into Swatara Creek. There are also a few smaller streams with populations of native brook trout. Non-powered boats are permitted on the creek, as long as they have one of the following permits: a state park launching permit, a state park mooring permit, or a current Pennsylvania boat registration. (There's no park office on-site. The park office is located at Memorial Lake State Park. To get there, take Exit 29 off Interstate 80 and drive north on Pennsylvania 934 for about a mile, following the signs.)

The multi-use trail runs 10 miles, from Lickdale at Exit 30 off Interstate 81 to Exit 30 at Pine Grove. Swatara State Park ends before the trail goes

MilesDirections

0.0 START from the access gate on PA 443 at the intersection with Moonshine Road and abandoned Old State Road.

0.6 Trail turns left.

0.8 Stay to the right at a fork in the trail.

1.1 Turn right onto the paved road.

1.3 Turn left onto the Waterville Bridge and cross over Swatara Creek. On the other side, turn left onto the trail walkway.

1.4 Turn left onto the paved road and walk past the bulletin board. Note the stone ruins on your left. Turn left into an open area alongside Swatara Creek; you'll find more stone ruins on your left.

1.5 Leave the open area and turn left onto the paved road. Note the second ruins on your left. Turn around and walk back toward Waterville Bridge.

1.6 Pass Waterville Bridge on you right.

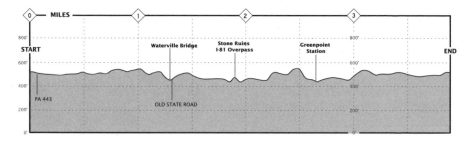

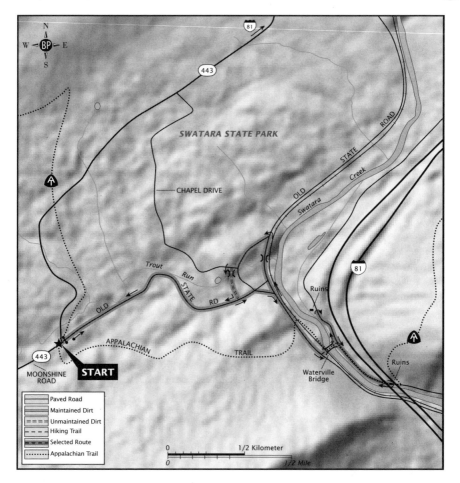

1.9 Arrive at the stone ruins under I-81. Turn around and retrace your steps back to the Waterville Bridge.

2.1 Cross Waterville Bridge and turn right onto the trail.

2.3 Stay to the right at the fork in the trail.

2.4 Pass a woods trail on your right. Pass an intersection with abandoned Old State Road.

2.6 Cross Trout Run on an old concrete bridge.

2.7 Arrive at open area on your right; this is where Greenpoint Station was located. Turn left at the intersection.

3.0 Turn left onto a shale road and cross Trout Run a second time on an old concrete bridge.

3.1 Pass under a power line and turn right onto abandoned Old State Road.

3.9 Arrive back at your vehicle.

An Appalachian Trail signpost on PA 443. Turn left for Maine, right for Georgia.

under Interstate 81, but the trail continues. Here's a popular loop ride within the park: Start at the Waterville Bridge and ride east on the trail for about five miles to Swopes Valley Road; return on the abandoned Old State Road. This route gives riders (or hikers) a chance to visit the Suedberg Fossil Pit, a terrific side trip. (To get to the fossil pit by car, drive east on Pennsylvania 443 about four miles to Swopes Valley Road. Turn right on Swopes Valley Road, cross over Swatara Creek, then turn right on Old State Road (which is a dirt road at this point), and drive about a quarter mile to the pit on your left.)

The fossil pit provides evidence that 375 million years ago—during the Middle Devonian Period of the Paleozoic Era—a shallow ocean covered this area. The fossils found here are casts and molds of marine animals with names like asteroids, trilobites, brachiopods, gastropods, cephalopods, and pelecypods. While a typical fossil is the remains of a prehis-

Did You Know?

- Pennsylvania produces over 30,000 tons of potato chips a year, enough to fill 81 million 12-ounce bags.
- Pennsylvania's hardwood forests are the most productive in the nation, with revenues of $5 billion per year.
- Pennsylvania has spent over $60 million in the past 20 years to rid its forests of gypsy moth and other pests.
- During World War I, 400,000 Pennsylvania coal miners provided 227 million tons of coal a year to defense industries.
- If all the coal still underground in Pennsylvania were piled into a one-square mile area, it would be five miles high.
- Pennsylvania applies 5,640 paint-miles every year when it re-lines the Pennsylvania Turnpike.
- Pennsylvania's population is nearly 12 million. Native Pennsylvanians are more likely to stay in the state where they were born than residents anywhere else in the nation. One-third of Pennsylvania's residents live in rural surroundings, representing the largest non-urban population in the nation.
- Pennsylvania has 225 colleges and universities.
- No matter where you are in the state, you're never more than 25 miles from a state park.
- Pennsylvania has 739,200 acres of lakes, ponds, reservoirs, streams, and rivers. There are 57,000 bridges in Pennsylvania—more than any area on earth its size.

toric plant or an animal buried and preserved in sedimentary rock, here at the Suedberg site the organisms' original shells were buried and dissolved by groundwater, leaving only impressions or molds. Some impressions were filled with new deposits, creating a replica of the shell, or what are called casts. Fossils range in age from the 3.5-billion-year-old blue-green algae cyanobacteria to 10,000-year-old animals from the last ice age.

As for the future of the park, the new dam was to be built about 700 feet upstream from the Waterville Bridge. In preparation for that dam, the roads used on this hike are closed to traffic. If and when the dam is built, the abandoned roads on the north side of Swatara Creek will be underwater. In the meantime, all the roads along this hike (within the park) are closed to traffic, except for DCNR vehicles.

Pennsylvania Symbols

State Dog: *Great Dane*
State Insect: *Firefly*
State Tree: *Hemlock*
State Flower: *Mountain Laurel*
State Fish: *Brook Trout*
State Animal: *White-tailed Deer*
State Bird: *Ruffed Grouse*
State Beverage: *Milk*
State Beautification Plant:
   Crownvetch
State Steam Locomotive:
   K4s Steam
State Electric Locomotive:
   GG1 4859 Electric
State Ship:
   United States Brig Niagara
State Fossil: *Phacops Rana*
State Song: *"Pennsylvania"*

Hike Information

🕔 Trail Contacts:
Swatara State Park, c/o Memorial Lake State Park, Grantville, PA (717) 865–6470

🕐 Schedule:
Open year round

💲 Fees/Permits:
No fees or permits required

❓ Local Information:
Schuylkill County Visitors Bureau, Pottsville, PA (570) 622–7700

💡 Local Events/Attractions:
Bloomsburg Fair, last week in September, Bloomsburg, PA (570) 784–4949

🛏 Accommodations:
Stone House Bed & Breakfast, Schuylkill, PA (570) 385–2115 • **Timber Hill Camping Resort,** Pine Grove, PA (570) 345–2400

🍴 Restaurants:
All American Family Restaurant, Pine Grove, PA (570) 345–4416

🎣 Local Outdoor Retailers:
En-Kay Sporting Goods, Palmyra, PA (717) 838–8324

🗺 Maps:
USGS maps: Indiantown Gap, PA

Honorable Mentions

Southeast Pennsylvania

Compiled here is an index of great hikes in the Southeast region that didn't make the A-list this time around but deserve recognition. Check them out and let us know what you think. You may decide that one or more of these hikes deserves higher status in future editions or, perhaps, you may have a hike of your own that merits some attention.

(A) John Heinz National Wildlife Refuge/Lagoon Loop

Part of the 1,200-acre Tinicum Marsh, the John Heinz National Wildlife Refuge is the largest remaining freshwater tidal wetland in Pennsylvania. The refuge seems wild and remote, yet it's less than a mile from the Philadelphia International Airport and just a few miles from downtown. The hike is an 8.9-mile loop on a wide gravel path that circles the Impound Area. Allow three to four hours or more; there's plenty of wildlife viewing here. (*See Hike 1*)

To get there from Philadelphia, drive south on I-95 to the Bartram Avenue exit. Drive west on Bartram Avenue to 84th Street. Turn right onto 84th Street and drive to Lindbergh Boulevard. Turn left onto Lindbergh Avenue and follow the signs to the John Heinz Visitor Contact Station; park in the lot just beyond the visitor center. For more information call The John Heinz Visitor Contact Station at (215) 365–3118. *DeLorme: Pennsylvania Atlas & Gazetteer:* Page 96 A1

(B) Wissahackon Gorge South Loop

Wissahackon Gorge is located in Fairmount Park in Northwest Philadelphia. (*See Hike 2*) There are two hike options: You can make your hike a 5.5-mile loop by following Forbidden Drive downstream and return-

ing on the trail closest to Wisshackon Creek, or you can do a nine-mile loop that also begins downstream but follows a network of connecting trails that take you farther away from Wissahickon Creek. Either way, you'll see plenty of natural and American history.

To get there from Philadelphia, drive west on I-76 to I-476. Drive north on I-476 to the Germantown Avenue exit. Drive east on Germantown Avenue for 6.1 miles to Springfield Avenue. Turn right onto Springfield Avenue and travel 0.7 miles. Bear right on Valley Green Road and drive 0.4 miles to the parking area on your right. For more information call the Fairmount Park Rangers at (215) 685–2172. *DeLorme: Pennsylvania Atlas & Gazetteer:* Page 82 D2

Ⓒ Ridley Creek State Park

This park is just 16 miles from downtown Philadelphia, but when you explore the colonial setting here, it feels like you're in another country. On this easy five-mile loop hike, you have a chance to visit a circa 1700 Quaker farm, complete with period-dressed interpreters and farm animals. There's a $3 fee for adults and $1.50 for children. There's also the Tyler Arboretum, home to over 1,000 varieties of native and exotic trees and shrubs. This hike is great for seniors and children.

To get there from Media, take U.S. 1 (Media Bypass) to PA 252 (Providence Road) for 2.4 miles. Turn left on Gradyville Road and drive for 1.1 miles. Bear left onto Sandy Flash and drive for 1.5 miles, then turn right, following the signs to Parking Area 15. For more information call Ridley Creek State Park at (610) 892–3900. *DeLorme: Pennsylvania Atlas & Gazetteer:* Page 95 A7

Ⓓ The Shippack Creek Trail

This trail is within the Evansburg State Park in Montgomery County, six miles north of Norristown. The trail is a 5.0-mile loop that runs 2.5 miles along each side of picturesque Shippack Creek. The hike includes a nature trail, visits to the Nature Center and the Friedt Visitor Center, where you can see an herb garden, root cellar, and well—all built by German Mennonites in the early 1700s.

To get there from Allentown, drive south about 20 miles on I-476 and take Exit 30. Drive east on PA 63 to PA 363; turn right on PA 363 and drive 8.5 miles to Germantown Pike. Make a right on Germantown Pike and drive 2.7 miles over Shippack Creek; turn right onto Shippack Creek Road. Continue on Shippack Creek Road to Mill Road and at the Mill Road intersection, get on May Hall Road and follow it into the park. For more information call Evansburg State Park at (610) 409–1150. *DeLorme: Pennsylvania Atlas & Gazetteer:* Page 81 C7

Ⓔ Delaware Canal State Park

This park, in Upper Black Eddy (Bucks County), is one of scores of access points to the 60-mile-long Delaware Canal. Design your own hike and walk alongside the last remaining intact canal system of the great towpath building era of the early and mid-nineteenth century. Examine 23 locks, 10 aqueducts, four river islands, locktenders' houses, spillways, and historical houses. Learn how barges carried 33-million tons of anthracite on the canal.

To get there from Easton, drive south on PA 611 into Bucks County. Continue on PA 611 for about five miles past the county line to PA 32. Turn left onto PA 32 and drive about eight miles to Upper Darby and the park office, which is right at the canal. For more information call the Delaware Canal State Park at (610) 982–5560. *DeLorme: Pennsylvania Atlas & Gazetteer:* Page 68 D3

Ⓕ Jacobsburg State Park

Jacobsburg is situated on the eastern fringes of the Lehigh Valley. There are over 12 miles of hiking trails in the park; loop hikes can be designed to run from four to about 8.5 miles, depending on how energetic you feel that day. There are two highlights: a highly rated environmental center (one of only four) run by the Department of Conservation and Natural Resource, and the Jacobsburg Historical District, which showcases the weapons manufactured here by the Henry family and used in the Revolutionary and Civil Wars.

To get there from Allentown, follow U.S. 22 to PA 33. Drive north on PA 33 to the Belfast exit. Turn left on Henry Road and drive 1.1 miles to Jacobsburg Road, then another 1.2 miles to Belfast Road. Turn left onto Belfast Road and continue for 0.7 miles to the parking area on the right. For more information call Jacobsburg State Park Office, Nazareth, PA at (610) 759–7616. *DeLorme: Pennsylvania Atlas & Gazetteer:* Page 68 B1

Ⓖ French Creek State Park: Red & White Loop

This 6.2-mile loop includes a visit to historic Hopewell Furnace, a once-thriving industrial plantation built on the border of Berks and Chester counties in 1771. Visit a restored iron-maker's village, complete with implements and tools, sheds, furniture, and houses.

To get there from Philadelphia, drive west on U.S. 30 to Exton and PA 100. Head north on PA 100 for 7.8 miles, then drive west on PA 401 for 6.4 miles to PA 345. Go north on PA 345 for 5.6 miles, past the park entrance, to Shed Road and a pull-off parking area on the right. For more information call the French Creek State Park Office at (610) 582–9680. *DeLorme: Pennsylvania Atlas & Gazetteer:* Page 81 C4

Ⓗ Middle Creek Wildlife Area

Middle Creek Wildlife Area is 6,000 acres of state game lands in Lancaster and Lebanon Counties, north of Lititz. The area is a great spot for viewing wildlife in its natural habitat: over 250 bird species have been noted here. There is a network of trails, a lake, picnic area, visitor center, and theatre. A map of the trails and a brochure is available at the visitor center. Suggestion: Visit the MCWA from January to March and you'll see 50,000 or more greater snow geese on their winter migration. (In the winter of 1995–96, 150,000 geese were counted.) These geese are unusually large, weighing up to 30 pounds, with a four- to five-foot wingspan.

To get there from Reading, drive south on U.S. 222 to the U.S. 322 exit near Ephrata. Drive west on U.S. 322 through Ephrata; from downtown Ephrata, continue west on U.S. 322 for 4.3 miles to the village of Clay. In Clay, turn right on North Clay Road at the sign for the Middle Creek Wildlife Management Area. Drive 1.1 miles on North Clay Road and turn right onto Hopeland Road; continue 0.6 miles and turn left onto Kleinfeltersville Road. Drive 2.3 miles on Kleinfeltersville Road to Museum Road and the MCWA. For more information call the Middle Creek Wildlife Management Area at (717) 733–1512. *DeLorme: Pennsylvania Atlas & Gazetteer:* Page 79 C7

Ⓘ Susquehannock State Park

The park overlooks the Lower Susquehanna River in southern Lancaster County. There are just five miles of hiking within this 224 acre-park, but the Bureau of Parks includes this tiny park on its list of the best-kept secrets of Pennsylvania State Park System. Highlights include views of the Susquehanna River, a visit to the Lock No. 12 Historic Area, cliffs, and views of islands that were created by the Conowingo Dam in Maryland.

To get there from Lancaster, drive south on PA 272 for about 12 miles to the PA 372 exit at the village of Buck. Head west on PA 372 for about five miles, then turn left onto Susquehannock Drive and drive for four miles to the Susquehanna State Park sign. Turn right at the sign and continue 0.8 miles to the parking area near the Landis House. For more information call the Gifford Pinchot State Park at (717) 432–5011. *DeLorme: Pennsylvania Atlas & Gazetteer:* Page 93 B7

Northeast
PENNSYLVANIA

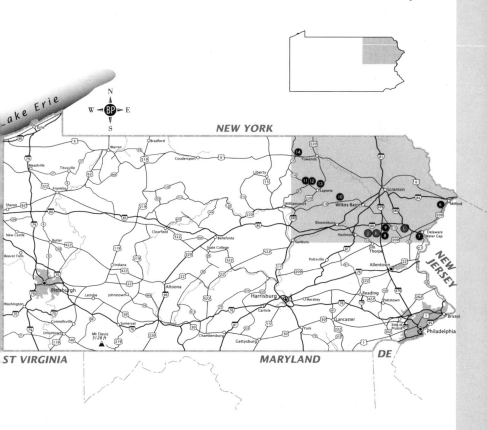

The Hikes

Dingmans Falls **6.**
Mount Minsi **7.**
Hawk Falls **8.**
Hickory Run Boulder Field **9.**
Ricketts Glen **10.**
Canyon Vista **11.**
Worlds End State Park **12.**
Haystacks **13.**
Mount Pisgah State Park **14.**

Honorable Mentions

J. Lehigh Gorge State Park
K. Drake's Creek
L. Big Pocono State Park

Northeast Pennsylvania

L ook at a road map of northeastern Pennsylvania and it looks like any other. Look at topographic maps of the area, however, and you'll see that northeastern Pennsylvania is made up of three different mountain systems. From the south, the first of these is the Pocono Plateau, a section that includes all or part of Pike, Monroe, Wayne, Lackawanna, and Luzerne Counties. Roughly speaking, the plateau is bordered by Interstate 81, from the tiny village of Temaqua (north of Pottsville) to Scranton, Interstate 84 into Pike County, and Pennsylvania 209.

There's not a city or town on the Pocono Plateau with a population over 5,000. The name of the game in this part of the state is tourism—specifically outdoor vacation and recreation sites. The terrain here is mostly rolling hills with lakes, wetlands, and bogs. The Hickory Run Boulder Field—a must-see natural phenomenon (*See Hike 09*)—is here, part of the 15,000-acre Hickory Run State Park.

The Glaciated Low Plateau comprises an odd-shaped section that begins in Monroe County and runs northeast through Pike County to the Delaware River. In the other direction, it cuts north of Scranton into Susquehanna County, then cuts south to northcentral Luzerne County, before it runs snake-like across the Northern tier through Lycoming County, zig-zags into Bradford County, then exits the state in Tioga County. It derives its name from the geologic phenomenon glaciation, which occurs when a glacier melts, or retreats, and changes the topography by creating lakes, bogs, ravines, and in some cases, reversing the flow of water as a result of moraines, created by the debris left behind. Like the Pocono Plateau, this area is not heavily developed: the largest town is Sayre, with a population of less than 10,000. There are plenty of wooded areas, fishing streams, lakes, and creeks—what more could you want?

The Valley and Ridge Province passes through northeastern Pennsylvania as it makes its way northeast to the border. This system runs north and south of the Pocono Plateau; on a map, it looks like a thumb and a forefinger holding the Pocono Plateau in its grip. If all this sounds confusing, it is. Pennsylvania's mountains are difficult to get a grip on. Suffice it to say that the Valley and Ridge Province covers 25 percent of the state, covering all or part of 27 counties, and provides some of the most dramatic views, waterfalls, and plunging ravines around.

The biggest thing going in northeastern Pennsylvania, however, is the Delaware Gap National Recreation Area, a 70,000-acre recreation paradise that runs for 40 miles on both the Pennsylvania and the New Jersey sides of the Delaware River. It hosts over four million visitors a year, and there's everything here from canoe-camping to rock climbing to mountain biking, and of course—our favorite—hiking.

Overview

Dingmans Falls

This is a fun hike and a great place to be on a hot summer day. Wooden walkways, steps, and a series of wooden footbridges lead through the bottom of a deep hemlock ravine to two dramatic and distinctly different waterfalls, where the mist and the shade from the hemlocks cool the air. Follow a trail that parallels Dingmans Creek to another spot with three more dramatic waterfalls, old factory ruins, and a picnic area. *(See page 48)*

Mount Minsi

This a bold hike that uses a stretch of the Appalachian Trail (AT) as it weaves along the ridge of the Delaware Water Gap, at one point taking hikers to an overlook 1,000 feet above the Delaware River. This is one of the most—if not the most—rugged section of the AT in Pennsylvania. There are heart-stopping views of the Delaware Water Gap, the Delaware River, and the Interstate 80 bridge across the Delaware. From the summit, look across the Gap to Mount Tammany and Kittatinny Ridge in neighboring New Jersey. *(See page 52)*

Hawk Falls

The highlight of this hike is the spectacular and unusual Hawk Falls. The falls occur when Hawk Run, which is 40 feet above Mud Run, empties into the lower creek at a three-sided canyon. The water cascades down the center of the canyon, ever widening, from one ledge to the next and empties into a deep pool of crystal-clear water.

The trail passes through a huge rhododendron tunnel to the magnificent Mud Run Natural Area in the bottom of Mud Run Gorge. The trail turns downstream and runs alongside Mud Run, one of the top trout streams in the state. There are plenty of streamside boulders and smaller waterfalls along the way. *(See page 58)*

45

Hickory Run Boulder Field

This hike is designed to give hikers a chance to explore the Hickory Run Boulder Field Natural Area, a 16-acre, 12-foot-deep phenomenon created during the last ice age. The Boulder Field—the only geological formation of this type in the East—has been studied by scientists for over 100 years; the core of their studies is displayed on bulletin boards in the on-site educational area. *(See page 62)*

Ricketts Glen

Here's the bottom line: Ricketts Glen is the best hike in Pennsylvania. It may also be one of the top hikes in the East. There are 22 named waterfalls, and the tallest, Ganoga Falls, is 94 feet. The other 21 falls range from 15 to 49 feet, plus, there are a dozen or more waterfalls that are unnamed. At the center of the hike is Kitchen Creek, a torrential mountain stream that drops 1,000 feet down the face of the Allegheny Front.

Starting at the bottom of the ravine, the trail runs a short ways then it's up one branch of Kitchen Creek, a mile across the top, then down the other. The man-made pathway is stone steps, ledges, and wooden bridges, made of timbers the size of telephone poles. On your way through the bottom of the ravine, you pass through Glens Natural Area, where there is exotic flora growing beneath 500-year-old hemlocks, pines, and oaks. *(See page 66)*

Canyon Vista

This hike provides one of the premier vistas in the state, but you do have to work for it—the climb to the summit is over one mile. The Rock Garden is a boondoggler's delight, as you make your way over and around the huge sandstone boulders. *(See page 72)*

Worlds End State Park

The trail on this hike runs alongside Loyalsock Creek, where hikers can do a low-grade boondoggle among the boulders. From there, it's a challenging climb up out of the gorge, through a boulder field to a 30-foot waterfall, followed by a steep hand-over-hand climb across a talus slope. The next section is a short—but precarious—walk along the edge of the ridge to an impressive overlook. *(See page 76)*

Haystacks

This is an easy, pleasant hike along Loyalsock Creek to the Haystacks boulders area and Dutchman Falls. At the falls, you can explore the site where the falls empties into the creek. With its deep, hemlock-shaded valleys and plenty of pine needles covering the ground, this area could justly be described as picturesque. *(See page 82)*

Mount Pisgah State Park

If you do this hike in summer, be sure to take your camera and plenty of water. There are plenty of steep, Ironman-type ascents, the last of which lands you at the top of Mount Pisgah for an impressive view of the surrounding valley. As for photo ops, the trail passes through a number of wildflower meadows bursting with the vibrant colors of nature in bloom. These meadows are not only breathtakingly beautiful, they'll also

provide an excuse for the much-needed rest after the climb. *(See page 86)*

6

Dingmans Falls

Hike Specs

Start: From the Dingmans Falls Visitors Center parking lot
Length: 5.0-mile out-and-back
Approximate Hiking Time: 3 hours
Difficulty Rating: Easy. The trail is mostly level, with a short climb out of a ravine.
Terrain: Follow a mountain stream through a hemlock ravine to explore five distinctly different waterfalls. The trail itself is a combination of wooden walkways, wooden steps, and pine needle paths.
Elevation Gain: 558 feet
Land Status: National recreation area
Nearest Town: Milford, PA
Other Trail Users: Tourists
Canine Compatibility: Leashed dogs permitted

Getting There

From Wilkes-Barre: Drive south on PA 9 and get on I-80 heading east toward Stroudsburg. From I-80 take Exit 52 and drive north on PA 209 for four miles to the intersection of Business PA 209 and PA 209. Turn right at the stoplight to stay on PA 209. Drive north on PA 209 for 20 miles and turn left onto Johnny Bee Road, then turn right at the sign for Dingmans Falls. *DeLorme: Pennsylvania Atlas & Gazetteer:* Page 55 C5

This hike is located within the Delaware Water Gap National Recreation Area, a 70,000-acre watershed atop the Pocono Plateau that stretches for forty miles on both the Pennsylvania and New Jersey sides of the Delaware River. The trail begins on a wooden walkway that takes you to the foot of Silver Thread Falls, where water from a tributary to Dingmans Creek drops 80 feet through a narrow shale crevasse, cascading over a series of ledges.

At Dingmans Falls, rushing waters leap from one shale ledge to the next, creating a dramatic 130-foot drop. The walkway leads to a viewing platform at the base of the falls. From the viewing platform there are steps, which take you to a higher viewing ledge, then on to a rock outcrop above the falls. For the non-hikers, this is the end of the tour. There are three more falls to visit, but they can return to their cars and drive to the upper falls area.

Our hike continues with a short climb into the forest on a well-worn, root-covered path beside the rock outcrop above Dingmans Falls. From this point, the trail essentially follows the creek-side through a hemlock ravine for two miles to our destination, the George Childs Recreation Area.

As you walk through the ravine, it's easy to see why the Eastern hemlock is Pennsylvania's state tree. With its shallow root system, the hemlock can grow just about anywhere. In fact, it thrives in damp ravines. (And, as experienced hikers know, you can't walk a mile in any direction in Pennsylvania's mountains without running into a ravine.) Native Americans and early settlers ground hemlock bark into a powder that was used to stop bleeding. They made tea from hemlock bark and used it as a remedy for sore gums and other ailments. Tannin from the hemlock bark was used in tanning leather.

Check out the hemlocks for round or oblong holes; this is the work of the pileated woodpecker. At a foot and a half long, it's the largest woodpecker in North America and easy to spot: it has black and white neck stripes and a flaming red crest on its head. And although hikers may not see one, naturalists have observed the short-tailed shrew in the ravine. These gray, mole-like rodents tend to be about four inches long with an inch-long tail. Their diet consists of worms, insects, snails, amphibians, and mice.

Hike Information

● Trail Contacts:
Delaware Gap National Recreation Area, Bushkill Falls, PA (570) 588–2451 or *www.nps.gov/dewa*

● Schedule:
Open year round

● Fees/Permits:
No fees or permits required

● Local Information:
Pocono Mountains Vacation Bureau, Stroudsburg, PA (570) 421–5791 or 1–800–762–6667 or *www.800poconos.com*

● Local Events/Attractions:
Bushkill Falls, Bushkill, PA (570) 588–6682 • **Delaware State Forest** (570) 895–4000 – *over 30 miles of mountain biking trails*

● Accommodations:
Graerock Bed & Breakfast, Milford, PA (570) 296–7273 • **Ken's Woods Campground,** Bushkill, PA (570) 588–6381

● Restaurants:
Waterwheel Café & Bakery, Milford, PA (570) 296–2383

● Local Outdoor Retailers:
Sportsmen's Rendezvous, Milford, PA (570) 296–6113

● Maps:
USGS maps: Lake Maskenozha, PA

Hikers may not see a black bear either (many life-long outdoorsmen have never seen one in the wild), but they're alive and well in the Delaware Gap National Recreation Area. These opportunistic feeders—which are primarily nocturnal—tend to raid campers' and picnickers' food stashes and garbage. Although it'd be hard to mistake one for just about anything else, the adult black bears in Pennsylvania are anywhere from 50 to 85 inches long and stand about 30 inches at the shoulder. Weights for adults range

MilesDirections

0.0 START at the gravel path from the parking lot. Walk past the information booth. Cross Dingmans Creek on a wooden footbridge and continue on the wooden walkway to Silver Thread Falls.

0.2 Stay on the walkway. Cross Dingmans Creek on a second bridge.

0.3 Arrive at Dingmans Falls. Walk to the viewing platform. Retrace your steps and turn right onto the wooden steps.

0.5 Cross Dingmans Creek on a wooden bridge.

0.6 Arrive above Dingmans Falls at the fenced viewing area and educational plaque. This is the end of the walkway at this section. Turn left onto a worn path and climb uphill over the roots. Enter a forest of hemlock and rhododendron.

0.7 Cross Doodle Hollow Road. Note the blocked bridge on your right. Continue on the south side of the creek.

1.4 An abandoned railroad grade comes in from your left and merges with the trail. The trail turns right.

1.6 Cross the paved SR 20001.

1.7 The trail becomes an abandoned logging road. Turn right onto an earthen mound and walk to the creek. Turn left at the creek.

2.0 Cross a pipeline swath.

2.1 Cross a wooden bridge over Dingmans Creek and arrive at Deer Leap Falls. Walk through the picnic area and turn left onto the wooden steps.

2.2 Pass a set of steps on your right. Turn left onto a bridge above Dear Leap Falls.

2.3 Turn right onto the wooden walkway.

2.4 Cross the creek on a wooden bridge at Fulmer Falls. Turn left and walk through the picnic area to Factory Falls.

2.5 Arrive at Factory Falls. View the falls and retrace your steps.

5.0 Arrive back at the parking lot and your vehicle.

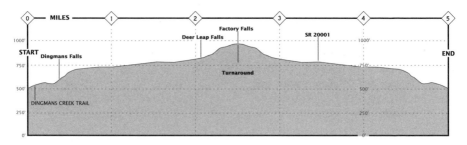

from 140 to 400 pounds, with rare individuals weighing 800 pounds. They walk in a shuffling, flat-footed manner and while most are black with a tan muzzle and white mark on their chests, a few are cinnamon-colored.

Statewide, the black bear population is estimated between 8,000 and 9,000. To control the population, there's a three-day hunting season, monitored by the Pennsylvania Game Commission, in late November. In 1998 the harvest was 2,598; in 1999 it was 1,740; and in 2000 it was a record-setting 3,070. Here in Pike County, 170 bears were harvested in 2000.

Along this section, the trail is a pleasant stroll through open woods. At times you'll have to climb out of the ravine, away from the stream, but these jaunts are short. Most of the time, you walk beside the creek until you reach the Childs Recreation Area, where once again you'll find yourself in a somewhat touristy area. There is a network of walkways and wooden steps,

complete with viewing platforms that lead from the parking lot to the picnic area and to the falls.

There are three falls here: Deer Leap, Fulmer, and Factory, one right above the other, and each uniquely different from the others. There's also a stone ruin, a reminder that the waters from Dingmans Creek have run a number of mills throughout the years.

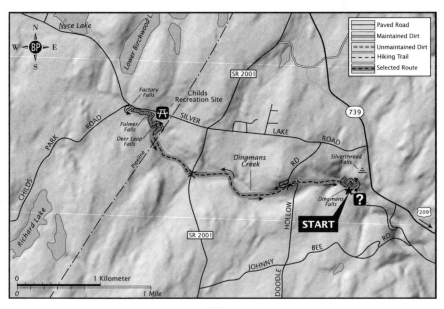

Mount Minsi

Hike Specs

Start: From the parking lot for Lake Lenape

Length: 4.9-mile loop

Approximate Hiking Time: 3 hours

Difficulty Rating: Moderate, due to plenty of climbing over boulders and a rocky trail

Terrain: Follow a typical mountain footpath over rocks and through outcroppings; climb along the rocky edge of a water gap for impressive views.

Elevation Gain: 1,221 feet

Land Status: National recreation area

Nearest Town: Stroudsburg, PA

Other Trail Users: Backpackers

Canine Compatibility: Leashed dogs permitted

Getting There

From Scranton: Drive south on I-380 and connect with I-80, heading east toward Stroudsburg. Take Exit 53 and drive south on PA 611 for 0.6 miles to the stoplight in the town of Delaware Water Gap. At the stoplight, turn left onto PA 611 South. Drive 0.3 miles and turn right onto Mountain Road. Drive 0.1 miles and turn left at the fork in the road and drive to the Lake Lenape parking lot. **DeLorme: Pennsylvania Atlas & Gazetteer:** Page 68 A2

> *Note: Most hikers want to get away from traffic and noise. On this hike you will. You're high enough that even though you can see the traffic, you can't hear it.*

The town of Delaware Water Gap has the air of an alpine skiing village. The town is small and its outskirts look like any other small Pennsylvania town, but as soon as you reach the downtown area, you get the feeling something outdoorsy is happening around the place.

Something is happening: the Appalachian Trail passes through town. You get the feeling that residents are used to seeing weary hikers plodding into their town for a little R&R. One café on the main street sums up the feeling with its name, the Trails End Café.

The town of Delaware Water Gap is also the southern terminus of the Delaware Water Gap National Recreation Area, a 70,000-acre recreation paradise that runs for 40 miles on both the Pennsylvania and the New Jersey sides of the Delaware River, and hosts over four million visitors a year.

At the center of all this activity is the Delaware River. Even though it's just the 25th largest river in the country, its importance cannot be overstated. Despite its relative size, the Delaware provides ten percent of the nation's population with water. And even more remarkable, its water is clean and it's one of the few remaining free-flowing rivers in the country. To recognize this small miracle, this section of the Delaware has been designated a Middle Delaware Scenic and Recreation River and a National Scenic River.

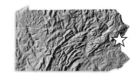

One of the popular activities here is river camping, which, for those unfamiliar with it, involves canoeing a stretch of the river, stopping for the night at one of the many riverside campsites along the way. Within the park boundaries, the river is a series of shallow riffles and quiet pools, with no difficult rapids. There are access points every eight to 10 miles, which allow for easy day trips, or boaters can camp (for one night only) in one of the primitive campsites along the river. Tubing and rafting are allowed as well. There are a number of local liveries that rent tubes, rafts, and canoes, and have a launch and pickup service.

Boulders along the Appalachian Trail on Mount Minsi.

53

Whether it's a leisurely sightseeing tour along the Delaware or a more aggressive ride on a mountain bike, there are a number of bicycle trails inside and outside the park. The longest touring route is the Old Mine Road, which is on the New Jersey side and runs the length of the park. Mountain bike riders can check out the Zion Church Road for a ride past Hidden Lake and the historic Zion Church and cemetery.

There are over 20 ice climbs and 200 rock-climbing sites in the park, ranging in level from novice to advanced. Climbers don't have to register with the park, but park officials recommend that climbers tell a friend where they intend to climb, and leave them the park's 24-hour emergency number (1–800–543–4295).

MilesDirections

0.0 START at the parking lot. Walk to the iron access gate across the Mount Minsi Fire Road and the trailhead bulletin board. Turn left onto a paved path and follow the white blazes of the Appalachian Trail.

0.1 Cross the breast of Lake Lenape. Start an uphill climb.

0.2 Note the massive boulder cliffs on your right.

0.3 Turn left at the double white blazes. Note the blazes are on a tree on your right. Stay to the left at the fork in the trail.

0.4 Arrive at the first outcropping for a view of I-80.

0.5 Come to an outcropping with a sign that reads "Council Rock."

1.1 Cross a stream with a sign "Eureka Creek."

1.2 Turn right at the View Trail sign.

1.9 Reach a flat area. Turn left onto the Mount Minsi Fire Road for 50 feet then turn right onto the white-blazed Appalachian Trail.

2.2 Reach the summit of Mount Minsi. Retrace your steps back to the Mount Minsi Fire Road.

2.5 Turn right onto the Mount Minsi Fire Road. Begin descent.

2.6 Pass the Appalachian Trail on your left, then again on your right. Continue straight on the fire road.

4.6 Pass the Appalachian Trail on your right.

4.8 Arrive at Lake Lenape.

4.9 Arrive back at the parking lot and your vehicle.

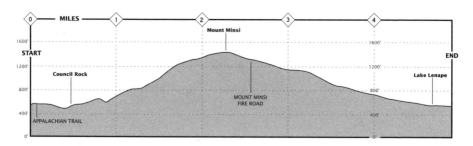

This hike starts at the trailhead for the Appalachian Trail, just a few blocks south of town at the parking lot of tiny Lake Lenape. This is a popular spot for tourists and locals, so when you start out, you get the feeling that the trail will be crowded. But as soon as you begin the first serious climb, you realize that your fellow hikers have opted to stay low. It's just you and the boulders, proving once again what all serious hikers have always known: When the air gets thin, so does the crowd.

Just a half-mile into the hike you'll get your first vista. Standing on an outcrop, you can see the cars and 18-wheelers whizzing along Interstate 80. Interestingly, while you can see the traffic, you won't hear it. There are not only no crowds this high up, but there is no traffic noise either. As you climb higher and higher up the rocky cliff edge of Mount Minsi, each time you stop for a view, the trucks and cars get smaller and smaller, until when you reach the summit, the vehicles are indistinguishable from the roadway.

After hugging the cliff edge for a mile, you turn onto the View Trail. From this point, the trail cuts away from the rim and into the forest for your

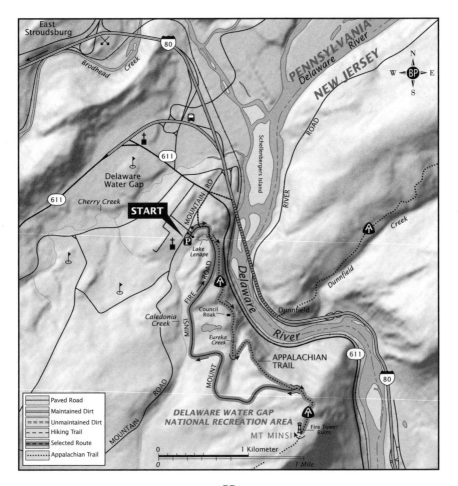

View from Mount Minsi of I-80 crossing the Delaware River.

last, short climb to the summit of Mount Minsi, a flat open area where a fire tower once stood. All that remains of the tower is a set of stone steps and the concrete pylons where the tower legs were anchored into the earth. When you feel the force of the wind as it whips up out of the gap, you get an idea of what it must have been like in that tower. But like all the other fire towers in the state, this one was shut down when the Forest Service began using small airplanes to monitor forest fires.

It's lonely at the top. There's not much else up here but the wind and a fenced-in microwave tower, hanging on the edge of the cliff. There's a grove of table mountain pine trees. And in one of them there's a sign that says Mount Minsi.

Hike Information

● Trail Contacts:
Delaware Gap National Recreation Area, Bushkill Falls, PA (570) 588–2451 or *www.nps.gov/dewa* • **Kittatinny Mountain Bike Association,** Flanders, NJ (973) 584–2210 or *www.nps.gov/dewa/expbike.html*

● Schedule:
Open year round

● Fees/Permits:
No fees or permits required

● Local Information:
Pocono Mountains Vacation Bureau, Stroudsburg, PA (570) 421–5791 or 1–800–762–6667 or *www.800poconos.com*

● Local Events/Attractions:
Water Gap Trolley, Delaware Water Gap, PA (570) 476–9766 – *tour points of interest on antique-style trolley* • **Quiet Valley Living Historical Farm,** Stroudsburg, PA (570) 992–6161

● Accommodations:
Shepard House Bed & Breakfast, Stroudsburg, PA (570) 424–9779 • **Mountain Vista Campground,** Stroudsburg, PA (570) 223–0111

● Restaurants:
Trails End Café, Delaware Water Gap, PA (570) 421–1928

● Local Outdoor Retailers:
Ramsey Outdoor Store, Ledgewood, NJ (973) 584–7799

● Maps:
USGS maps: Stroudsburg, PA

8

Hawk Falls

Hike Specs

Start: From the Hawk Falls Trail trailhead parking lot on the south side of PA 534 just east of I-476

Length: 3.1-mile loop

Approximate Hiking Time: 2.5 hours

Difficulty Rating: Easy, due to mostly level trail with one short switchback climb

Terrain: This hike follows paved and forest roads through delightful rhododendron tunnels and alongside a rushing mountain stream to visit a unique waterfall.

Elevation Gain: 424 feet

Land Status: State park

Nearest Town: Wilkes-Barre, PA

Other Trail Users: Tourists, campers, and anglers

Canine Compatibility: Leashed dogs permitted

Getting There

From Wilkes-Barre: Drive south on PA 9 to I-80. Get on I-80 heading west and take Exit 41. Drive south on PA 534 for 1.8 miles to the town of Lehigh Tannery. Turn left at the stop sign in town and drive east on PA 534 into Hickory Creek State Park. Drive past the park office and continue about four miles until you pass under I-476. Park on your right immediately after passing under I-476. *DeLorme: Pennsylvania Atlas & Gazetteer:* Page 53 D5

> **Note:** At Hawk Falls, hikers can see the Interstate 476 bridge that spans Mud Run Gorge, but the bridge is high enough and far enough away that there's no traffic noise at the falls.

There are two misnomers on this hike. First off, the waters of Mud Run are astonishingly clear. Secondly, you won't see any hawks or other raptors diving for fish at Hawk Falls. The creek and the falls are named after the Hawk family that once owned the property on which the eponymous creek and falls are located.

Of the 22 hikes in the 15,500-acre Hickory Run State Park, Hawk Falls is the most popular with both locals and tourists. The majority of these hikers take the direct route from the parking lot, across Hawk Run, and on to the falls. Some may wander upstream along Mud Run for a ways, then return the way they came. Fishermen, on the other hand, generally drive through the campground and park at the parking lot just before the closed access gate. (This way they only have to carry their gear about a half-mile.)

But fishermen and tourists miss the pine forest and thriving rhododendron tunnels. Rhododendron, some as tall as 15 feet, line both sides of the forest road that leads into a pristine forest of pines, beech, maple, and oak to Mud Run. Mud Run is popular with fly fishermen angling for a chance to hook a native trout or a brook trout. If you do this hike in fishing season,

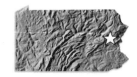

Hike Information

📞 Trail Contacts:
Hickory Run State Park, White Haven, PA (570) 443–0400

🕐 Schedule:
Open year round

💲 Fees/Permits:
No fees or permits required

❓ Local Information:
Carbon County Tourist Promotion Agency, Jim Thorpe, PA (570) 325–3673

💡 Local Events/Attractions:
Steamtown National Historic Site, Scranton, PA: 1–888–693–9391 • **Electric City Trolley Station & Museum,** Scranton, PA: 1–888–229–3526

🛏 Accommodations:
Harry Packer Mansion Inn, Jim Thorpe, PA (570) 325–8566 • **Hickory Run State Park Campgrounds,** White Haven, PA (570) 443–0400

🍴 Restaurants:
Black Bread Café, Jim Thorpe, PA (570) 325–8957

🏬 Local Outdoor Retailers:
National Sporting Goods, Scranton, PA (570) 343–3970

🗺 Maps:
USGS maps: Blakeslee, PA; Hickory Run, PA

you'll almost certainly be able to watch a fly fisherman in waist-high boots wading into the stream and flicking his line about. He's aiming toward one of the deep, shaded pools where he's convinced an enormous, cagey old trout is just waiting to take his bait.

There is one short switchback climb out of the steepest section of the ravine. Once you make the summit, the yellow-blazed trail divides: One branch continues across the plateau; the other turns left. You must take the branch that turns left to descend the ravine and make your way back to Mud Run. Look for a sheared-off stump that is taller than you, with a yellow

MilesDirections

0.0 START at the trailhead parking lot on PA 534. Walk east alongside PA 534.

0.1 Hawk Run passes under PA 534. Note the small dam on your left.

0.4 Turn right at the Organized Group Camping sign onto the forest road. Follow the yellow blazes.

0.5 Pass bathrooms on your right.

0.6 Pass water hand pump on your left.

0.7 Pass a second bathroom on your right.

1.0 Come to an access gate across the road.

1.4 Pass an unmarked footpath on your right.

1.5 Turn right into a rhododendron tunnel.

1.6 Arrive at Mud Run and turn right.

2.0 The trail turns right to climb out of the ravine.

2.2 Trail turns left at the edge of the plateau. Turn left and begin your descent back down the ravine to Mud Run. Look for the yellow blaze on a large stump. (Note, another set of yellow blazes for the Orchard Trail continues across the plateau.)

2.5 Arrive at a trail intersection. Turn left and follow Mud Run to Hawk Falls.

2.6 Arrive at Hawk Falls. Retrace your steps back to the trail intersection.

2.7 Arrive at the trail intersection. Continue straight.

2.8 Turn left on a short side trail to an overlook above Hawk Falls. Retrace your steps back to the trail and turn left.

2.9 Ford across Hawk Run.

3.1 Arrive at PA 534 and turn right to the parking lot and your vehicle.

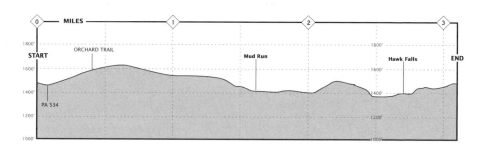

blaze. Back at the creek, it's a short side trek to Hawk Falls, at the juncture where Hawk Run empties into Mud Run, which continues west until it empties into the Lehigh River.

Aside from the wonders of nature, hikers on this trail can marvel at the wonders of man's ingenuity. When you're at Hawk Falls, you are almost directly under the Interstate 476 bridge that spans this gorge. From this vantage point, you have a clear view of the underside of the bridge, which is high enough and far enough away that there is no traffic noise in the gorge.

After visiting the falls, the trail takes you out of the ravine bottom and on to a very short side trail where you can view Hawk Falls from above. From there, the trail continues to Hawk Run, where, depending on the water level, you can either ford the creek on exposed rocks or simply wade through it.

Wet feet or not, you are soon back to Pennsylvania 534 where you turn right to your vehicle.

In contrast to its name, the waters of Mud Run are quite clear.

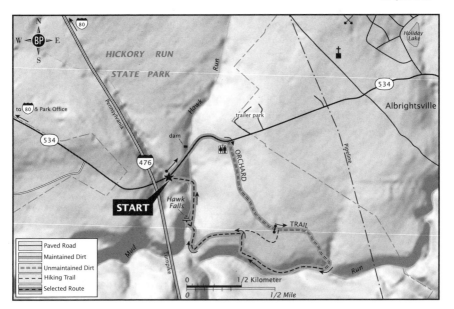

Hickory Run Boulder Field

Hike Specs

Start: From the Boulder Field Trailhead parking lot on the north side of PA 534 just east of I-476

Length: 7.0-mile out-and-back

Approximate Hiking Time: 3 hours

Difficulty Rating: Easy, due to a level trail

Terrain: This hike follows a meadow path and abandoned forest roads through a pine forest to the Hickory Run Boulder Field, the only natural phenomenon of this type east of the Mississippi.

Elevation Gain: 550 feet

Land Status: State park

Nearest Town: Wilkes-Barre, PA

Other Trail Users: Tourists and hunters (in season)

Canine Compatibility: Leashed dogs permitted

Getting There

From Wilkes-Barre: Drive south on PA 9 to I-80. Get on I-80 heading west and take Exit 41. Drive south on PA 534 for 1.8 miles to the town of Lehigh Tannery. Turn left at the stop sign in town and drive east on PA 534 into Hickory Creek State Park. Drive past the park office and continue about four miles until you pass under I-476. Park on your left immediately after passing under I-476. *DeLorme: Pennsylvania Atlas & Gazetteer:* Page 53 D5

At 15,500 acres, Hickory Run State Park is one of Pennsylvania's largest state parks. It's also one of the most picturesque. Its forests are a mixture of second-growth white pine and hemlock, mixed oak, and northern hardwoods. Sand Spring Lake, the largest of the four dams in the park, has a swimming beach. Two clear mountain streams, Sand Run and Hickory Run, intersect in the center of the park, at the site where a booming 19th-century logging mill and village once stood. A few of the village buildings remain and are used by the park service; one is the park office. From March to November, park environmental education specialists can help you fully appreciate the natural beauty of the park through their hands-on activities, guided walks, and presentations on natural and historical resources.

For hikers, there's a 40-mile network of well-maintained trails leading through dense mountain laurel and rhododendron patches, along the pristine streams to dams and rustic spillways, and through to scenic areas like the Shades of Death Trail. (Early settlers named the trail because the dense forests of virgin white pine and hemlock were so thick they blocked the sun from reaching the forest floor.) But for many, the major attraction in

Hickory Run State Park is the Hickory Run Boulder Field, a geological formation of boulders created during the Pleistocene Epoch or, as it's commonly referred to, the last ice age.

Scientists who have studied the Boulder Field believe it was created 15,000 years ago as a result of the same glacial activity that created the Great Lakes in North America. During the Pleistocene Epoch, huge ice sheets covered most of the earth. [Referring to the last and most recent ice age, the term Pleistocene Epoch is, quite logically, derived from the Greek words *pleistos* (most) and *kainos* (recent). That "recent" thing is a relative term, though: The Pleistocene Epoch lasted from about 1.6 million to 10,000 BC.] In North America, the latest ice sheet—the Wisconsin—stretched across most of the northern United

Hike Information

● Trail Contacts:
Hickory Run State Park, White Haven, PA (570) 443–0400

● Schedule:
Open year round

● Fees/Permits:
No fees or permits required

● Local Information:
Carbon County Tourist Promotion Agency, Jim Thorpe, PA (570) 325–3673

● Local Events/Attractions:
The Mauch Chunk Museum & Cultural Center, Jim Thorpe, PA (570) 325–9190 • **Rail Tours, Inc.,** Jim Thorpe, PA (570) 325–4606

● Accommodations:
Blueberry Mountain Inn Bed & Breakfast, Blakeslee, PA (570) 646–7144 • **Hickory Run State Park Campgrounds,** White Haven, PA (570) 443–0400

● Restaurants:
Bagel Gourmet, Albrightsville, PA (570) 722–3600

● Local Outdoor Retailers:
Soccer Mania, Wilkes-Barre, PA (570) 821–0848

● Maps:
USGS maps: Blakeslee, PA; Hickory Run, PA

States, creating a climate similar to that of Greenland. This ice sheet reached its southernmost point in northeastern Pennsylvania, about one mile north and one mile east of the Boulder Field.

When the sheet retreated (melted), it left behind a moraine—an accumulation of boulders, stones, and debris. Meltwater from the glacier produced a freeze-thaw cycle that heaved the earth and split the caprocks. This action, repeated over thousands of years, carried the rocks and boulders farther and farther downslope, until the cycle stopped 15,000 years ago. The boulders' rough edges were rounded as they shifted. The resulting fine gravel, clay, and sand deposited around the boulder were washed away by glacial meltwater. Because there is no soil around the boulders, the field is more or less devoid of vegetation. But with every passing year, the red maple, alder, hemlock, and spruce that surround the field drop their foliage and contribute to humus capable of supporting small plants and trees.

The boulders, which are red sandstones at the north end and red conglomerates with white quartz pebbles in the south end, vary in size from four to 25 feet in length. The field is 400 feet wide on an east-west axis and 1,800 feet long north to south. It's remarkably level and at least 12 feet deep. There are holes, what geologists call reliefs, that look as though someone had fashioned the holes around giant bowls.

The hike to and from the field itself is a pleasant walk through a pine forest. At a little over a mile and a half, you'll cross the Stage Trail, originally the stage coach route that ran from Bethlehem to Wilkes-Barre and stopped at the once bustling sawmill town of Saylorsville, just north of the center of the park.

MilesDirections

0.0 START at the trailhead parking lot on the north side of PA 534. Walk to the trail sign and a set of wooden steps, then on to a path through an open field.

0.1 Come to the Boulder Field Trail sign. Follow the yellow blazes.

0.8 Cross a washout stream.

1.7 Cross the Stage Trail.

3.4 Arrive at the boulder field. Walk across the field to the educational bulletin boards.

3.5 Arrive at the bulletin boards. Retrace your steps back to the trailhead.

5.3 Cross the Stage Trail.

7.0 Arrive at the parking lot and your vehicle.

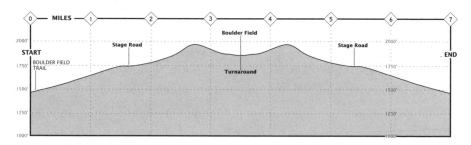

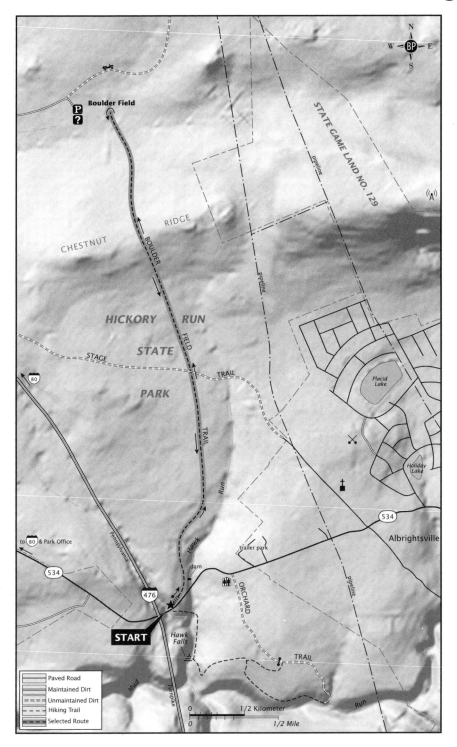

Boulder Field

STATE GAME LAND NO. 129

RIDGE

CHESTNUT

BOULDER

HICKORY RUN

STATE FIELD

PARK

STAGE TRAIL

80

TRAIL

Run

Placid Lake

Holiday Lake

534

Albrightsville

to 80 & Park Office

534

Pennsylvania

Hawk

trailer park

ORCHARD

476

dam

START

Hawk Falls

TRAIL

Mud

Turnpike

Run

pipeline

| Paved Road |
| Maintained Dirt |
| Unmaintained Dirt |
| Hiking Trail |
| Selected Route |

0   1/2 Kilometer

0   1/2 Mile

65

Ricketts Glen

Hike Specs

Start: From the Ricketts Glen Natural Area parking lot on PA 118
Length: 7.1-mile loop
Approximate Hiking Time: 5 hours
Difficulty Rating: Moderate, due to the extensive, steep climb and stone steps
Terrain: Follow a well-worn forest path, shale walkways, and dirt roads through a natural area of 500-year-old trees; walk alongside a raging mountain stream past 22 named waterfalls.
Elevation Gain: 1,081 feet
Land Status: State park
Nearest Town: Williamsport, PA
Other Trail Users: Tourists
Canine Compatibility: Leashed dogs permitted

Getting There

From Williamsport: Drive east on I-180/U.S. 220 approximately 15 miles and take the U.S. 220 exit. Continue on U.S. 220 about 10 miles to Beech Glen and the intersection with PA 42. Turn right onto PA 42 South and drive 4.5 miles to PA 239. Continue on PA 239 for 5.1 miles to PA 118 East. Continue on PA 118 for 12 miles, past the village of Red Rock and past the (first) Ricketts Glen State Park sign. Continue 2.3 miles on PA 118 to the Ricketts Glen sign and parking lot on your right.
DeLorme: Pennsylvania Atlas & Gazetteer: Page 51 B7

> **Note:** *Regardless of the season, the stone steps can be wet and slippery. Hiking boots with good tread are strongly advised. The weather in the ravine can change abruptly—usually to a cold rain—so foul-weather gear is also recommended. On the plus side, take your swimming suit: there are shallow pools where hikers can walk under the falls.*
>
> *Because of the heights and the slippery stones and (sometimes) muddy and slippery walkway, this hike is not recommended for children or those who are not physically fit.*

At Ricketts Glen, history meets geology, and the result is a truly unique hike. This is not only the most magnificent hike in the state, but it ranks up there with the top hikes in the East.

This hike has everything: It is a National Natural History Area, with trees estimated to be up to 900 years old. There are breathtaking waterfalls, pristine settings boasting unique flora and fauna, and mammoth trees strewn along the trail and across the creeks. Here at Ricketts Glen, even the drainage streams that pour into Kitchen Creek produce picture-postcard waterfalls.

The majesty of 22 waterfalls, ranging in height from 15 to 94 feet, makes this hike one of the top hikes in the state.

67

Ricketts Glen State Park encompasses 13,050 acres along the Allegheny Front in Sullivan, Colombia, and Luzerne Counties. It's named after Colonel Robert Bruce Ricketts, a veteran of the Civil War who enlisted in the army as a private, and after leading a battery of men at Gettysburg was awarded the rank of colonel upon his discharge. But Ricketts's greatest impact on this area was as a businessman, not a colonel. When the railroad reached the area, Ricketts began a major logging industry, at one point employing over 1,000 men. To more easily move the massive logs, two lakes were built on the plateau above the glen; Lake Jean and Mountain Stream Lake still exist today. The 245-acre Lake Jean is used for recreation and fishing. The Pennsylvania Fish & Boat Commission owns Mountain Stream Lake and the land around it. It too is open for fishing.

Kettle Creek drains Lake Jean and drops 1,000 feet down the ravine. A little over halfway down, it's joined by its eastern branch, which drains the other side of the ravine. Together, they form the "Y" around which the hike is formed. You'll hike uphill along one branch, then downhill along the other.

The Glens Area is remote, and is believed by scholars to be just as it was when Europeans first came to America; this remoteness has yielded an ecosystem free of introduced species. The glen is home to a wide variety of mosses and lichens, false nettle (also called bog hemp), ferns, and wild sarsaparilla—a member of the ginseng family. Throughout this forest, there are 100-foot tall hemlock and oaks boasting five-foot diameters, as well as birch, ash, and striped maple. The trail itself is over 100 years old; workers employed by Ricketts built it to make a path along the falls. The trail is mostly placed stone steps, which, because of the spray of the falls, can be wet and muddy even on a sunny day.

The forces of nature are hard at work in the glen. Huge fallen trees criss-cross Kitchen Creek at every turn. A heavy rain sometimes obliterates steps. Walkways are frequently washed away. But the repair work is ongoing. There are a number of newly built bridges, and the entire walkway to Onondaga Falls, which was washed out during a storm, has been rebuilt.

Ricketts Glen is a haven for hikers, photographers, botanists, outdoor lovers, and tourists; it is not, however, suitable for small children. For those who can't make this hike, there is an excellent waterfall south of PA 118, adjacent to the parking lot. Adams Falls cascades 36 feet into a deep bowl formed by the shale bottom. The trail to it passes through a stand of pictur-esque pines, where there are picnic tables and benches.

Hike Information

● Trail Contacts:
Ricketts Glen State Park, Benton, PA (570) 477–5675 or *www.dcnr.state. pa.us*

● Schedule:
Open year round

● Fees/Permits:
No fees or permits required

● Local Information:
Luzerne County Convention and Visitors Bureau, Wilkes-Barre PA (570) 819–1877 or 1–888–905–2872 or *www.tournepa.com* • **Lycoming County Visitors Bureau,** Williamsport, PA (570) 327–7700 or 1–800–358–9900 or *www.vacation pa.com*

● Local Events/Attractions:
Lycoming County Fair, second week in July, Hughesville, PA (570) 784–0487

● Bus Service:
Fullington Trailways, Clearfield, PA (814) 765–7871 or 1–800–252–3893 – *There is a bus stop in Red Rock, 1.25 miles west of the trailhead. The bus schedule dic-*tates an overnight stay in the park. Since Red Rock is a flag stop, it's best to call Fullington for more information before traveling.

● Accommodations:
Snyder House Victorian Bed & Breakfast, Williamsport, PA (570) 326–0411 or (570) 494–0835 – *for reservations* • **Ricketts Glen State Park,** Benton, PA (570) 477–5675 – *camping*

● Restaurants:
Buckeyes, Hughesville, PA (570) 584–4090

● Organizations:
Alpine Club, P.O. Box 501, Williamsport, PA 17703

● Local Outdoor Retailers:
Country Ski & Sports, Montoursville, PA (570) 368–1718 or 1–877–669–9966 or *www.country skiandsports.com* • **Jocks Sports Center,** Williamsport, PA (570) 326–2000

● Maps:
USGS maps: Red Rock, PA

MilesDirections

0.0 START at the parking area. Cross PA 118 at the crosswalk and walk to the trailhead and Glens Natural Area Falls Trail sign.

0.1 Arrive at the Falls Trail map and bulletin board.

0.2 Turn right onto a footbridge across Kitchen Creek.

0.3 Turn left onto a dirt road.

0.5 Cross a tributary on the footbridge. Arrive at a trail sign and turn right.

0.8 Turn left onto a footbridge and cross Kitchen Creek.

0.9 The trail veers left away from the creek. Look for the yellow arrow signpost.

1.3 Arrive at Murray Reynolds Falls.

1.5 Arrive at Sheldon Reynolds Falls.

1.6 Arrive at Harrison Wright Falls.

1.8 Turn right on Waters Meet Bridge and onto the Glen Leigh Trail.

1.9 Arrive at Wyandot Falls. Turn right onto the footbridge.

2.1 Arrive at B. Reynolds Falls. Turn left onto the footbridge and arrive at B. Ricketts Falls.

2.2 Arrive at Ozone Falls.

2.3 Turn right onto the footbridge and arrive at Huron Falls.

2.4 Arrive at Shawnee Falls.

2.6 Turn left onto the footbridge and arrive at F.L. Ricketts Falls. Climb the wooden steps.

2.7 Turn right onto the footbridge and arrive at Onondaga Falls.

2.8 Turn left onto a wooden bridge.

2.9 Cross a feeder stream.

3.0 Turn left onto the Highland Trail. At the trail fork, stay to the right.

3.4 Pass through Midway Crevasse.

4.0 Turn left onto the Ganoga Glen Trail.

4.2 Cross the West Branch Kitchen Creek on a large wooden bridge. Pass the intersection with the Old Beaver Dam Road Trail. Turn left at sign for Falls Trail and arrive at Mohawk Falls.

4.4 Arrive at Oneida Falls.

4.5 Arrive at Cayuga Falls.

4.6 Arrive at Ganoga Falls. Pass the Ganoga Falls View Trail on your right.

4.8 Arrive at Seneca Falls and Delaware Falls.

4.9 Arrive at Mohican Falls.

5.0 Arrive at Conestoga Falls.

5.2 Arrive at Tuscarora Falls and Erie Falls.

5.3 Arrive at the Meeting Waters Bridge and retrace your steps toward PA 118.

7.1 Cross PA 118 to the parking lot and your vehicle.

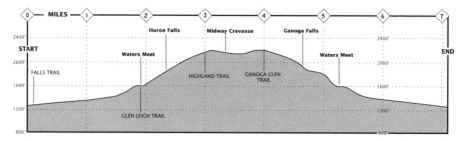

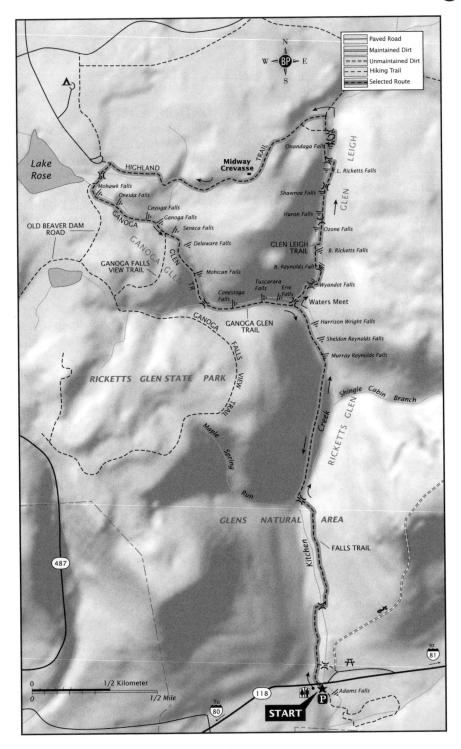

Paved Road
Maintained Dirt
Unmaintained Dirt
Hiking Trail
Selected Route

Lake Rose

HIGHLAND

Midway Crevasse

Onandaga Falls

F.L. Ricketts Falls

Mohawk Falls

Oneida Falls

Cayuga Falls

Ganoga Falls

Seneca Falls

Delaware Falls

Mohican Falls

Conestoga Falls

Tuscarora Falls

Erie Falls

GANOGA GLEN TR

Shawnee Falls

Huron Falls

Ozone Falls

GLEN LEIGH TRAIL

B. Ricketts Falls

B. Reynolds Falls

Wyandot Falls

Waters Meet

GANOGA GLEN TRAIL

Harrison Wright Falls

Sheldon Reynolds Falls

Murray Reynolds Falls

OLD BEAVER DAM ROAD

GANOGA FALLS VIEW TRAIL

GANOGA FALLS VIEW TRAIL

RICKETTS GLEN STATE PARK

Shingle Cabin Branch

RICKETTS GLEN

Creek

Maple Spring Run

GLENS NATURAL AREA

Kitchen

FALLS TRAIL

487

0   1/2 Kilometer
0   1/2 Mile

118

To 80

to 81

Adams Falls

START

P

Canyon Vista

Hike Specs

Start: From the Worlds End State Park Family Campground parking lot on PA 154
Length: 4.2-mile loop
Approximate Hiking Time: 3 hours
Difficulty Rating: Moderate, due to an extensive uphill climb
Terrain: Typical forest footpath and shale roads cut through a mixed hardwood forest. Mostly uphill switchback climb, followed by a steep descent.
Elevation Gain: 744 feet
Land Status: State park
Nearest Town: Laporte, PA
Other Trail Users: Tourists
Canine Compatibility: Leashed dogs permitted

Getting There

From Williamsport: Drive east on U.S. 220/I-180 for 12 miles to the U.S. 220 exit. Take the U.S 220 exit and continue on U.S. 220 for 24 miles to Laporte. Drive through Laporte for less than a mile to the intersection with PA 154. Turn left onto PA 154 and drive 6.5 miles to the family campground and turn left into the campground. *DeLorme: Pennsylvania Atlas & Gazetteer:* Page 51 A5

I f you want to do some hiking in the Worlds End region, you should know that hiking here means climbing, and Canyon Vista is a good example of a typical out-of-the-gorge trek. The summit is 1,750 feet above sea level, but, because of the switchbacks and lengthy circumnavigation, you'll end up walking over a mile to reach the top.

But the top is where the views are, and here are some of the best in the state. It's difficult to describe a vista. It's like trying to describe a song, or describing a hole-in-one. Canyon Vista is one of those things you have to experience to appreciate. The view seems to stretch forever—one deep hollow and ridge after another, all the way to the seemingly endless horizon. Try to keep this appreciation and peace of mind when you leave the vista and head for the Rock Garden. It's here you'll discover that while you were huffing and puffing and sweating on your way to the top, most of the people who are milling around the summit drove up in their air-conditioned cars.

Next, visit the Rock Garden. Here, enormous, boxy boulders of coarse-grained sandstone and conglomerate litter the landscape and serve little purpose other than as a playground for visitors. So take advantage of them. Frost action in the vertical rock joints has created deep, narrow crevices known as fissures. These fissures are interconnected and create passageways, so that children and (thin) adults can walk through the maze.

Visitors with an interest in plant life can examine the moss, lichen, and liverwort that live on the rocks. In late spring and early summer, bird-

watchers can sit quietly and listen for the songs of the breeding warbler, or walk into the forest in hopes of encountering a wood thrush or a hermit thrush or a veery—also a thrush.

Although the trail on the way up is steep, it's hiker-friendly; the trail back down is another story. It's rocky, and in sections, it bristles with thorny blackberry and cat briar. And in some sections, the canopy is so dense the path is actually dark, even at midday. There

Hike Information

Trail Contacts:
Worlds End State Park, Forksville, PA (570) 924–3287 or www.dcnr.state. pa.us

Schedule:
Open year round

Fees/Permits:
No fees or permits required

Local Information:
Eagles Mere Village Incorporated, Eagles Mere, PA (570) 525–3503 or www.eaglesmerevillage.com • Endless Mountains Visitors Bureau, Tunkhannock, PA (570) 836–5431 or 1–800–769–8999 or www.endless mountains.org

Local Events/Attractions:
Festival in the Park, second week in August, Route 42, Laporte, PA 18626 Steamtown National Historic Site, Scranton, PA (570) 340–5200 or 1–888–693–9391

Accommodations:
Balzer's Cabins, Forksville, PA (570) 924–3962 • Worlds End State Park Campgrounds, Forksville, PA (570) 924–3287

Restaurants:
Laporte Hotel & Motel, Laporte, PA (570) 946–7921 • Laporte General Store, Laporte, PA (570) 946–7141

Organizations:
Alpine Club, P.O. Box 501, Williamsport, PA 17703

Local Outdoor Retailers:
Country Ski & Sports, Montoursville, PA (570) 368–1718 or 1–877–669–9966 or www.countryskiand sports.com • North Mountain Sportsman, Muncy Valley, PA (570) 482–2980

Maps:
USGS maps: Eagles Mere, PA

are numerous patches of striped maple, as well as plenty of hemlock, pines, oaks, beech, and birch.

But you eventually leave the bushes behind and concentrate on making your way down an extremely steep gorge. There are switchbacks to make it easier going, and every so often you get lucky and find a sturdy sapling just when you need something to hold on to. Once on the valley floor of the gorge, the trail becomes an access road through the campgrounds on back to the trailhead where you started out.

MilesDirections

0.0 START at the Family Campground parking area. Turn right on the campground access road. Pass the contact station, and then turn left onto Mineral Spring Road. Walk across the road to the Canyon Vista Trailhead.

0.1 The trail cuts uphill away from road. Follow the blue blazes.

0.4 Come to an intersection with the Loyalsock Trail. Continue straight.

0.5 Reach an open plateau.

0.7 Pass through a stand of eastern hemlock.

1.0 Begin a serious climb. Trail makes a switchback to the left. At this point the trail merges with the Link Trail.

1.4 Reach the summit. Arrive at Canyon Vista. Walk up the wooden steps, through the parking area to the Rock Garden sign.

1.6 Arrive at the Rock Garden. Retrace your steps back to Canyon Vista and turn right. Come to a sign for the Loyalsock

Trail & Link Trail, which merge into the Canyon Vista Trail. Follow the blue blazes.

1.7 Arrive at a fork in trail. Turn left, following the blue blazes.

1.9 Pass through a rock outcropping.

2.1 Pass an intersection with the Loyalsock Trail. Continue straight.

2.2 Cross an open plateau.

2.6 Pass through a boulder outcropping.

2.8 Trail turns right through a boulder outcropping. Begin your descent.

3.2 Trail turns left.

3.5 Pass the state park boundary.

3.7 Enter the campground.

3.8 Turn left onto the shale road.

4.0 Pass the amphitheater.

4.1 Pass the Canyon Vista Trailhead on your left. Turn right on Mineral Spring Road, then, turn right again on the access road.

4.2 Arrive back at the parking lot.

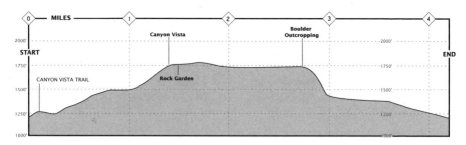

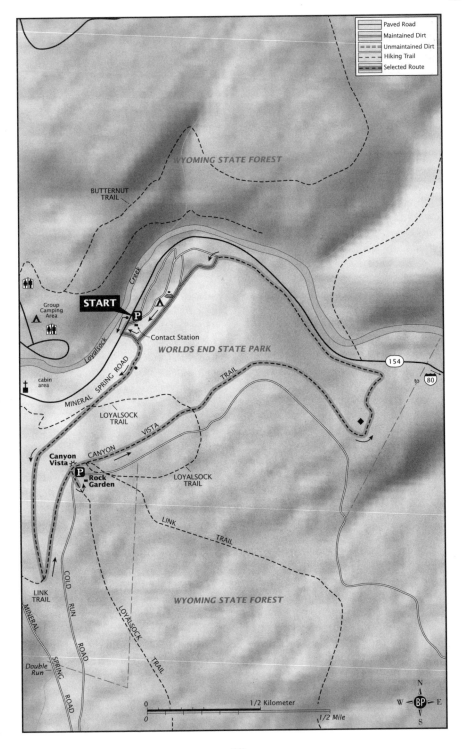

Worlds End
State Park

Hike Specs

Start: From the Double Run Nature Trail trailhead in Worlds End State Park

Length: 3.6-mile loop

Approximate Hiking Time: 3 hours

Difficulty Rating: Difficult, due a rocky climb out of the gorge [**Note.** *The High Rock Trail portion of this hike is not for children.]*

Terrain: A typical pine-needle nature trail winds alongside a mountain stream to a waterfall, over creekside boulders, up a steep gorge, along boulder outcroppings, and down park roads.

Elevation Gain: 1,133 feet

Land Status: State park

Nearest Town: Laporte, PA

Other Trail Users: Backpackers, tourists, and anglers

Canine Compatibility: Leashed dogs permitted

Getting There

From Williamsport: Drive east on U.S. 220/I-180 for 12 miles to the U.S. 220 exit. Take the U.S. 220 exit and continue on U.S. 220 for 24 miles to Laporte. Drive through Laporte for less than a mile to the intersection with PA 154. Turn left onto PA 154 and drive 6.7 miles to the Double Run Nature Trail parking lot on your left. *DeLorme: Pennsylvania Atlas & Gazetteer:* Page 51 A5

> **Note:** *There are signs along the High Rock Trail that advise hikers to stay on the trail. If you're new to hiking or afraid of heights, you may want to skip the High Rock Trail. If you want to get to High Rock Vista without the rocky climb, enter the trail below the swimming beach on Pennsylvania 154.*

Hikers, intent on their agendas, sometimes miss the highlights of an area. Fortunately, that won't happen here. This hike was designed to incorporate Worlds End highlights, such as Loyalsock Creek and High Rock Vista, with a vigorous workout.

As soon as you enter Worlds End State Park, you hear it: the never-ending rush of the waters of Loyalsock Creek. These are the waters that have created (over the past 200 million years or so) the 1,600-foot-deep gash known as Loyalsock Gorge. This hike provides the opportunity to see Loyalsock Creek up close, and if you do this hike in early spring or late fall, you may see kayakers maneuvering through the whitewater rapids. The abundance of boulders in the creek creates some appreciable rapids, as well a few treacherously deep spots. For this reason swimming is permitted only at the swimming beach area. If you need further deterrent, summer water temperatures range from the low 50s to the mid 60s.

After the creek, you'll arrive at the High Rock Trailhead; here you'll find signs warning that the trail is not suitable for children. The first stop up the

gorge is at High Rock Run and Falls, a drainage stream that cascades over an outcrop. There is evidence that hikers have climbed down alongside the falls, but the payoff isn't worth the danger. In fact, there are signs at the trailhead warning hikers to stay on the trail.

It's less than a half-mile from the falls to High Rock Overlook, but there's a short stretch along the edge of the gorge subject to washouts. Use extra caution along this section.

Backpackers from all corners of the state come to hike Worlds End State Park.

High Rock Vista provides a striking view of the gorge, the serpentine creek, and the surrounding mountains. After the vista, life gets easy again. The trail is a typical hardwood forest trail, through a dense canopy of shade, and, of course, it's all downhill. When you reach Pennsylvania 154 and turn left, look on your left for a jungle of blackberry bushes, loaded with dark, juicy fruit.

As you walk along Pennsylvania 154, you can see that the creek has been dammed and a sand beach has been created for a swimming area. The dam spillway is a favorite photo opportunity. The trail winds through the park, and passes the park office and park store along the way. The park office has outdoor exhibits, maps, trail updates, and a bulletin-board size map of the entire Loyalsock Trail.

The trail leads you through a picnic area and back to the paved park road where you came out earlier—after you walked alongside Loyalsock Creek. Once you're at this juncture, you retrace your steps until you get to Pennsylvania 154, where you can turn left and walk to your vehicle.

MilesDirections

0.0 START at the Double Run Nature Trail parking lot. Walk under the arch into the forest. Look for white, rectangular blaze with a green cross-member.

0.1 Go up the wooden steps.

0.2 Note the stream branches come together. Meet Loyalsock Trail: yellow rectangular blaze with red cross-member. Turn right onto the plank footbridge and cross the stream. Turn left onto the Double Run Trail. The stream is on your left.

0.4 Arrive at Cottonwood Falls. Walk beyond falls and ford easily across the stream on the exposed rocks.

0.5 Turn left onto the Link Trail. Look for yellow blazes with a red "X."

0.7 Arrive at a trail intersection. The trail turns left toward the stream at the double X blazes. Turn left at the stream, then turn right and retrace your steps across the stream on the same plank footbridge, going in the same direction you crossed it the first time. This time on the other side of the stream, turn right at the yellow arrow and follow the Link Trail. *[Note. Three trails merge for about 30 feet]*

0.8 Cross a stream branch on a wooden footbridge and turn right onto the Link Trail, following the yellow blaze with a red "X."

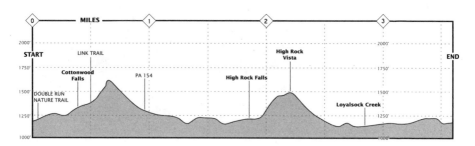

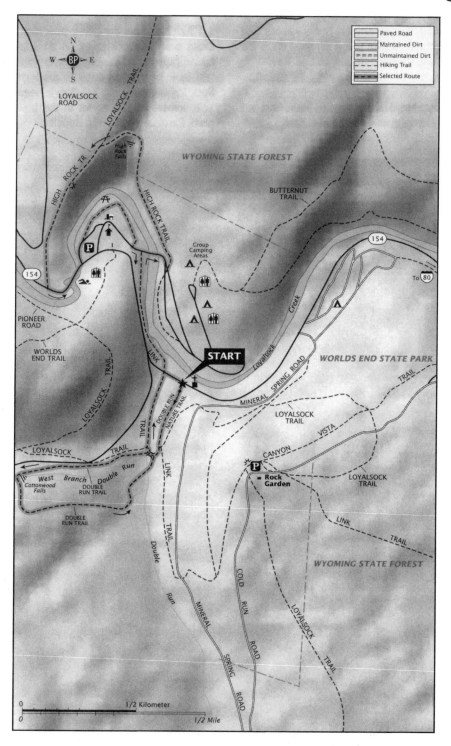

0.9 The trail divides. The Loyalsock Trail (red blaze with yellow LT) goes off to the left. Continue straight on Link Trail.

1.0 Cross PA 154.

1.1 Arrive at Loyalsock Creek. Turn left and walk along the stream bank.

1.4 Turn right onto the paved park road. Cross over Loyalsock Creek on an auto bridge. Note the small picnic area on your left. Look for a yellow arrow to the High Rock Trail and Butternut Trail. Turn left and walk across the parking lot to the trailhead. Continue on the High Rock Trail.

1.8 Pass through a boulder outcropping and arrive at High Rock Falls.

2.0 The Loyalsock Trail veers off to the right. Continue straight on the High Rock Trail, following the yellow blazes.

2.2 Arrive at High Rock Vista.

2.3 Come to a trail intersection sign for the Loyalsock Trail. Continue on the High Rock Trail.

2.6 Pass under the telephone lines.

2.7 Turn right at a trail fork. Turn left onto PA 154.

2.8 Cross the bridge over Loyalsock Creek. Turn left into the parking lot and walk to the picnic area. Stay on road nearest Loyalsock Creek.

3.0 Walk past the park store. Reach the Loyalsock Trail sign beside the store. Turn left down the steps. Turn right at the bottom of the steps and walk through the picnic area.

3.1 Turn left onto the paved park road.

3.2 Turn right onto the Link Trail and retrace your steps. Look for yellow blazes with a red "X."

3.6 Cross PA 154. Turn left and arrive back at the Double Run Nature Trail parking area.

Hike Information

☎ Trail Contacts:
Worlds End State Park, Forksville, PA (570) 924–3287

☉ Schedule:
Open year round

$ Fees/Permits:
No fees or permits required

❓ Local Information:
Eagles Mere Village Incorporated, Eagles Mere, PA (570) 525–3503 or *www.eaglesmerevillage.com* • **Endless Mountains Visitors Bureau,** Tunkhannock, PA (570) 836–5431 or 1–800–769–8999 or *www.endless-mountains.org*

◉ Local Events/Attractions:
Flaming Foliage Show and Sale, first weekend in October, Forksville Fairgrounds, Forksville, PA • **Sullivan County Fair Association,** last week in August, Forksville, PA

⊜ Accommodations:
Montvale Bed and Breakfast, Forksville, PA (570) 924–3574 • **Worlds End State Park Campgrounds,** Forksville, PA (570) 924–3287

🍴 Restaurants:
Sweet Shoppe, Eagles Mere, PA (570) 525–3525 • **Laporte General Store,** Laporte, PA (570) 946–7141

👫 Organizations:
Alpine Club, P.O. Box 501, Williamsport, PA 17703

🚴 Local Outdoor Retailers:
Country Ski & Sports, Montoursville, PA (570) 368–1718 or 1–877–669–9966 or *www.countryskiandsports.com* • **Benton Sports Center,** Benton, PA (570) 925–6001

Ⓝ Maps:
USGS maps: Eagles Mere, PA

Haystacks

Hike Specs

Start: From the Loyalsock Trail trailhead parking lot on U.S. 220

Length: 4.5-mile loop

Approximate Hiking Time: 3 hours

Difficulty Rating: Easy, with short, steep ascents

Terrain: Follow a cinder railroad grade, shale roads, and pine needle paths through a shaded forest to a streamside hemlock grove for views of the rapids and a waterfall.

Elevation Gain: 648 feet

Land Status: State forest

Nearest Town: Laporte, PA

Other Trail Users: Backpackers

Canine Compatibility: Leashed dogs permitted

Getting There

From Williamsport: Drive east on U.S. 220/I-180 for 12 miles to the U.S. 220 exit. Take the U.S. 220 exit and continue on U.S. 220 for 24 miles to Laporte. Drive through Laporte for approximately 3.5 miles and turn left onto Mead Road. Drive 0.25 miles and turn right into the parking lot. *DeLorme: Pennsylvania Atlas & Gazetteer:* Page 51 A6

T his hike got its name from a section of Loyalsock Creek where sandstone boulders—which are said to look like haystacks—create a series of rapids in an otherwise calm creek. The best time to see these rapids is when the water level is high, in spring after the winter melt off, or late fall, after the area's rainy season.

Haystacks is the eastern terminus of the 59.3-mile long Loyalsock Trail. The name Loyalsock is derived from the Native American term *Lawi-Saquick*, meaning "middle creek." In this case, Loyalsock Creek runs between Muncy and Lycoming Creeks on its way to the Susquehanna River at Montoursville. The trail, which is described as a wilderness footpath, runs alongside Loyalsock Creek through Worlds End State Park and ends on Pennsylvania 87 a few miles north of Montoursville. It's broken up into eight sections, each with road access at both ends.

The beginning of this hike is a mile-long section of abandoned railroad grade. Here, during the summer months, you'll pass families with children rolling tubes they've brought from home, heading for the Haystacks rapids. This section of the hike is popular and very easy; you may even see parents pushing strollers. Of course, these walkers go in and come out on the rail-road grade and the improved shale road.

At the Haystacks area, the trail follows the creek upstream. Walking the gorge bottom is easy and relaxing: Eastern hemlocks provide plenty of shade, the trail is covered with pine needles, and the rushing waters of Loyalsock Creek create a hypnotic spell that makes you forget you're just a few miles from civilization. Along this section you can see where visitors

Loyalsock Creek, viewed from Dutchman Falls.

have built fire rings and spent some time enjoying the tranquility. (There are seasonal and conditional bans on fires in Wyoming State Forest. For more information, call the Hillgrove Ranger Station at (570) 924–3501.)

Before the parking lot was built, hikers parked on U.S. Route 220, walked in on the railroad grade to Dutchman Falls, then continued their trek. If you park in the parking lot off Mead Road, you are west of the falls. That's why, when the hike is almost completed, you have to walk a short distance past your starting point on the railroad grade and turn left to see the falls.

In order to appreciate Dutchman Falls, it's necessary to climb down the gorge to the streambed where the water from the falls empties into Loyalsock Creek. You can go down either side of the waterfalls, making your way from one flat boulder to the next.

MilesDirections

0.0 START from the trailhead parking lot. There are two paths to get to the trailhead: one at each end of the parking lot. Take the one nearest to Mead Road. Walk to the sign: "Alternative Hiking and Biking Trail to Loyalsock Trail & Haystacks" and walk between the two boulders.

0.4 Turn left onto the abandoned railroad grade. Look for the round red blazes with yellow LT.

1.6 Turn right at the Haystacks ½ Mile sign. Follow the round yellow blaze with a red "X."

2.0 Arrive at Loyalsock Creek and the Haystacks area. Turn right and follow the yellow rectangular blaze with red cross-member and red round blaze with yellow LT.

2.7 Pass Mile Marker 58.

3.4 Begin a climb up gorge.

3.6 Turn left onto the railroad grade and retrace your steps.

3.9 Pass Mile Marker 59 and walk past the parking lot sign. Walk past the trail blazed with "XX." Turn left onto the trail blazed with a single "X." Look for the Dutchman Falls sign.

4.0 Arrive at Loyalsock Creek. Retrace your steps out of the gorge.

4.1 Turn right onto the railroad grade. Turn left onto the alternative path to parking lot where you started out and retrace your steps.

4.5 Arrive back at the parking lot.

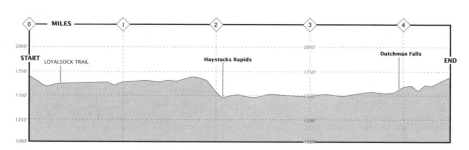

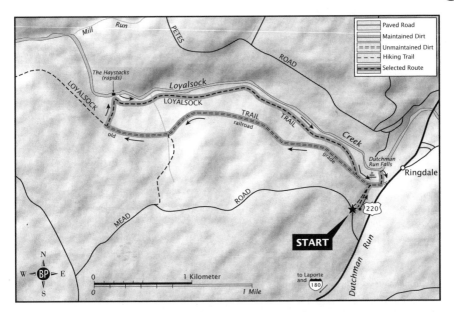

Hike Information

📞 Trail Contacts:

Wyoming State Forest, Bloomsburg, PA (570) 387–4255 • **Hillgrove Ranger Station:** (570) 924–3501 • **Alpine Club,** P.O. Box 501, Williamsport, PA 17703

🕐 Schedule:

Open year round

💲 Fees/Permits:

No fees or permits are required

❓ Local Information:

Endless Mountains Visitors Bureau, Tunkhannock, PA (570) 836–5431 or 1–800–769–8999 or *www.endless mountains.org*

💡 Local Events/Attractions:

Sullivan County Historical Museum and Baldwin House, Laporte, PA (570) 946–5020 • **Endless Mountains Majesty Photographic Wildlife Preserve and Retreat,**

Sullivan County, PA (570) 928–7582 or 1–888–625–5251 or *www. emmajesty.com*

🛏 Accommodations:

Eagles Mere Inn, Eagles Mere, PA 1–800–426–3273 or *www.eaglesmere inn.com* • Worlds End State Park Campgrounds, Forksville, PA (570) 924–3287

🍴 Restaurants:

Eagles Mere Inn, Eagles Mere, PA 1–800–426–3273 or *www.eagles mereinn.com*

🎒 Local Outdoor Retailers:

Country Ski & Sports, Montoursville, PA (570) 368–1718 or 1–877–669–9966

🅝 Maps:

USGS maps: Laporte, PA

Mount Pisgah State Park

Hike Specs

Start: From the fishing area parking lot on Stephen Foster Lake (in Mount Pisgah State Park)
Length: 7.9-mile loop
Approximate Hiking Time: 4 hours
Difficulty Rating: Moderate, with steep, strenuous climbs
Terrain: Follow a typical pine needle trail and boardwalk along a lake inlet and stream, through wildflower meadows, and climb a very steep dirt road to a microwave tower.
Elevation Gain: 1,732 feet
Land Status: State park and county park
Nearest Town: Troy, PA
Other Trail Users: Picnickers and anglers
Canine Compatibility: Leashed dogs permitted

Getting There

From Williamsport: Drive north on U.S. 15 for 47 miles to U.S. 6 in Mansfield. Turn right onto U.S. 6 and drive east for 17 miles through Troy and East Troy to the Mount Pisgah State Park sign at SR 3019. Turn left on SR 3019 and drive two miles to the park and Stephen Foster Lake. *DeLorme: Pennsylvania Atlas & Gazetteer:* Page 37 B4

Mount Pisgah State Park is a 1,302-acre, day-use park. There's no overnight camping, and the park isn't near anything. Some might say Mount Pisgah is remote and inconvenient. It is. But this kind of isolation ensures a pristine park, and for many hikers and outdoors-people, Mount Pisgah is a favorite.

The centerpiece of the park is the 75-acre Stephen Foster Lake, created in 1979 when Mill Creek was dammed. There's a large swimming pool in the park, so the lake is used primarily by recreational boaters and fishermen. There's a boat rental shed on the north side of the lake for pedal boats, V-bottom aluminum boats, and canoes. There's also a single-lane boat-launching ramp, seasonal mooring area, and a courtesy dock for loading and unloading.

Since power boats aren't allowed on the lake, fisherman—especially bass anglers—use electric trolling motors on their boats to get to their favorite spots (the shallow and weedy areas where bass hang out). In addition to the bass, perch, bluegill, and crappies are sometimes planted in the lake. There are plenty of spots for shoreline fishing, making this a popular spot for children to learn to fish.

The lake is named after Stephen Foster (1826–1864), a Pittsburgh native and former resident of this region. He was the composer of popular nine-

teenth century songs like "Oh! Susanna" (his first hit) and "De Camptown Races," which immortalized the horse races run from nearby Camptown to Wyalusing. Foster composed 285 songs, hymns, arrangements, and instrumental works; some of these, such as "Old Folks at Home," "Jeanie with the Light Brown Hair," and "Old Black Joe," are considered the most popular songs ever written. Unfortunately for Foster, nineteenth century copyright laws offered little protection and he received minimal income from his work. The last three years of his life he lived alone in New York City, where he died of a fever in the charity ward of Bellevue Hospital.

The trail begins across the street from the fishing area parking lot and makes its way along Mill Creek. You're in a pine plantation as you walk along the inlet. There is an abundance of vegetation, such as cattails and Queen Ann's Lace, throughout the marshy area. As the trail enters the forest canopy, you can see the ruins of stone fences, which were, when this area was first settled, boundary lines. This type of fence accomplished two

Hike Information

● Trail Contacts:
Mount Pisgah State Park, Troy, PA (570) 297-2734 or *www.dcnr.state.pa.us*

● Schedule:
Open year round

● Fees/Permits:
No fees or permits required

● Local Information:
Central Bradford County Chamber of Commerce, Towanda, PA (570) 268-2732

● Local Events/Attractions:
Antique Carriage and Sleigh Festival, third weekend in September, Bradford County Heritage Museum, Troy, PA (570) 297-3410 or *www.endless-mountains.org*

● Accommodations:
Golden Oak Bed and Breakfast, Troy, PA (570) 297-4315 or *www.bbonline.com/pa/goldenoak* • **Worlds End State Park Campgrounds**, Forksville, PA (570) 924-3287

● Restaurants:
Edgewood Family Restaurant, Troy, PA (570) 297-4784

● Local Outdoor Retailers:
Troy Sports Store, Troy, PA (570) 297-2367

● Maps:
USGS maps: East Troy, PA

MilesDirections

0.0 START from the fishing area parking lot on Stephen Foster Lake. Turn right onto the park road and walk to a split-rail fence on the left side of the road. Turn left onto the Mill Stream Trail, then veer right.

0.2 Come to a marshy area on your right.

0.4 Arrive at a meadow.

0.6 Turn right onto the Pine Tree Trail. Pass through the stone wall ruins.

0.7 Begin an uphill climb.

0.8 Turn right onto Ridge Trail. Pass through a meadow and join up with an abandoned jeep road.

0.9 *[FYI. Notice the stone wall ruins on your right.]*

1.0 Begin a steep climb.

1.3 Pass a bench on your right. Notice the huge oak trees.

1.4 Begin an extremely steep climb. Note the faded red blaze on your right.

1.5 Pass through a clearcut area.

1.8 The Hicks Hollow Trail goes off to your right. Continue straight past the Ridge Trail sign and enter a wildflower meadow.

2.0 *[FYI. Notice the stand of quaking aspen.]* Re-enter the forest. Note the faded red blaze with black arrow.

2.1 Pass a bench on your right.

2.6 Arrive at an alpine meadow.

2.8 Begin a serious uphill climb.

3.0 Come to an access gate.

3.1 Reach another flat, open area, and pass an abandoned building.

3.5 Come to a cable gate across the trail. Turn right onto the paved road. Note the picnic table and viewing area on your right. Continue uphill on the paved road.

3.7 Turn left onto a dirt road and pass a red concrete building on your left.

3.8 Pass through a small picnic area on your right.

3.9 Turn left to an overlook, then retrace your steps and turn left onto the road.

4.0 Turn left and walk uphill through a children's wooden playground.

4.3 Walk to two viewing areas on your left. Walk the loop around the tower.

4.7 Arrive at a viewing area on your left, then continue downhill on the paved road.

4.8 Come to the cable gate across the trail. Turn left onto Ridge Trail and retrace your steps.

6.5 Pass unmarked footpath on your right.

7.3 Arrive at an intersection with the Pine Tree Trail on your left. Continue straight.

7.5 Pass through a small meadow and turn right at a sign for snowmobiles and the Ridge Trail.

7.7 Cross the park road and turn left onto the Oh! Susanna Trail.

7.9 Walk on the boardwalk parallel to lake back to the parking area and your car.

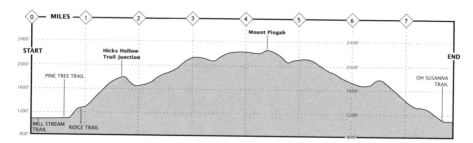

things: it set the boundary between farms, and it was a convenient way for farmers to get rid of the stones from their fields.

The trail is not blazed in the state park, but it is well maintained. Along the way, you pass from the state to the county park; you can tell when you begin the county park section because you'll notice the faded red blazes. After you make your first serious climb in the forest, you enter into a meadow on a mowed path. You continue on this trail to a larger meadow filled with Black-eyed Susans, Queen Ann's Lace, common goldenrod, and wild bergamot.

Enjoy the leisurely stroll through the meadows for as long as you can; the climb to the summit is next on your agenda. It's over a mile to the top, and it varies between being steep and being very steep. Once at the summit, though, you can eat your lunch and take in one of the many vistas of the Bradford County farmlands and valleys. For your convenience, there are bathrooms and a number of strategically placed picnic tables set alongside natural overlooks.

If you were smart and planned ahead, you would have a cold chicken dinner, a thermos of coffee, and your fishing rod waiting for you in your vehicle. You would have rented a boat with a trolling motor and had it waiting for you so you could slip into the lake and let the cool afternoon breeze and gentle rocking of the boat lull you into a much-needed rest.

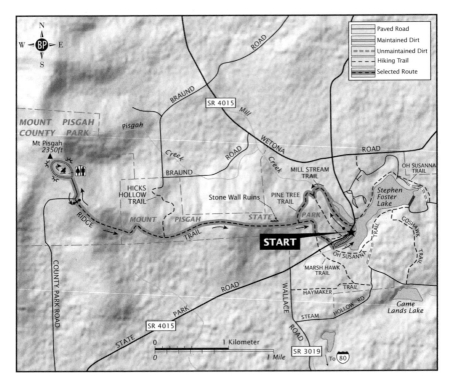

Northeast Pennsylvania

Compiled here is an index of great hikes in the Northeast region that didn't make the A-list this time around but deserve recognition. Check them out and let us know what you think. You may decide that one or more of these hikes deserves higher status in future editions or, perhaps, you may have a hike of your own that merits some attention.

J Lehigh Gorge State Park

Lehigh Gorge State Park is in Carbon County near the crossroads of I-80 and I-476. (*See Hike 8 and Hike 9*) The trail is an abandoned railroad grade that parallels the Lehigh River, stretching 30 miles from White Haven in the north to Jim Thorpe in the south. There are a number of access points along the way in this stunning gorge, so you can plan your hike accordingly. Expect to see plenty of mountain bicyclists and whitewater rafters: the Lehigh River is one of the top whitewater rivers in the country and the bike trail is considered by Outside magazine to be Pennsylvania's best biking trail.

To get there from Jim Thorpe, drive south on PA 209 to PA 903. Turn right onto PA 903 and drive across the Lehigh River to a stop sign. At the stop sign, go straight onto Coalport Road for 0.4 miles to the park entrance. For more information call Lehigh Gorge/Hickory Run State Park at (570) 443–0400. *DeLorme: Pennsylvania Atlas & Gazetteer:* Page 67 A5

K Drake's Creek

Drake's Creek lies on the western edge of the Pocono Mountain Range near the crossroads of I-80 and I-476. There's an extensive trail network, so you can map out your own route according to your energy level. The Poconos got its name from the Lenni-Lenape Indians word pohoqualine, which means "a river between two mountains." The Nature Conservancy has called the Poconos one of the "Last Great Places" in America. Bring the family: there are tourist attractions galore, golf courses, and ski resorts.

To get there from Jim Thorpe, drive south on PA 209 to PA 903. Follow PA 903 north for 9.5 miles to Unionville Road. Turn left and drive 2.5 miles to the parking lot on your left. For more information call Northeast Pennsylvania Game Commission at (570) 675–1143. *DeLorme: Pennsylvania Atlas & Gazetteer:* Page 67 A5

(L) Big Pocono State Park

The park is located just south of I-80 and just east of the site where I-80 and I-380 connect in Monroe County. There are 10 miles of trails here; two of these, the Indian and North Trails, are not for inexperienced hikers. Climb famous Camelback Mountain for a visit to the fire tower that has been declared a historical structure, and for world-class views. For those who want to see the views without hiking, there's a 1.4-mile paved auto road that girdles the mountaintop, providing views in all directions.

To get there from Scranton, drive south on I-380 and connect with I-80 heading east. Take Exit 44 and follow the signs to the park. For more information call the Big Pocono State Park c/o Tobyhanna State Park at (717) 894–8336. *DeLorme: Pennsylvania Atlas & Gazetteer:* Page 54 D1

Northcentral
PENNSYLVANIA

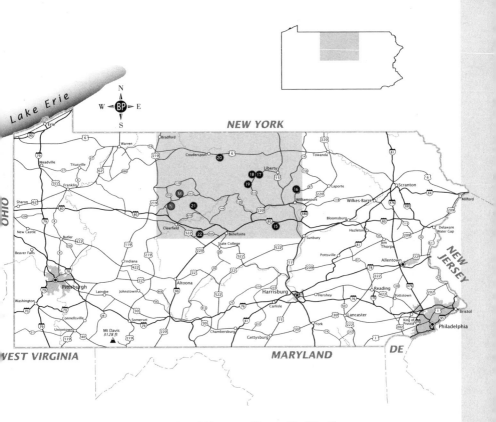

The Rides

R.B. Winter State Park **15.**
Loyalsock Trail **16.**
Gillespie Point **17.**
Bohen Run Falls & West Rim Trail **18.**
Pine Trail & Hemlock Mountain **19.**
Splash Dam Hollow **20.**
Wykoff Run Natural Area **21.**
Black Moshannon State Park **22.**

Honorable Mentions

M. The Elk Trail
N. Parker Dam State Park

Northcentral Pennsylvania

Northcentral Pennsylvania is big country. It's sparsely populated and remote. One local legend says that in Potter County there are more deer than people. That could be: there are 1.5 million deer in Pennsylvania and, as a weekday hiker, you'll see more deer on the trail than people. You'll also see huge ravines, some so steep, you'll wish you had climbing gear in your pack instead of that wrinkled peanut-butter-and-jelly sandwich.

Nature has been busy on the Allegheny High Plateau. The Plateau, which includes the highest point in Pennsylvania's Appalachian Plateau range, borders on the Valley and Ridge Province to the south along the escarpment known as the Allegheny Front—and that's where the fun begins.

Want to see the Allegheny Front in action? Visit Ricketts Glen and witness the awesome spectacle of a raging mountain stream as it sends water down the Front, for a plunge of 1,000 feet in two miles. Many would say that Ricketts Glen is the number one hike in the state (and I agree). Still others would say the top hike is the majestic Pine Creek Gorge—better known as Pennsylvania's Grand Canyon. At over 5,000 feet wide, 800 feet deep, and 47 miles long, it's the most spectacular gorge in the state. In fact, *Outdoor Magazine* named one of the gorge hikes "one of the best trails in Pennsylvania". (*See Hike 15*)

It's difficult to think of northcentral Pennsylvania as a plateau—with all its deep ravines, snake-like creeks, cliffs, and boulder outcrops—but it is. It started out with somewhat level terrain, but what with tectonic shifts and erosion and water running everywhere, it got to be, well, inhospitable to foot travel. If you generally try to avoid a little suffering, don't try these hikes. But if you like big challenges and big rewards, this region's for you.

Nowhere is the out-and-out ornery-"ness" of the region more obvious than at Worlds End State Park. Even getting to the area is a trip. In fact, legend has it that the narrow, snake-like roads scared the early settlers so much many wondered if they'd ever make it home: They didn't know if their world would end on even the shortest trip.

Overview

R.B. Winter State Park

This hike uses a challenging, and little known, cross-country skiing trail to take you across the ridgetops and in and out of the 500-foot deep hemlock valleys. It connects with an abandoned narrow-gauge railroad bed that runs for two miles over extremely rocky terrain. From there, it runs up another ridge to an overlook 300 feet above the valley, and then down the ridge to a nature trail through a second-growth pine and hemlock forest. *(See page 98)*

Loyalsock Trail

This begins with a difficult, steep climb up the side of a gorge. It's a challenging climb with short switchbacks and rock and root handholds. Once on top, you cross a plateau with huckleberry bushes and pine plantations. From the plateau's edge, there are spectacular views and a cool breeze that sweeps up the gorge. *(See page 104)*

Gillespie Point

This hike asks only one question: Would you climb a little over a mile up the side of a gorge to take in a once-in-a-lifetime view? Begin on an improved forest road, climb to the viewing area, and then loop back to this same forest road for an easy walk back to the starting point. *(See page 110)*

Bohen Run Falls & West Rim Trail

There is one world-class view of Pennsylvania's Pine Creek Gorge on this section of the West Rim Trail, and there are legions of hikers who consider the climb out of the gorge worth it. Along the way to the top, there are views of Pine Creek and sparkling mountain waterfalls. The final leg is on the Pine Creek Rails-To-Trails Bicycle Path. *(See page 114)*

Pine Trail & Hemlock Mountain

This hike begins with an easy walk alongside majestic Pine Creek, followed by a trek out of the gorge. Near the top of the gorge, the foot-path narrows as it passes through an outcropping of boulders that force hikers to bend over at points, and although it's not a dangerous spot, you may have to hold onto the boulders to keep your balance. There is a rough 0.7-mile climb through a steep, rocky washout to the mountaintop, where an unused forest road leads from one spectacular view of Pine Creek Gorge to the next. In fact, because of the enormity of the gorge and the high visibility, many hikers contend these are the best views in the state. *(See page 120)*

Splash Dam Hollow

A short bushwhack section makes this a challenging hike. The trail begins on a major hiking system, but soon connects with lesser-used trails, as it descends one hollow and meets a narrow stream whose banks are now overgrown. Beaver dams aggravate an already marshy area, and at one point a beaver dam blocks the trail. The trail leads up a second hollow to the ridge, where you bushwhack for a few tenths of a mile until you reconnect with the main trail. *(See page 124)*

Wykoff Run Natural Area

This is an easy hike through stands of white birch, mountain laurel, and meadows teeming with blueberry bushes. You're at an elevation of 2,000 feet—not the highest point in the state, but high enough to sense you're on top of a mountain. At times, as you hike through a meadow to the tree forest canopy, it feels surprisingly like an alpine forest. *(See page 130)*

Black Moshannon State Park

This is an easy hike that provides a tour of popular Black Moshannon State Park. It starts on the bridge across majestic Black Moshannon Lake and continues along the lakeside and past the dam spillway; then follows Black Moshannon Creek, as it meanders through the forest at the north end of the park. The trail leaves the stream and loops back to the bridge across the lake, where you cross the lake a second time and head toward the south end of the park, where you can explore the bog and its wildlife and exotic flora from an elevated boardwalk. *(See page 136)*

R.B. Winter State Park

Hike Specs

Start: From the R.B. Winter State Park parking lot on PA 192

Length: 7.5-mile loop

Approximate Hiking Time: 4 hours

Difficulty Rating: Moderate, due to uphill climbs and rocky footpaths

Terrain: Utilize a rocky footpath, cross-country skiing trails, a power line service road, improved roads, and a nature trail while encountering a pristine mountain lake, a mixed hardwood forest, rock outcrops, and pine and hemlock stands.

Elevation Gain: 898 feet

Land Status: State park

Nearest Town: Lewisburg, PA

Other Trail Users: Hikers, cross-country skiers, and hunters (in season)

Canine Compatibility: Leashed dogs permitted

Getting There

From Williamsport: Drive south on U.S. 15 for 33 miles to Lewisburg. In Lewisburg, turn right onto PA 192 and drive 17 miles west to R.B. Winter State Park. Park in the parking lot on your right, next to Halfway Lake. **DeLorme: Pennsylvania Atlas & Gazetteer:** Page 63 A7

The 695-acre R.B. Winter State Park lies within the Bald Eagle State Forest—195,000 acres of some of the most rugged and remote land in the state. The park sits in a narrow valley between two ridges, part of the Valley and Ridge Province—a series of parallel ridges that arcs from Maryland to the New Jersey border. The ridges were created by an upheaval, which folded, or faulted, the earth. As a result, the ridges and valleys produce two distinctly different environments: lush, marshy valleys carpeted with immense pines, and drier, rocky ridges and slopes with an abundance of deciduous hardwoods. You'll have an opportunity to sample a bit of each—or at least what's left of the original habitat—along this trail.

In earlier times, the best way to travel across this region was to travel in the valleys. In the 1700s, a wagon road was built through the narrow valley to haul produce from the agricultural region of Centre County to the Susquehanna River, where it was loaded onto barges. The road—which is now Pennsylvania 192—was called, appropriately, Narrows Road.

Halfway Lake at R.B. Winter State Park.

Logging began here in the late 1800s and ended in 1910, when there were no more trees to cut. A sawmill was set up and a log dam was built across Rapid Run, on the site where Halfway Lake is today. The forest was once so thick with white pine and hemlock—some over six feet in diameter and reaching heights of 200 feet—that it was referred to as the shrouded forest, because the forest canopy virtually blocked the sun, keeping the forest in semi-darkness.

MilesDirections

0.0 START at the steps in the Halfway Lake parking lot on PA 192 near the breast of the dam. Walk east alongside PA 192 and cross the bridge.

0.1 Turn left at the end of the guardrails and walk toward the dam spillway. *[Note. Look for the orange blaze on a large hemlock tree near the spillway.]*

0.2 Turn right at the double orange blazes near the spillway and begin an uphill climb. Cross Boyer Gap Road and arrive at the trailhead for the Bake Oven Trail. The trail sign reads "Mid State Trail & Sand Mountain Tower." Continue straight.

0.4 The trail levels. Note the blue signs indicating this trail is also used for cross-country skiing.

0.8 Pass the Old Boundary Trail on your left.

1.2 Pass under the power line.

2.3 Arrive at a trail intersection. Cross Boyer Gap Road and continue straight on the Mid State Trail. (The Bake Oven Trail goes off to your right.)

2.8 Arrive at a trail intersection. Turn left onto the blue-blazed Buffalo Path Trail. *[FYI. The Mid State Trail continues straight toward the (now closed) Sand Mountain Tower.]*

2.9 Pass the remains of a rock quarry on your left.

3.0 Turn right onto Boyer Gap Road.

3.2 Cross Sand Mountain Road. Continue straight onto the red-blazed Cracker Bridge Trail.

3.3 The cross-country skiing trail goes off to your left. Continue straight up a rocky knoll.

3.4 Come to an intersection with the cross-country skiing trail. Continue straight.

3.6 Arrive at a trail intersection. Turn left onto the Tram Road Trail.

3.7 Cross Spruce Run on a series of wooden footbridges.

5.4 Come to a sign that reads "Old Tram Trail." Pass Boiling Spring Trail on your left. Continue straight.

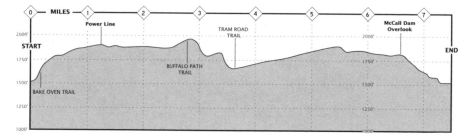

5.8 Turn left onto a jeep road. Make an immediate right turn to get under the power line. Make an immediate left onto the power line service road and walk along the road under the power line.

5.9 [**Note.** *Look for the red blaze and blue cross-country sign on a power line pole.*]

6.0 Turn right at a power stanchion with double red blazes and a white arrow.

6.6 Turn left onto McCall Dam Road and arrive at the McCall Dam Overlook. Turn left on the viewing platform to the man-made steps, and then begin your descent on a series of switchbacks.

7.0 Cross Sand Mountain Road and turn left at the sign for the nature trail.

7.1 Come to the "Nature Trail & Beach" sign; follow the yellow arrow. Pass through a hemlock stand and come to a trail intersection. Continue straight. Follow the white blaze. (The Rapid Run Nature Trail goes off to your right.)

7.2 Pass under a power line.

7.3 Turn right onto a shale road. Cross the bridge over Rapid Run, and then turn left and walk along the edge of Halfway Lake.

7.5 Arrive at the parking lot steps and your vehicle.

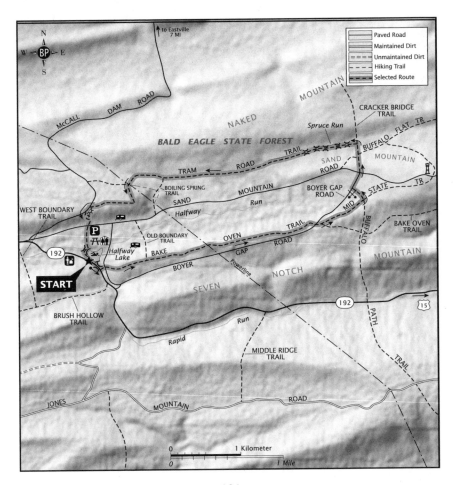

Starting at Halfway Lake, this hike trail begins with a brisk uphill warm-up. In less than a half mile, the trail levels out and you begin to see cross-country skiing signs. There are a few stretches so thickly strewn with rocks that you wonder how anyone could ski over this terrain. Needless to say, in order to ski over such a trail, there needs to be at least 10 inches of snow.

At a little over a mile, you cross under a power line. Here, in the clearing that runs under the power line, there's a clear view across the valley to Naked Mountain. In a little over five and a half miles, you'll be standing on that site, under the power line that looks impossibly far away.

The next section, the Tram Road Trail, runs for a little over two miles—and a good portion of the trail surface is rocky, rocky, rocky. As you walk this section you've got to wonder who would build a railroad over such rocky, rough terrain. Indeed, there are reports of such bumpy rides that cargo bounced off the train. Such was the case when a cracker barrel bounced off and rolled down the mountainside at a site now called Cracker Bridge.

After a view from the overlook, the trail leads down to the 34-acre natural area, a pristine second-growth pine-hemlock forest in the Rapid Run Valley. The area was set aside to give visitors an idea of what the forest looked like before it was clearcut. And although it may not be quite as good as the original, it's not a bad substitute.

Hike Information

🕐 Trail Contacts:
R.B. Winter State Park, Mifflinburg, PA (570) 966–1455

🕐 Schedule:
Open year round

💲 Fees/Permits:
No fees or permits required

❓ Local Information:
Susquehanna Valley Visitors Bureau, Lewisburg, PA (570) 524–7234 or 1–800–525–7320 or *www.svvb.com*

💡 Local Events/Attractions:
Mifflinburg   Buggy   Museum, Mifflinburg, PA (570) 966–1355

🛏 Accommodations:
Pineapple Inn B & B, Lewisburg, PA (570) 524–6200 • **R.B. Winter State Park,** Mifflinburg, PA (570) 966–1455 – *camping information*

🍴 Restaurants:
Brookpark Farm, Lewisburg, PA (570) 523–0220

🎒 Local Outdoor Retailers:
W.L. Donehower, Lewisburg, PA (570) 524–4408

🅽 Maps:
USGS Maps: Carroll, PA; Hartleton, PA

16

Loyalsock Trail

Hike Specs

Start: From the Loyalsock Trail trailhead on PA 87

Length: 6.9-mile loop

Approximate Hiking Time: 5 hours

Difficulty Rating: Difficult, with very steep ascents and rugged descents

Terrain: Traverse along a rocky switch-back footpath, an open plateau trail, a very rugged and rocky washout, and a shale road. You'll climb a sheer cliff to reach a plateau for outstanding views along the Allegheny Front.

Elevation Gain: 1,430 feet

Land Status: State forest

Nearest Town: Montoursville, PA

Other Trail Users: Hikers

Canine Compatibility: Leashed dogs permitted

Getting There

From Williamsport: Drive approximately seven miles east on U.S. 220 and take the Montoursville exit. Get on PA 87 and drive north for 8.8 miles to the Loyalsock Trailhead and parking area on your right. *DeLorme: Pennsylvania Atlas & Gazetteer:* Page 50 A2

This hike is the western terminus of the 59.3-mile Loyalsock Trail, which parallels the Loyalsock Creek, passes through the Worlds End State Park, and eventually empties into the Susquehanna River. The name is taken from the Native American reference *lawi-saquick*, or "middle creek," since it flows between Muncy and Lycoming creeks. The trail is well marked and well cared for, with convenient access trailheads every four to 10 miles, dividing the hike into eight sections. In fact, as you leave the forest on this hike, you pass the access point of next section of the trail, which leads to Smiths Knob.

There is no warm-up period on this hike; it's an assault from the very first step. As soon as you sign in at the trail register, you begin a 0.7-mile climb up the side of Loyalsock Gorge. The climb is steep—if it were any steeper, you'd need to trade in your hiking boots for mountain climbing gear.

At the summit, you'll come out onto a plateau. Interestingly, you're on top of the Allegheny High Plateau, which comprises the northern and western region of the Appalachian Plateau. The plateau, which is also called Allegheny Mountain, stretches north to the New York border and south to meet the Ridge and Valley Province—creating an escarpment called the

Looking south from the Allegheny Front.

Allegheny Front. It's difficult to think of any area with such deep gorges as a plateau. But as you listen to the never-ending rush of Loyalsock Creek, you begin to understand that, for over 200 million years, waters have been draining this area and cutting streambeds into the rock.

This hike is your chance to walk right to the edge of the Allegheny Front and take in the vistas of the valley below and the ridge tops off in the dis-

MilesDirections

0.0 START from the trailhead on PA 87. Walk to the Loyalsock Trail trailhead sign and trail register. Begin an uphill climb. Turn right at the yellow arrow.

0.2 The trail turns left.

0.6 Come to a round, blue sign ("Sock Rock") above a sandstone boulder—that supposedly looks like a sock. Follow the yellow arrow to the right.

0.7 Arrive at the top. The trail levels out on a plateau.

0.8 Enter the forest canopy.

1.4 Enter a white pine plantation.

1.5 Arrive at an intersection with an abandoned jeep road. Continue straight, and then veer right. Cross a small stream. *[**Note.** Look for red "LT" blazes and yellow rectangular blazes with red cross-member.]* Cross a second stream. The trail becomes a jeep road.

1.8 Turn left at the yellow arrow, and then turn left again.

2.0 Pass the two-mile marker. Begin a gradual ascent through boulders.

2.1 Arrive at the Allegheny Front. The trail parallels the cliff edge.

3.0 Pass the three-mile marker.

3.5 Turn right onto a jeep road.

3.7 The trail turn turns left, then left again.

4.1 Enter the forest canopy. The trail becomes a washout. Look for the yellow and red blazes.

5.3 Ford a small washout stream.

5.6 Pass through the Tiadaghton State Forest maintenance parking lot and cross a bridge over Bear Creek. On the other side turn left onto the shale road. *[**Note.** Look for the blazes along the road.]*

5.7 Pass the Loyalsock Trail sign on your right. Continue straight on the shale road.

6.3 Turn left at PA 87 and walk alongside the road.

6.9 Arrive back at the trailhead and your vehicle.

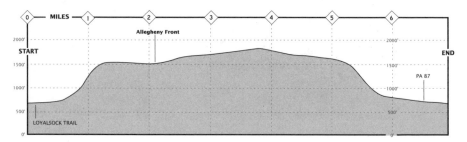

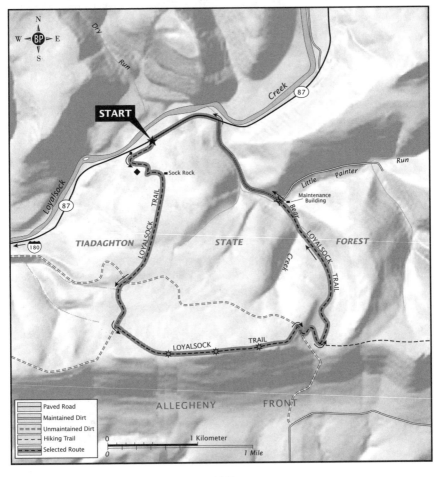

This trail follows the very edge of the Allegheny Front.

tance. A cool wind sweeps up from the ravine, cooling you as you walk through huckleberry bushes to rock outcroppings, where you can rest, take in the scenery, and eat your lunch.

Once you leave the ridge top, you're on your way down into Pete's Hollow. This trail back to civilization may challenge most hikers belief that going down is always easier than going up. Calling the steep, rocky washout into the hollow a trail is being generous. It's well marked like the rest of the trail, but for over a mile, you're boondoggling from one slippery boulder to the next.

The trail levels out in a hemlock valley beside Bear Creek. There's a dam just below the bridge where you can splash water on your face or take off your boots and give your feet a dip. From there, it's a level walk on a forest road beside Bear Creek. Along the way, you pass rustic cabins, set in deep shade on both sides of the road.

Hike Information

🌐 Trail Contacts:
Tiadaghton State Forest, South Williamsport, PA (570) 327–3450 or *www.dcnr.state.pa.us* • **Wyoming State Forest,** Bloomsburg, PA (570) 387–4255 • **Alpine Club,** P.O. Box 501, Williamsport, PA 17703

🕐 Schedule:
Open year round

💲 Fees/Permits:
No fees or permits required for hikers. There is a no-charge permit required for through-hikers who plan to primitive camp along the trail. Call the Tiadaghton State Forest at (570) 327–3450 or the Hillgrove Ranger Station (for the Wyoming State Forest section of the trail) at (570) 924–3501. Overnight hikers within the Worlds End State Park must register at the park office: (570) 924–3287

❓ Local Information:
Lycoming County Visitors Bureau, Williamsport, PA (570) 327–7700 or 1-800–358–9900 or *www.williams port.org/visitpa*

💡 Local Events/Attractions:
Lycoming County Historical Society Museum, Williamsport, PA (570) 326–3326 or *www.lycoming.org/ lchsmuseum*

● Accommodations:
The Bodine House Bed and Breakfast, Muncy, PA (570) 546–8949 or *www.bodinehouse.com* • **Worlds End State Park Campgrounds,** Forksville, PA (570) 924–3287 • **Almost Heaven Campgrounds,** Forksville, PA (570) 924–3458

🍽 Restaurants:
Family Afare, Montoursville, PA (570) 368–1181

🎒 Local Outdoor Retailers:
Country Ski & Sports, Montoursville, PA (570) 368–1718 or 1-877–669–9966 or *www.coun- tryskiandsports.com*

🅝 Maps:
USGS maps: Montoursville North, PA; Huntersville, PA

Gillespie Point

Hike Specs

Start: From the Blackwell Boaters Access Area parking lot on PA 414
Length: 4.9-mile loop
Approximate Hiking Time: 3 hours
Difficulty Rating: Moderate, due to a short, steep climb
Terrain: Climb along a shale road, a forest footpath, and rock outcroppings to the top of a mountain for an impressive view.
Elevation Gain: 1,159 feet
Land Status: State forest
Nearest Town: Wellsboro, PA
Other Trail Users: Hikers
Canine Compatibility: Leashed dogs permitted

Getting There

From Williamsport: Drive north on U.S. 15 for 26 miles to the village of Liberty. Look for the PA 414 sign. Turn left onto PA 414 and drive west 15 miles to the village of Blackwell and the Blackwell Boaters Access Area parking lot on your left. *DeLorme: Pennsylvania Atlas & Gazetteer:* Page 35 D5

T ioga State Forest consists of 160,000 acres of mountains and valleys, with a range in elevation from 780 feet to over 2,500. Unlike the Valley and Ridge Province of the state, faulting or the folding of the earth didn't create this area. It was formed during the last ice age when a glacier blocked the northerly flowing water, creating a glacial pond. When the glacier retreated, glaciation occurred, leaving behind a moraine of gravel, clay, and sand that reversed the flow of the water. Over the next 10 million years, this stream, now known as Pine Creek, carved out the gorge. And from Gillespie Point, you can have a commanding view of this project, eons in the making.

The 12,163-acre Pine Creek Gorge, which at its widest point is over 5,000 feet across, is commonly referred to as *The Grand Canyon of Pennsylvania*. Because of its beauty and distinct natural characteristics, the gorge was declared a National Natural Area in 1968. Two state parks, Colton Point and Leonard Harrison, claim the northern end of the gorge,

but this hike doesn't include them. These parks are not only more touristy—with over 300,000 annual visitors, wooden steps, guardrails, and viewing platforms on the trails—but also, neither offers anything near the views you'll experience at Gillespie Point.

Because of its conical shape, the apex of Gillespie Point is not very big—no bigger, say, than a full-size car. The viewpoint is nothing more than an outcropping that hangs over the cliff edge like a shelf. When you walk out onto it, snug down your hat—the wind whips up out of the gorge and whistles through the trees with appreciable force, just as it has for millions of years. (This is the vista you've come for, but there's a second view to the south of Big Run Valley and Oregon Hill, which is also impressive.)

Before this area was settled and seriously logged, the forests were predominately white pine, red maple, chestnut, and hemlock. Today, the forest is made up of two communities: one dominated by hardwoods, such as yellow birch, sugar maple, beech, and black cherry, and the other by white pine.

For the wildflower enthusiast, spring is the best time to visit. More than 50 species of wildflower bloom in April and May. Among them are

Hike Information

◑ Trail Contacts:
Tioga State Forest, Wellsboro, PA (570) 724–2868

◔ Schedule:
Open year round

◐ Fees/Permits:
No fees or permits required

❓ Local Information:
Wellsboro Area Chamber of Commerce, Wellsboro, PA (570) 724–1926

◔ Local Events/Attractions:
White water rafting and canoeing, Wellsboro Area Chamber of Commerce, Wellsboro, PA (570) 724–1926 – *call for detailed information*

◒ Accommodations:
Country Owl Getaway B&B, Morris, PA (570) 353–2540 • **Twin Stream Campsites,** Morris, PA (570) 353–7251

◉ Restaurants:
Wellsboro Diner, Wellsboro, PA (570) 724–3992

◍ Local Outdoor Retailers:
Davis Sporting Goods, Wellsboro, PA (570) 724–2626

Ⓝ Maps:
USGS maps: Cedar Run, PA; Morris, PA

columbine, jack-in-the-pulpit, wild ginger, false Solomon's seal, and the Canada mayflower. In summer look for the wild orchid helleborine, white snakeroot, hairy beardtongue, and red bee balm.

For birdwatchers spring is also the best time to see the osprey (also called the fish hawk) migrating north. This giant raptor, with a wingspan of five to six feet, was once almost wiped out by DDT, but it has rebounded well since the banning of the pesticide.

In addition to wildlife viewing from the trails, some birdwatchers go a step farther: They head out on the water in canoes for a chance to view the bald eagles that nest around the tiny village of Blackwell. If you're interested, you too can launch your canoe from the Blackwell boat access and comb the river, possibly witnessing one of these raptors diving into the waters to pluck a fish.

MilesDirections

0.0 START at the Blackwell Boater's Access Area. Turn right onto PA 414 and walk through the village of Blackwell.

0.2 Cross over Babb Creek on the one-lane traffic bridge.

0.3 Turn right onto Big Run Road.

0.4 Arrive at the Mid State Trail sign and a sign for Gillespie Point and Little Pine State Park. Begin an uphill climb, following the orange blazes.

1.0 The trail turns left at the double orange blazes.

1.3 Arrive at Gillespie Point Overlook.

1.7 The trail turns right and you pass through an open area.

1.9 Cross a washout stream and an abandoned logging road. Note the clear-

cut area on your left.

2.0 Cross a second washout stream.

2.2 Cross a third washout stream.

2.3 The trail turns right.

2.8 Turn right onto Big Run Road. Arrive at the Mid State Trail and a sign that reads: "Mid State Trail, Brill Hollow, and Gillespie Point."

4.5 Pass a sign marking the Tioga State Forest boundary. Pass the Mid State Trailhead where you first left Big Run Road.

4.6 Turn left onto PA 414 and retrace your steps across the traffic bridge.

4.9 Turn left into Blackwell Boating Access Area and arrive at your vehicle.

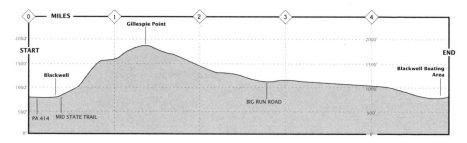

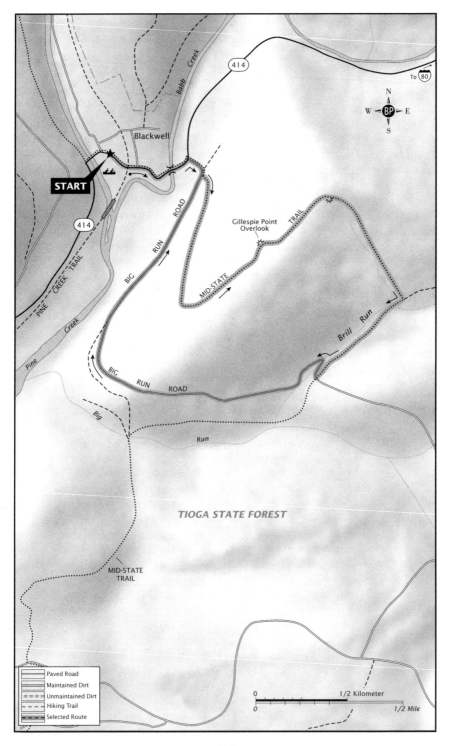

18

Bohen Run Falls & West Rim Trail

Hike Specs

Start: From the Blackwell boater access parking lot on PA 414

Length: 8.5-mile loop

Approximate Hiking Time: 5 hours

Difficulty Rating: Moderate, due to the extensive uphill climbs

Terrain: Utilize abandoned logging roads, mountain footpaths, a wheat grass meadow, and a shale bicycle path. Tour a hemlock-lined stream in a gorge bottom, passing waterfalls and culminating with a natural boulder overlook.

Elevation Gain: 859 feet

Land Status: State forest

Nearest Town: Wellsboro, PA

Other Trail Users: Hikers

Canine Compatibility: Leashed dogs permitted

Getting There

From Williamsport: Drive north on U.S. 15 for 26 miles to the village of Liberty. Look for the PA 414 sign. Turn left onto PA 414 and drive west 15 miles to the village of Blackwell and the Blackwell boater access parking lot on your left.

DeLorme: Pennsylvania Atlas & Gazetteer: Page 35 D5

This hike comprises sections of two of the state's most popular backpacking trails: the West Rim and the Mid State trails. The West Rim Trail stretches 30 miles along the western rim of Pine Creek Gorge—Pennsylvania's *Grand Canyon*. The Mid State Trail runs 189 miles across the state, from the village of Water Street on U.S. Route 22 to its connection with the West Rim Trail near Bohen Run in the north. Regardless of where you enter this gorge, you'll be struck by the sheer strength of the force that turned a mountain plateau into a corrugated landscape that, seen from an adjoining mountain peak, looks like a giant green washboard.

On this hike, you achieve not only the northern terminus of the Mid State Trail, but you also walk the final leg of the West Rim Trail to its southern terminus on Pennsylvania 414. More importantly, if you are new to this area, these hikes will afford you a quality Pine Creek Gorge experience, far from the tourist-friendly Leonard Harrison and Colton Point state parks in the northern end of the gorge.

But hikers are not the only ones who sing the praises of this rugged wilderness. In 1968 Congress declared an 18-mile stretch of the gorge—from Ansonia in the north to Blackwell in the south—a National Natural

Bohen Run Falls.

Landmark. Our hike takes you into the southern tip of this 12,163-acre natural wonderland.

You begin at ground zero, Pine Creek, the lowest point in the gorge. Keep your eyes open for bald eagles as you walk along the creek side. Sightings are common along Pine Creek, especially around Blackwell. You may also see a bald eagle taking a swan dive into the water and emerging with his dinner between his talons.

Run-off waters from the mountaintops cut gashes in the hollow bottoms, as they make their way to the bottom of the gorge. Once you have climbed up the face of Pine Creek Gorge, you encounter your first run-off streams, Jerry Run and Bohen Run.

If you do this hike early in the spring, the waterfalls will be dancing and the trails will be slippery. If you come later in the year or during a dry season, you're unlikely to find waterfalls—and if it has been an extended dry season, there may be no water at all. This is important to note if you're one of the many hikers who use waterfalls and streams as reference points.

The Mid State Trail ends at its junction with the West Rim Trail. From there it's a short climb to the West Rim Overlook, a great place to eat your lunch, stretch out on the grassy flat area for a snooze, or just to sit on a rock and listen to the wind.

The Rattlesnake Rock access area to the Pine Creek Rails-to-Trails is directly across Pennsylvania 414. Bathrooms and seasonal water are here. The trail, which has a crushed limestone base, is being completed in sections. The first section to be finished is the 19 miles from Ansonia to Blackwell. When the trail is finished it will run a total of 62 miles, from Ansonia in the north to Jersey Shore in the south. Lucky for you, the weary hiker, you only have to walk a scant mile and half to your car.

Hike Information

● Trail Contacts:
Tioga State Forest, Wellsboro, PA (570) 724–2868

● Schedule:
Open year round

● Fees/Permits:
No fees or permits required

● Local Information:
Wellsboro Area Chamber of Commerce, Wellsboro, PA (570) 724–1926

● Local Events/Attractions:
Tioga County Fair, second week in August, Whitneyville, PA (570) 724–3196 or (570) 549–8176

● Accommodations:
The Four Winds B & B, Wellsboro, PA (570) 724–6141 • Stony Fork Creek Campground, Wellsboro, PA (570) 724–3096

● Restaurants:
Penn Wells Hotel, Wellsboro, PA (570) 724–2111

● Organizations:
Keystone Trails Association, P.O. Box 251, Cogan Station, PA 17728

● Local Outdoor Retailers:
Pine Creek Outfitters, Wellsboro, PA (570) 724–3003

● Maps:
USGS maps: Cedar Run, PA

MilesDirections

0.0 START at the Blackwell boater access parking lot. Turn left onto PA 414 and cross the traffic bridge over Pine Creek.

0.1 Turn right at the double orange blazes painted on the backside of a street sign. You must step over the guardrail.

0.2 Arrive at stone steps and a trail sign for the Mid State Trail, Jerry Run Falls, Bohen Run Falls, and the West Rim Trail.

0.8 Cross a deep washout.

1.0 Arrive at a rock outcropping and a view area.

1.2 Arrive at a natural overlook and Jerry Run Falls.

1.3 Trail turns right onto an old logging road at the double orange blazes.

1.5 Pass a trail that goes off to the right, down the gorge to campsites. Continue straight.

1.6 Arrive at double orange blazes. Trail turns uphill onto an old logging road.

2.3 Arrive at Bohen Run, visible to your right.

2.8 Arrive at the intersection with the West Rim Trail and trail register. Make a severe left turn and begin climbing on the West Rim Trail.

3.6 Arrive at the West Rim Trail Overlook.

4.1 Pass a hunting camp on your left.

4.4 Cross West Rim Road and arrive at a sign: "West Rim Trail to PA 414—2.3 Miles."

4.5 Pass an abandoned dynamite shed on your left.

4.7 Pass an intersection with a woods road then turn right into the forest canopy.

4.9 The trail turns left onto a dirt road, then becomes rocky footpath.

5.1 The trail turns left at Lloyd Run stream.

6.4 Arrive at fork in the trail. Go to the right, following the orange blazes.

6.6 Arrive at the West Rim Trail register.

6.9 Cross PA 414 to Rattlesnake Rock Access Area parking lot. Walk on the path past the bathrooms and turn left onto the Pine Creek Bicycle Trail.

8.4 Cross Pine Creek on the wooden Rails-to-Trails bridge.

8.5 Pass the auto access gate and turn left onto PA 414. Shortly afterward, turn left into the Blackwell boater access parking lot and find your vehicle.

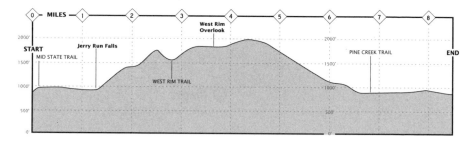

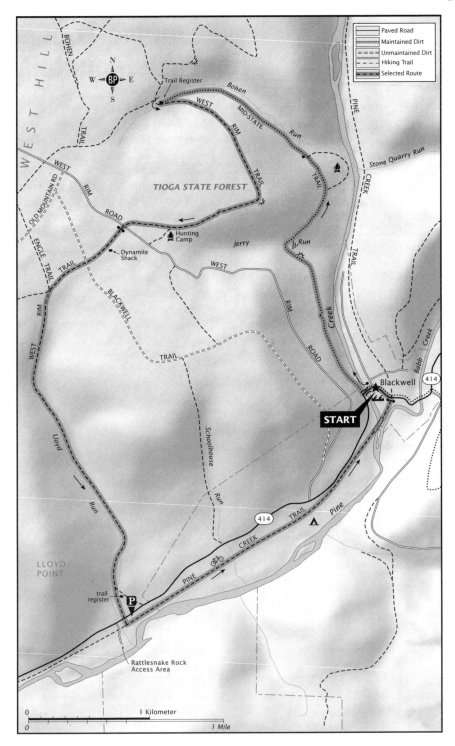

Pine Trail & Hemlock Mountain

Hike Specs

Start: From the Pine Trail Trailhead at the end of Naval Run Road in the Tiadaghton State Forest

Length: 8.3-mile loop

Approximate Hiking Time: 6 hours

Difficulty Rating: Difficult, due to a steep, 0.75-mile climb out of a hollow on a rocky washout

Terrain: Follow abandoned logging roads, a typical mountain footpath, a narrow cliff-side path, rocky washouts, and out-croppings. You'll walk alongside a wide creek, cut uphill to a man-made footpath that makes its way past giant boulders, climb to the mountaintop for sweeping views, and then descend into the gorge for a view of a waterfall.

Elevation Gain: 2,006 feet

Land Status: State forest

Nearest Town: Wellsboro, PA

Other Trail Users: Hikers

Canine Compatibility: Leashed dogs permitted

Getting There

From Williamsport: Drive west on U.S. 220 to Exit 24. Take Exit 24 and drive north on PA 44 about 12 miles through the village of Waterville to the intersection of PA 44 and PA 414. At this intersection, PA 44 becomes PA 414. Drive north on PA 414 for approximately 15 miles to the village of Slate Run. Just 0.1 miles before Wolfe's General Store, turn left onto Slate Run Road and cross over Pine Creek. You'll know you've gone too far if you wind up in downtown Slate Run (which consists of the Wolfe's General Store & Gas Station). Once across Pine Creek, turn left onto Naval Run Road and drive 1.3 miles to the picnic area and cul-de-sac at the end of Naval Run Road. *DeLorme: Pennsylvania Atlas & Gazetteer:* Page 49 A4

Pennsylvania's Grand Canyon, Pine Creek Gorge, runs 47 miles on either side of Pine Creek, from Ansonia in the north to Jersey Shore—that's Pennsylvania, not *the* Jersey Shore—in the south. The gorge is a result of a glacial melt that left behind a natural dam of gravel, sand, and clay. The dam, which geologists call a *moraine*, not only stopped the northerly flow of water, but also reversed the flow from north to south. That mass of water, raging southward for millions of years, formed the gorge, which is at some points 1,000 feet deep and one mile wide. Today, it's Pine Creek that flows through the bottom of the gorge.

Pine Trail is one of the best ways to appreciate Pine Creek Gorge, though it will involve a bit of pain and suffering. When you've climbed 200 feet up the face of the gorge, the trail guides you past an outcropping of giant boulders, where, if you let your imagination take over, you might think you're exploring the Anasazi cliff dwellings of the American Southwest. The trail, which is man-made, is comprised of a well-maintained, red clay base with

sideboards in the spots that are prone to washout. Despite the construction effort, you'll find yourself holding onto the boulders and doing a little ducking and weaving as you traverse the face of this steep ravine.

Once you've completed your first climb, you enter the canopy of the Black Forest. When the first Europeans settled the area, the stands of pine and hemlock were so dense within these 750,000 acres that they essentially blocked all the sunlight from the forest floor.

Calling the section of *trail* that leads you out of Riffle Run Valley a trail is generous. It's well marked, but it is rough going. It's obvious that this three-quarter of a mile section is subject to perennial washouts. When you see mountain laurel, you can relax; you're out of Riffle Valley and soon you'll turn onto a wide, flat road that leads across the top of Hemlock Mountain. Along this road, you'll pass four vistas. This stretch of the hike is the easiest, but the best is yet to come.

When you turn right onto the Old Cutoff Trail, it's pretty much like any other mountain trail. But hold on. Just before you begin your descent back

Hike Information

🟤 Trail Contacts:
Tiadaghton State Forest, Williamsport, PA (570) 327–3450

🕐 Schedule:
Open year round

🟤 Fees/Permits:
No fees or permits required

❓ Local Information:
Lycoming County Visitors Bureau, Williamsport, PA 1–800–358–990

🟤 Local Events/Attractions:
Mountain Bike Challenge, in September, Asaph State Forest, U.S. 6, west of Wellsboro, PA (570) 724-1926

🟤 Accommodations:
Cedar Run Inn B&B, Cedar Run, PA (570) 353-6241 • **Pettecote Junction Campgrounds**, Cedar Run, PA (570) 353-7183

🍴 Restaurants:
The Steak House, Wellsboro, PA (570) 724-9092

🟤 Organizations:
Mid State Trail Association, P.O. Box 167, Boalsburg, PA 16827

🟤 Local Outdoor Retailers:
Davis Sporting Goods, Wellsboro, PA (570) 724-2626 • Wolfe's General Store & Slate Run Tackle Shop, Slate Run, PA (570) 753-8551

🟤 Maps:
USGS maps: Slate Run, PA

MilesDirections

0.0 START at the picnic area at the dead-end of Naval Run Road. Walk to the Pine Trail trailhead and turn right at the sign that points you toward Callahan Run, Riffle Run, and Big Trail Run. Follow the blue blazes.

0.1 Cross Naval Run and turn left on the other side for a short uphill climb.

0.2 Arrive at an open area. Trail veers to the right and enters a pine plantation.

0.9 Come to Callahan Run. Cross the stream and turn right at the double blaze. Ascend a knoll to a flat area. Turn left at the double blue blaze and stay on the Pine Trail. (Callahan Run Trail continues straight.)

1.0 Pass through an open area.

1.2 The trail becomes a narrow footpath. Pass through a boulder outcropping.

1.6 Arrive at Half Dome Mountain Vista. The trail turns right and parallels Riffle Run.

1.8 The trail becomes a rocky washout. Look for the blue blazes on the rocks.

2.5 Turn right onto Big Trail Road.

2.6 Arrive at Riffle Run Valley & Slate Run Vista on your right.

2.8 Pass the road to Stone Quarry Hollow & Trout Run on your left.

4.0 Pass the road to Big John Hollow on your left.

4.2 Pass the orange-blazed Black Forest Trail intersection on your left. Arrive at the viewing area of Hemlock Mountain on your right. Pass an intersection with Black Forest Trail on your right.

4.4 Pass an unnamed trail on your left.

4.9 Turn right at the log gate onto the Old Cutoff Trail.

5.4 Connect with the Black Forest Trail. The trail turns right. Follow the orange blazes.

5.7 The trail descends into a hollow.

6.2 Climb a rocky outcropping.

6.3 Reach the top of outcropping and a vista.

6.4 Walk across the narrow ridge top.

6.5 Arrive at the vista to the north.

6.6 Trail begins a descent and makes a series of switchbacks.

7.0 Enter a hemlock canopy. The trail turns right at the double blue blazes and begins another series of switchbacks.

7.6 Arrive at an intersection. (The Black Forest Trail turns to the left.) Continue straight as the trail becomes the Naval Run Trail Horse Path.

7.7 Turn right onto Old Naval Run Road.

8.0 Pass a waterfall.

8.2 Turn left and cross Naval Run stream. *[**Note.** This is where you crossed Naval Run at the beginning of this hike.]* Stay left for uphill climb.

8.3 Arrive at the trailhead and your vehicle.

to civilization, you come to one of the top views in the state. Looking north from this natural overlook, you take in Pine Creek as it winds its way through the endless series of ridges and valleys within the gorge. At the bottom of the mountain, along Old Naval Run Road, keep an eye out for a waterfall.

At a little over eight miles the trail crosses Naval Run at the same point where you crossed the stream when you first started out. There was once a culvert here, so that Old Naval Run Road used to connect with Naval Run Road. But the infamous Hurricane Agnes of 1972 washed it out. Today, Naval Run Road dead-ends, and there's no visible attempt to reconnect the two roads. Once you cross the stream, you merely retrace your beginning steps up a small incline to the trailhead and your vehicle.

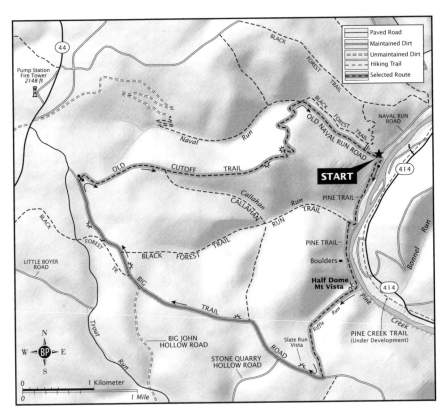

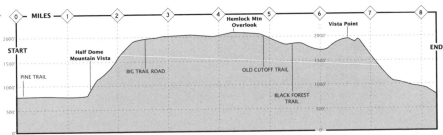

Splash Dam Hollow

Hike Specs

Start: From the Susquehannock State Forest District Office parking area

Length: 7.8-mile loop

Approximate Hiking Time: 4–4.5 hours

Difficulty Rating: Moderate, due to bush-whacking and the steep climb out of a hollow

Terrain: Follow old fire trails, abandoned logging roads, cross-country ski trails, a paved road, overgrown marshes, and hollow bottoms. Hike through a high plateau forest, deep hollows, and a marshy area beside a narrow stream.

Elevation Gain: 1,124 feet

Land Status: State forest

Nearest Town: Coudersport, PA

Other Trail Users: Hikers, cross-country skiers, and hunters (in season)

Canine Compatibility: Leashed dogs permitted

Getting There

From Dubois: Drive north on U.S. 219 for 48 miles to the intersection with U.S. 6. Turn right onto U.S. 6 and drive 53 miles to the Susquehannock State Forest Office and parking lot on your right. **DeLorme: Pennsylvania Atlas & Gazetteer:** Page 34 B2

The Susquehannock Trail System (STS) is a popular 85-mile loop that runs through the Susqhehannock State Forest— 262,000 acres of deeply cut ravines and plateaus. Though the trail is well maintained and well marked, the hike is not without its challenges. The first challenge is right at the trail sign-in station (cue 0.4). You can avoid any confusion by making the hairpin right turn at the fork about 20 feet before the sign-in station. If you find yourself at the log book, however, follow these directions: Looking ahead, it appears that to turn right, you should continue following the trail, which does indeed veer off to the right. Actually, what you want to do is turn around and look back the way you came. The fork goes left and right. To the right is the blue-blazed trail that you started out on; to the left is the orange-blazed STS trail, which you want to take.

With that business taken care of, you can focus on the scenery around you. Follow the STS across a high plateau and into a deep ravine. This forest was logged extensively in the late 1800s and the early 1900s, and from the trail you can see evidence of the clearcutting. The recovering areas are mostly second-growth hardwoods, such as black cherry, beech,

and maple. (Second-growth pine and hemlock can be seen mostly in the lower wetlands.) Scattered throughout are black oak, pin oak, northern red oak, chestnut oak, and white oak; however, the bulk of the oak population has been destroyed by a caterpillar known as the oak leaf roller *[see Sidebar on page 127]*.

The trail descends along the slope of a ravine and onto the bottom of Splash Dam Hollow and an intersection with Lyman Run. The deep pools in the stream (or *splash dams*, for which this hollow was named) were built by loggers to temporar-

> *The National Register of Historic Places lists downtown Coudersport, Pennsylvania, as a well-preserved example of a 19th century small town.*

ily store their logs. When full, the dam was opened and logs were floated downstream to major centers of industry like Pittsburgh. The term *splash dam*, if not obvious, comes from the enormous splash that occurred when logs were rolled down the hollow into the dam. If you're looking for an example of such a damn, unfortunately none remain on Lyman Run.

When the loggers moved out, the beaver moved in. Along this following section, you'll notice beaver dams appearing across Lyman Run. Around the dams, there are areas where the beavers have done some clearcutting of their own.

The trail cuts away from the stream and intersects with an ATV road for a short one-tenth of a mile. (Here's evidence that hikers are not the only ones with trails in this forest: aside from ski trails, there is a 43-mile network of ATV and snowmobile trails. These roads are not marked on the state forest hiking maps, but ATV maps are available at the state forest office.) It's along this section that you'll need to be diligent to not lose your way. The trail leaves the road at a wooden post. The trail here is overgrown, but it does exist. Shortly after that, there is a beaver dam that blocks the trail. Before you get to it, while you are still on high ground, turn left and follow a fishermen's path that will take you across the stream. On the other side of the stream, make your way toward the edge of the dam and you'll pick up the trail again. If you look ahead at this point, you'll see Lyman Run Road.

The trail continues on Lyman Run Road, passing dozens of quaking aspens on the right. Even the slightest breeze causes its almost circular leaves to tremble, hence the name. Many of the forest animals graze on its twigs, and although its inner bark is bitter, it's a staple in the beaver diet. Aspen, which sprout quickly from a widespread root system, have the widest

Deep in the Susquehannock Forest. This is big country.

range geographically and ecologically of any species in North America. The aspen is also an important pioneer species—the first tree to invade an area that has recently been burned or cut.

When you leave Lyman Run Road, look for another wooden post. There is a trail, but before too long, it is obliterated by blow-down and lack of use. At this point, simply walk the hollow bottom. Like the first ravine, this cut is deep and steep. It's especially steep as you crest the ridge and intersect with another ATV road. From the ATV road, you bushwhack in the same northerly direction across a fern-covered open, flat area for roughly two-tenths of a mile. Hikers with a compass could practice using it here.

The STS cuts east and west across this plateau, so if you're heading north, you're sure to cross it. Turn left and return to the trail sign-in and retrace you steps to the parking area.

The Oak Leaf Roller

This mottled brown, half-inch long caterpillar seems to thrive on oak leaves. In satisfying this urge it severely reduces the trees' ability to perform photosynthesis. This defoliates and weakens the trees, so that when the roller returns year after year, the trees stand little chance of survival. The oak leaf roller began appearing in the state's forests in the 1960s and 1970s. There have been periodic outbreaks since, most recently in Cambria, Cameron, Clearfield, Clinton, and Warren counties.

Hike Information

● Trail Contacts:
Susquehannock State Forest, Coudersport, PA (814) 274–3600 • **Susquehannock Trail Club,** P.O. Box 643, Coudersport, PA 16915

● Schedule:
Open year round

● Fees/Permits:
No fees or permits required

● Local Information:
Potter County Visitors Association: 1–888–768–8372 or (814) 435–2290 or *www.pavisnet.com/pcva*

● Local Events/Attractions:
Pennsylvania Lumber Museum, Galeton, PA (814) 435–2652 • **God's Country Marathon,** first Saturday in June, Galeton, PA: *www.pavisnet.com/marathon – cash prizes*

● Accommodations:
Frosty Hollow Bed and Breakfast, Coudersport, PA (814) 274–7419 or *www.frostyhollowbandb.com* • **Lyman Run State Park,** Galeton, PA (814) 435–5010 – *for camping information*

● Restaurants:
Potato City Country Inn, Coudersport, PA (814) 274–7133

● Local Outdoor Retailers:
Mountain Ridge Sports, Coudersport, PA (814) 274–9494 or *www.mountainridgesports.com*

● Maps:
USGS maps: Brookland, PA; Cherry Springs, PA

Worth noting: Nearby Lyman Run State Park is open for camping and other activities, but the 45-acre Lyman Lake has been drained, so there is no swimming or fishing.

MilesDirections

0.0 START at the Susquehannock State Forest District Office parking area. Walk past the maintenance building on your left to the access gate and follow the orange blazes.

0.1 Cross over a small run and arrive at a blue trail sign with a black arrow. Turn right and climb the man-made steps.

0.4 Come to the trail register. Make a severe, hairpin turn to the right. *[Note. Read more about this turn in the hike description.]*

0.7 Cross an unpaved ATV/Maintenance Road.

1.3 Cross Lyman Run Road. *[Note. Notice the clear cutting on your left.]*

1.4 Come to a hand-carved, orange sign that reads STS.

1.8 Begin your descent into the hollow.

2.7 Come to the signpost: "STS trail to the right." You turn left.

2.9 *[Note. Notice the beaver dams.]*

3.4 Cross a small wash out.

3.8 Turn right onto an unpaved ATV road.

3.9 Leave the road and walk straight toward a wooden post.

4.3 Come to a stump on your right with thick wire cable around it. Turn left onto the fishermen's trail, and then turn right and cross Lyman Run. *[Note. The STS turns right at Lyman Run; our hike turns left. There are no blazes and the trail is overgrown, but the trail is there. At points it's high above Lyman Run, cutting across a slope and paralleling the stream.]*

4.4 Turn left onto Lyman Run Road. *[Note. Notice the quaking aspens on your right.]*

5.5 Lyman Run Road makes a sweeping curve. Turn right at the wooden post. There is no trail sign, but this is the Township Trail. The trail runs alongside, and then into the hollow bottom.

6.3 Cross at unpaved ATV road and continue walking in the same northerly direction across an open, flat area.

6.5 Come to the Susquehannock Trail and turn left.

7.4 Arrive back at the trail register. At the fork, follow the blue blazes to the right and retrace your steps.

7.8 Arrive back at the access gate and parking area.

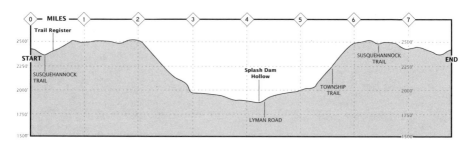

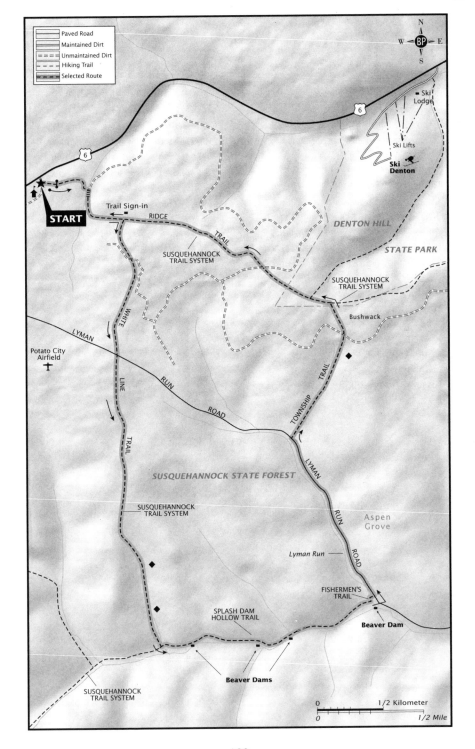

21

Wykoff Run Natural Area

Hike Specs

Start: From the Wykoff Run Natural Area trailhead on Quehanna Highway
Length: 4.8-mile loop
Approximate Hiking Time: 2.5 hours
Difficulty Rating: Easy, due to the level terrain
Trail Surface: Follow abandoned jeep roads, cross-country ski trails, and foot-paths through hardwood forest, stands of white birch, and meadows covered with blueberry bushes.
Elevation Gain: 342 feet
Land Status: State forest and natural area
Nearest Town: Clearfield, PA
Other Trail Users: Hikers, cross-country skiers, and hunters (in season)
Canine Compatibility: Leashed dogs permitted

Getting There

From Dubois: Drive east on I-80 and take Exit 19 at Clearfiled. Drive north on PA 879 for about 17 miles to Karthaus. In the village of Karthaus, take the Quehanna Highway and drive north 8.7 miles to the trailhead and parking lot on the right at the intersection with Wykoff Run Road. *DeLorme: Pennsylvania Atlas & Gazetteer:* Page 47 C6

Wykoff Run Natural Area is a 1,252-acre segment of the Elk State Forest section of the 48,000-acre Quehanna Wild Area. Ironically, this massive network of natural areas, wilderness, and state forest along the Allegheny High Plateau was once the site of oil and gas well drilling, as well as extensive logging. When the loggers pulled out, they left behind the limbs and waste wood, which fueled the wildfires that left this area treeless and devoid of vegetation.

In the years after World War II, Clearfield and Cameron counties suffered recession-level unemployment. In an effort to attract businesses and create jobs, the government promoted this barren land as an industrial site. Then, in 1955, the Curtiss-Wright Corporation opened a testing and manufacturing site on 50,000 acres, which they had either purchased or leased from the state. On this lonely site they built and operated a four-megawatt nuclear reactor, developed and tested jet engines, and experimented with nuclear engines for aircraft.

Curtiss-Wright felt that it would be advantageous to operate these types of projects in a remote area, far from any neighbors, and the Wykoff Run

area provided just that. Curtiss-Wright also needed a pool of workers to staff its plant; the depressed local economy could provide that too. But nuclear powered jet engines never came to be, and area coal miners and loggers didn't fit into the manufacturer's high-tech environment. Ultimately, the endeavor failed and the plant closed in 1963.

Evidence of the company's aborted projects can be found along the trail. Just three-quarters of a mile in from the trailhead you'll pass a concrete bunker-type building with slits for windows. The structure was built to test jet engines, but after the tests were discontinued, the company used the building to store hazardous and explosive material. Today, the building is covered in graffiti and looks like an apocalyptic-movie relic. Just past that, at about mile 1.0, there's an open area to the left. This is the site where the company buried beryllium oxide, an aluminum-like material widely used in the aircraft industry because of its rigid, lightweight, and heat-resistant properties.

Industry didn't end with Curtiss-Wright's collapse. After Curtiss-Wright left, the Piper Aircraft Company moved in and used some of the buildings.

MilesDirections

0.0 START at the trailhead on Quehanna Highway. Follow the blue blazes.

0.4 Cross a small run.

0.7 Come to an abandoned concrete building on your left. Cross a wide meadow.

0.8 The meadow ends and you enter the forest again.

1.1 Come to large, marshy meadow.

1.7 Turn right onto the Hoover Road. A sign reads "Old Wykoff Road."

1.9 Turn left onto a logging road.

2.0 Come to an access gate.

2.2 Turn right at the sign "Wykoff Road 1 Mile."

3.2 Cross Wykoff Run Road and come to the sign Ski Trails. Cross a wooden footbridge over Wykoff Run.

3.3 Begin a climb up the ridge.

3.9 Arrive at a trail intersection with multiple signposts. Turn right and follow the sign "Quehanna Highway 1 Mile."

4.0 Cross two small runs.

4.6 Pass through a clearing.

4.8 Turn right at the Quehanna Highway and walk about 300 feet to the trailhead parking area.

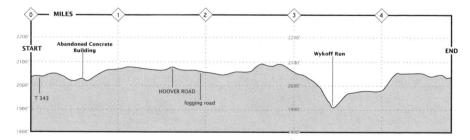

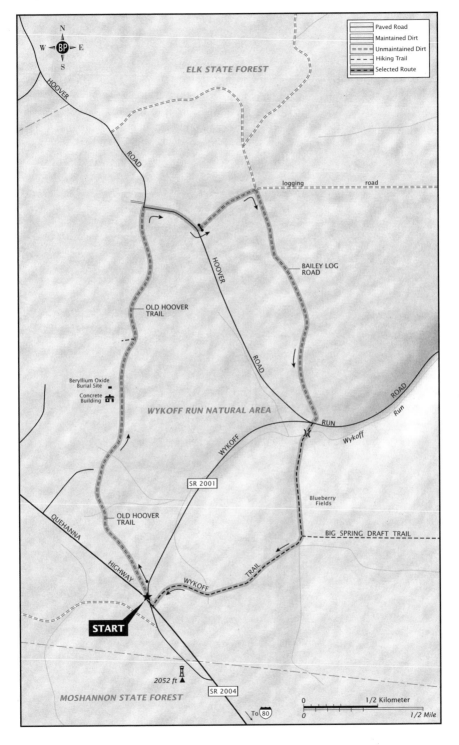

Paved Road
Maintained Dirt
Unmaintained Dirt
Hiking Trail
Selected Route

N
W BP E
S

ELK STATE FOREST

HOOVER ROAD

logging   road

HOOVER

BAILEY LOG ROAD

OLD HOOVER TRAIL

ROAD

Beryllium Oxide Burial Site
Concrete Building

WYKOFF RUN NATURAL AREA

RUN

Wykoff   Run

ROAD

WYKOFF

SR 2001

Blueberry Fields

OLD HOOVER TRAIL

BIG SPRING DRAFT TRAIL

QUEHANNA

HIGHWAY

TRAIL

WYKOFF

START

2052 ft

SR 2004

MOSHANNON STATE FOREST

To 80

1/2 Kilometer
1/2 Mile

But by the mid 1980s, they too had moved out. Today, these buildings are part of the 100-acre Quehanna Industrial Complex, located alongside Quehanna Highway.

Despite its past, this area is popular with hikers; it's also a favorite trailhead for backpackers who use this hike to connect with the Quehanna Trail, a 73-mile loop that covers some of the roughest, most remote terrain in the state. For the most part, this section of the mountains is like any other—except that you encounter magnificent stands of white birch trees, surrounded by typical northern hardwoods, hemlocks, and other conifers. One of the reasons the area was set aside was to protect the birch trees, a

Wykoff Run travels through this hemlock woodland.

species that thrives in upland forests and burned-out or clearcut areas.

Since reverting to a natural area, wildlife here is once again abundant. If you spent enough time here, you might catch a glimpse of the elusive wild turkey or a black bear at the blueberry patches—you almost surely will see the ubiquitous white-tailed deer. Take note: Hunting is permitted in the natural area and the surrounding forest. Always be aware of hunting season dates before going into the forest. (You may be relieved to know, however, that hunting the amphibians and reptiles, including snakes—permitted in some parts of the state—is forbidden in the natural area.)

The hike itself is pleasant. The abandoned jeep roads are groomed for cross-country skiing and along the footpaths, especially if you come in mid June, you'll see endless patches of mountain laurel. Wykoff Run is a typical Allegheny Plateau stream: the water is clear and cold, and the gorge it has created is evidence that Mother Nature, regardless of how she was abused, is alive and well…and busy.

Hike Information

● Trail Contacts:
Elk State Forest, Forest District Headquarters, Emporium, PA (814) 486–3353 • **Quehanna Trail and Wild Area,** Moshannon State Forest, P.O. Box 952, Clearfield, PA 16830

● Schedule:
Open year round

● Fees/Permits:
No fees or permits required

● Local Information:
Cameron County Tourist Promotion Agency, Driftwood, PA 1–888–252–2872 or (814) 546–2665 or *www.pavisnet.com/camtpa* • **Cameron County Chamber of Commerce,** Emporium, PA (814) 486–4314

● Local Events/Attractions:
Elk County Visitors Bureau, St. Marys, PA (814) 834–3723 or *www.elk-county.com – observe wild elk in their natural habitat*

● Accommodations:
Black Moshannon State Park, Phillipsburg, PA (814) 342–5960 or 1–888–727–2757 – *for information on camping and cabins*

● Restaurants:
Dutch Pantry Restaurant, Clearfield, PA (814) 765–2137

● Local Outdoor Retailers:
Bob's Army & Navy Store, Clearfield, PA (814) 765–4652 or *www.bobs armynavy.com* • **Jim's Sports Center,** Clearfield, PA (814) 765–3582

● Maps:
USGS maps: Devil's Elbow, PA; Driftwood, PA

Black Moshannon State Park

Hike Specs

Start: From the boat launch area No. 1 parking lot

Length: 7.3-mile loop

Approximate Hiking Time: 3 hours

Difficulty Rating: Easy, due to the level terrain

Terrain: Paved road, lakeside path, forest footpath, shale road, and elevated boardwalk. A mountain lake and stream, park road, elevated boardwalk leading into a bog and a wildlife-viewing platform

Elevation Gain: 581 feet

Land Status: State park

Nearest Town: Philipsburg, PA

Other Trail Users: Anglers, swimmers, and birdwatchers

Canine Compatibility: Leashed dogs permitted

Getting There

From Dubois: Drive east on I-80 and take Exit 21 (PA 53). Drive south on PA 53 for eight miles to Philipsburg. In the city of Philipsburg, turn left onto U.S. 322 and drive south one mile to South Philipsburg and the intersection with PA 504. Turn left onto PA 504 and drive 8.5 miles to the entrance of Black Moshannon State Park. Once in the park, drive over the bridge across Black Moshannon Lake and immediately turn right into the boat launch area No. 1 parking lot. *DeLorme: Pennsylvania Atlas & Gazetteer:* Page 61 A7

Pennsylvania has a number of interesting geological sites, but one thing it will never have is its own alpine lake—since, by definition, an alpine lake must be at least 10,000 feet above sea level. However, at the center of Black Moshannon State Park, you'll find the next best thing: Black Moshannon Lake, a 250-acre lake situated in a basin-shaped area high atop the Allegheny Front. The basin, at 1,900 feet above sea level, traps the cooler, heavier air, creating mild summers and longer-lasting winters. Over 350,000 people come to observe and indulge in this phenomenon each year.

Because of these cooler temperatures, the area is home to an array of plants and animals that are usually observed much farther north. The bog is also home to some peculiar vegetation, such as the insect-eating pitcher plant and the sundew. Carnivorous plants usually grow in nutrient-poor soil; they've evolved to supplement their diets by trapping insects. The pitcher plant has a 20-inch stalk with purplish-red, vase-like leaves that contain water (hence *pitcher* plant). Its color attracts insects into its curled leaves where tiny hairs hold them until they drown. The sundew is quite a bit smaller. It has an eight-inch stalk that supports a curved cluster of white-to pink-tinged flowers and sticky hairs that it uses to trap insects and digest them. Both are fascinating and unusual finds. Take the time to find a few and appreciate natures adaptive abilities.

The Bog Trail begins with this boardwalk that leads to a viewing platform.

Black Moshannon State Park comprises 3,394 acres of forests and wet-lands, surrounded by another 43,000 acres of the Moshannon State Forest. In 1994 the state designated 1,592 acres of swamps, bogs, marshes, and forests in the southern end of the park as the Black Moshannon Bog Natural Area.

Our hike begins with a walk alongside the dark waters of Black Moshannon Lake. The water appears almost black—hence the park's name. Indeed, the waters here are darker than usual, and that's pretty much due to the sphagnum moss. And the sphagnum moss, in case you're looking, is *everywhere*. Acres of sphagnum moss absorb the tannin from the decaying plant life and hold onto it; then, like a giant teabag, it releases the tannin into the water, making it the color of strong tea.

As for the park's unusual name: According to local legend, *moshannon* is derived from the Seneca Indian phrase *moss-hanne*, which means "moose

Sphagnum moss holds plant tannin like a tea bag, then releases it into the water of Black Moshannon Creek.

138

stream." However, since moose aren't native to Pennsylvania, what they called moose were most likely elk, which at one time were present throughout the state.

Walk along the shoreline to the Bog Trail, with its elevated boardwalk and wildlife-viewing platform. Be sure to take your binoculars and camera. Depending on the season and the time of day, you're liable to see beavers, porcupines, pickerel frogs, and even a black bear. Waterfowl you're likely to see include the migrating osprey, wood ducks, tundra swan, and the great blue heron. The best times for watching wildlife are mornings and evenings.

Feeding the wildlife is prohibited, and there are a number of reasons for this. Some are just nuisance issues: Feeding waterfowl like the Canadian geese ensures that they return to the same spot year after year, leaving enormous amounts of droppings. Some concerns are more serious: Black bears, searching for food, cause damage to park equipment and can even cause injuries to visitors. In any area where bear are present, keep food and food scraps in you car or camper. Never keep foodstuffs in a tent or put them in an open garbage can.

Hike Information

● Trail Contacts:
Black Moshannon State Park, Philipsburg, PA (814) 342-5960

◔ Schedule:
Open year round

⑨ Fees/Permits:
No fees or permits required

❷ Local Information:
Centre County Convention and Visitors Bureau, State College, PA (814) 231-1400 or 1-800-358-5466 or www.visitpennstate.org

◉ Local Events/Attractions:
Columbus Chapel and Boal Mansion Museum, Boalsburg, PA (814) 466-6210 or www.vicon.net/~boalmus – a collection of Christopher Columbus belongings • God's Country Marathon, first Saturday in June,

Galeton, PA: www.pavisnet.com/marathon – cash prizes

● Accommodations:
Centennial Rose B&B, Philipsburg, PA (814) 342-8239 or www.centennialrose.com • Black Moshannon State Park, Philipsburg, PA (814) 342-5960 – for information on camping and cabins

⑪ Restaurants:
Sarina's, Philipsburg, PA (814) 342-6237

⊛ Local Outdoor Retailers:
C&M Sports, Philipsburg, PA (814) 342-7323

Ⓝ Maps:
USGS maps: Black Moshannon, PA

MilesDirections

0.0 START at the boat launch area No. 1 parking lot. Walk to PA 504 and turn left to cross the bridge over Black Moshannon Lake. Once across the bridge, turn right onto the paved road at the campground sign. Then turn right again at the yellow Tent Hill Trail marker and walk toward the Environmental Learning Center building.

0.1 Arrive at the Environmental Learning Center building. Veer to the right—stay between the building and the shore of the lake. Walk through the picnic area to the "Tent Hill Trail" sign and yellow blazes.

0.2 Pass an unmarked trail on your left. Continue straight along the lake.

0.4 The Tent Hill Trail goes off to the left. Continue straight toward the dam and spillway.

0.5 Cross a shale access road and walk to the blue-blazed Shingle Mill Trail sign. Continue straight. *[**Note.** There's a water filtration plant on your left and Black Moshannon Creek on your right.]*

1.4 Cross a pipeline swath and arrive at an open, flat area.

1.6 Ford an unnamed tributary.

2.4 Turn right onto Huckleberry Road. Cross the bridge over Black Moshannon Creek and turn right onto Black Moshannon Road.

3.2 Cross the pipeline swath. *[**Note:** There are access gates on both sides of the road.]*

3.5 Pass the Short Trail and the Dry Hollow Trail trailhead on your left. Continue straight.

4.0 Pass the Ski Slope Trail on your left. Veer right into the picnic area. Walk through the picnic area.

4.2 Pass by the beach area on your right.

4.3 Turn right onto PA 504 and cross the bridge over Black Moshannon Lake. On the other side, turn left onto the paved walkway and walk through the picnic area.

4.4 Turn left onto the West Side Road.

5.5 Pass Hay Road Trail on your right. Continue straight.

5.6 Walk through boat launch area No. 3 to the Bog Trail. Follow the yellow blazes onto the boardwalk.

5.9 Arrive at the Bog Trail viewing platform. Retrace your steps to the boardwalk and turn left. Pass the Indian Trail and the Moss-Hanne Trail trailhead on your left. Turn right onto the West Side Road and retrace your steps to boat launch area No. 1 parking area.

7.3 Arrive back at your vehicle.

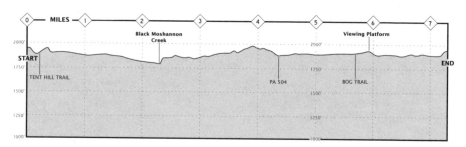

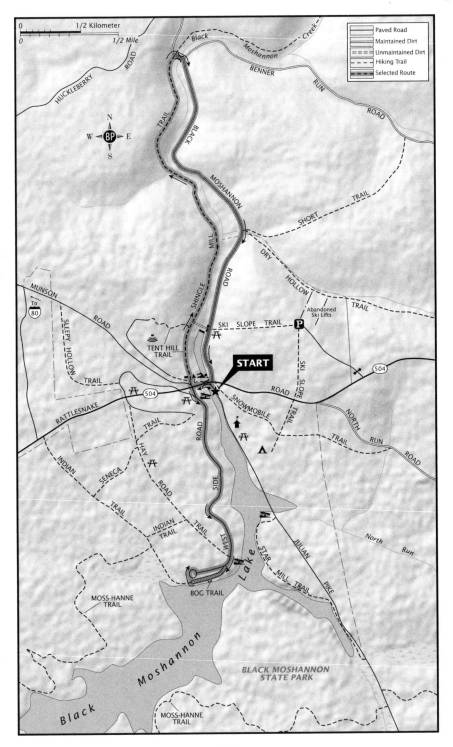

Northcentral Pennsylvania

Compiled here is an index of great hikes in the Northcentral region that didn't make the A-list this time around but deserve recognition. Check them out and let us know what you think. You may decide that one or more of these hikes deserves higher status in future editions or, perhaps, you may have a hike of your own that merits some attention.

(M) The Elk Trail

This 17-mile trail, in Elk County, is designed to show off the county's namesake. You can find the trail in the Elk State Forest, north of I-80, southwest of St. Marys, and south of Emporium. The trail is simply out in the middle of nowhere. And that's precisely why the herd of 650 to 700 elks was re-established here. These cousins of the white-tailed deer were native to the area, but by the mid 1800s they were wiped out by over-hunting and loss of habitat. From 1913 to 1926, elk were captured in Yellowstone National Park and reintroduced here. Even today, there's still a struggle going on between farmers, who suffer crop damage, and elk advocates, who want to see the herd preserved. To get there from Dubois, drive north on PA 255 about 18 miles to the village of Weedville. Turn right on PA 555 and drive about six miles to Benzette. In Benzette, turn north on the paved road opposite the Benzette General Store, pass the Benzette Hotel and drive to where the pavement ends and park. For more information call Parker Dam State Park (814) 765–0630 or Elk State Forest (814) 486–3353, or email: *fdl3.emporium@al.dcnr.state.pa.us*. **DeLorme:** **Pennsylvania Atlas & Gazetteer:** Page 47 B5

FYI:

There is an elk viewing area where you can view elk without hiking or walking. To get there from Benzette, drive north on Winslow Hill Road 3.5 miles to the parking and viewing area. The best time to see elk is at dawn or dusk during the mating season, September and October.

Ⓝ Parker Dam State Park

This park is in Clearfield County just north of I-80. The Keystone Trails Association calls Parker Dam "a hikers' park." It's that and more: This park is an outdoor lover's paradise. First, there's a network of trails that include the Beaver Trail—a boardwalk trail that takes you through a beaver propagation area. Then there are the trails that take you on an outdoor tour of the logging industry, where you can see the old tools and the ingenious way loggers had to transport logs over land. As for getting logs to market, William Parker built a number of splash dams to accomplish that. There's also fishing, a swimming beach, canoe rentals, rental cabins, camping, and a top-notch nature and education center in the park office.

To get there from Dubois, drive east on I-80 for about 17 miles to Exit 18 at Penfield. Drive north on PA 153 about 10 miles and turn right on Mud Run Road at the Parker Dam sign. Continue on Mud Run Road for two miles to the park and the park office on your right. For more information call Parker Dam State Park (814) 765–0630. *DeLorme: Pennsylvania Atlas & Gazetteer:* Page 46 C3

Southcentral
PENNSYLVANIA

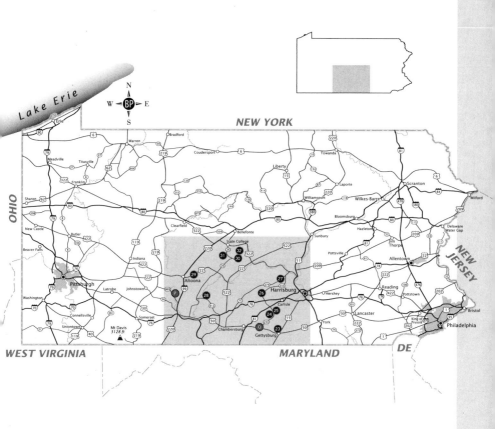

The Rides

Gettysburg **23.**
Sunset Rocks **24.**
Pole Steeple **25.**
Flat Rock **26.**
Little Buffalo State Park **27.**
Trough Creek State Park **28.**
Canoe Creek State Park **29.**
Greenwood Furnace State Park **30.**
Indian Steps **31.**
Alan Seeger NA to Greenwood Fire Tower **32.**

Honorable Mentions

O. Caledonia State Park
P. Blue Knob State Park

Southcentral Pennsylvania

Southcentral Pennsylvania has so much going for it, it's hard to imagine why anyone would want to go anywhere else. Let's review: There's Gettysburg National Military Park, an extremely user-friendly area, where all you have to do is park your car and start walking. Hikers can explore the battlefield and examine the relics of one of the bloodiest and most important battles of the Civil War.

The two highest peaks in the state, Mount Davis and Blue Knob, are also here—as is Raystown Lake, the largest body of water in the state. And you'll also see some of the state's oldest quartzite rocks (300 million years old) at Pole Steeple.

How about history? There are a number of state parks in southcentral Pennsylvania where historical iron furnaces, blacksmith shops, houses, and in some cases, entire villages have been restored to show a new generation what life was like when coal was king and manufacturing was the number one employer in the area. Hikers can explore iron furnaces and learn how just one furnace consumed over an acre of timber a day. (*See Hike 27*)

At Alan Seeger Natural Area in Centre County, visitors can marvel at how the giant hemlocks there survived the axe, while the entire area around them was clearcut. Not far from Alan Seeger there lies another mystery: The Indian Steps. No one knows who built them, but what we do know is that they lead to the top of Brush Mountain, through some of the rockiest mountain slopes in the state.

Many of the southcentral region's natural wonders are the handiwork of the mountain system known as the Valley and Ridge Province, a range of parallel ridges separated by valleys, covering 25 percent of the state and all or part of 27 counties. Looking like a giant washboard, this range begins at the Maryland border and arcs northeast to the New Jersey border at the Delaware Water Gap. Climb any mountain in southcentral Pennsylvania and you'll see one ridge after another and another, until they're lost to the horizon. But be careful: once you've seen this sight you may get hooked.

Overview

Gettysburg

When you've finished this hike, you'll have a comprehensive idea of what took place July 1st through July 3rd, 1863, at the Battle of Gettysburg, when over 150,000 troops clashed on the rolling hills surrounding this small Pennsylvania town. Considered by most historians to be the turning point of the Civil War, it was also one of the bloodiest conflicts in modern warfare. During the three-day battle, there were over 51,000 casualties.

Just like the auto and bus tours, this hike visits the important battle sites and monuments; however, the hike leads away from the paved roads and monuments and onto the battlefields. Hikers get a first-hand experience of what it was like for Confederate soldiers to charge through an open field with bullets whizzing by. Let your imagination take over as you position yourself behind a boulder on Little Round Top or walk along a line of cannons. *(See page 152)*

Sunset Rocks

Walk a section of the Appalachian Trail to the ruins of a top-secret World War II POW camp. Climb Little Rocky Ridge for an exciting, hands-on boondoggle through a narrow boulder outcrop for a mountaintop view. *(See page 158)*

Pole Steeple

The rugged quartzite cliffs that cap off this hike are estimated to be at least 300 million years old. Pole Steeple Cliffs sit 526 feet above a pristine mountain lake and provides a spectacular view. If you're lucky enough to come at the right time, you'll see rock climbers all roped up and doing their thing.

For hikers, there's a second highlight. This hike uses a section of the Appalachian Trail. Less than a mile from the start, hikers come to the halfway point of the 2,138-mile-long trail. Check out the trail register to see what weary hikers have to say. The last two miles of this hike are flat and popular with cyclists, but the bicycle traffic is modest and shouldn't be a concern. Also, the rustic buildings, the iron furnace, stables, and the iron-master's mansion have been designated a National Historic Area. *(See page 162)*

Flat Rock

A short, rocky climb leads to a spring house for an icy drink then continues up Blue Mountain to Flat Rock for one of the top views in the state. From this overhanging ledge—which is one flat rock no bigger than your SUV—there is a 180-degree view of the majestic Cumberland Valley and (on a clear day) South Mountain. Tiny cars whiz along the roads, while tiny farm tractors stir up the dust in the fields. Along the trip you'll cross the famous 248-mile-long Tuscarora Trail. *(See page 168)*

Little Buffalo State Park

Bring your camera on this hike. It starts out on an 82-foot-long covered bridge—and not just any covered bridge. This is a Burr Truss, patented by Theodore Burr of Connecticut, architect and builder of the longest, single-arch bridge in the world (also in Pennsylvania). How about a tour of a restored 19th Century gristmill, with one of the largest waterwheels east of the Mississippi?

Take a self-guided nature tour, then walk the path of a peculiar, narrow gauge railroad on your way to an inlet where you might see a little green heron, an egret, or a blue-winged teal. End your hike at the Blue Ball Tavern, built in 1811, now the local historical society headquarters. *(See page 174)*

Trough Creek State Park

Bring your camera on this hike and get a picture of the famous Balanced Rock, a rock hanging on the edge of the cliff and looking like it could topple into the valley at any moment. The trail climbs to the ridge top for a view of the largest body of water in Pennsylvania, Raystown Lake, and then descends into the valley for an exploration of a cave-like hole in the ground known as the Ice Mine. Along the way, it leads hikers to a bridge across Rainbow Falls for another great photo opportunity. *(See page 180)*

Canoe Creek State Park

This is an easy, pleasant hike where you can explore the limestone kilns used in the early 1900s to supply the limestone for the bustling iron and steel industries. Visit an abandoned quarry operation, now a bat colony, then make your way up a knoll for views of the valley. Walk alongside Canoe Creek on its way to Canoe Lake. Both bodies of water are good for fishing. *(See page 186)*

Greenwood Furnace State Park

This is simply a great hike. It starts in a restored 19th-century village that was once the company town for Greenwood Furnace Iron Works. The entire village has been designated a National Historic District. Old wagon roads and tramway trails lead hikers through the village and into the surrounding mountains where the remains of charcoal pads can still be seen. There are visits to a historic cemetery, a pristine mountain lake,

and, believe it or not, there's even a top-notch view. Bring your camera and your children on this one. *(See page 192)*

Indian Steps

The major highlight of this hike is the mystery of a series of large, stone steps erected on the side of a steep mountain. The second highlight is the views—in all four directions. The hike begins with a gradual ascent to the summit, where the clearings above talus slopes provide sweeping views. On the top the trail connects with a popular backpacking trail and skirts along the ridge flank. Your descent includes the mysterious Indian Steps. *(See page 200)*

Alan Seeger Natural Area to Greenwood Fire Tower

The hike begins as a gentle nature walk on a pine needle path that leads to some of the oldest trees in the state. You crisscross a delightful mountain stream as you wind your way through tunnels of rhododendron, some as high as 20 feet, with a four-inch diameter. You make a major climb as you ascend to the mountaintop and a fire tower, which provides a panoramic view. *(See page 206)*

Gettysburg

Hike Specs

Start: From the overflow parking lot between the visitor center and the Cyclorama off PA 134 at Gettysburg National Military Park

Length: 9.1-mile loop

Approximate Hiking Time: 5–6 hours

Difficulty Rating: Easy. The trail is flat, except for a few brief climbs.

Terrain: Paved roads connect a series of Civil War monuments placed around the Gettysburg Battlefield; follow an abandoned trolley grade, forest footpaths and traverse open fields to famous hillside and open meadow battle sites.

Elevation Gain: 597 feet

Land Status: National military park

Nearest Town: Gettysburg, PA

Other Trail Users: Tourists, students, history buffs, and equestrians

Canine Compatibility: Leashed dogs permitted. No pets permitted in the National Cemetery.

Getting There

From Philadelphia: Drive west on I-76 past Harrisburg to Exit 17. Drive south on U.S. 15 for about 30 miles and merge onto U.S. 15 Business. Drive to the traffic circle in the center of the city of Gettysburg. Once on the circle, turn right onto PA 15. Drive south for one mile, then turn right onto PA 134. Drive past the visitor center and turn right into the overflow parking lot. *DeLorme: Pennsylvania Atlas & Gazetteer:* Page 91 B7

After the Battle of Gettysburg

Over 172,000 men and 634 cannons were positioned in an area encompassing 25 square miles. It was estimated that 569 tons of ammunition was expended. There were over 5,000 dead horses left on the battlefield. In three days there were 51,000 casualties, the bloodiest battle of American history.

The extent of death and destruction stemming from the American Civil War is truly staggering. In the four years the war raged, over $5 billion in property was damaged and more than 600,000 lives were lost. One of the bloodiest battles of the war was fought from July 1st through July 3rd, 1863, on the rolling hills surrounding the city of Gettysburg in south-central Pennsylvania. A trip to Gettysburg National Military Park offers Americans the chance to look beyond the textbook accounts and numbers, and understand the devastation on a visceral level.

Most scholars consider the Battle of Gettysburg the turning point in the Civil War. The actions that set the stage for this momentous battle began about a month earlier with the Confederate victory at Chancellorsville, Virginia. On the strength of that victory, Confederate General Robert E. Lee decided to divide his army into three corps and invade Pennsylvania.

On June 30th, Confederate troops spotted Union troops on their way to Gettysburg, but there was no encounter that night. Forewarned and anticipating battle, troops from both sides set up their positions through the night. On July 1st the fighting began, and by day's end, over 7,000 Confederates were dead, wounded, or taken prisoner. The North's casualties were even higher, with over 4,000 men taken prisoner.

Full-scale firing didn't begin until late the next day. By that evening, Union General Daniel Sickles ordered his troops to abandon their post near Little Round Top and attack the Confederates at a wheat field and peach orchard. Sickles' troops were massacred; the losses were so great that the wheat field turned scarlet from the bloodshed.

But by the third and last day, the North was secure in its positions and the South had lost its offensive drive. Confederate troops made one final attempt to breach the North's line. General George E. Pickett and 15,000 troops led a charge across an open field toward the Northern stronghold of Cemetery Ridge. Pickett's men were slaughtered, the attack was repulsed, and the Battle of Gettysburg was over.

The next day, during heavy rains, Lee led his men in retreat to Virginia. During the three-day battle the Union Army had 23,000 casualties—the Confederates, at least 25,000.

Millions of people have visited Gettysburg National Military Park since it was dedicated in 1895, but the vast majority seldom ventures past the popular monuments. You will. At key sites, this hike leads away from the paved roads and monuments and onto the actual battlefields. (This hike follows the Gettysburg Heritage Trail Guide booklet, published by the

Abraham Lincoln & the Gettysburg Address

When the Battle of Gettysburg was over many of the dead were buried in hastily dug, inadequate graves, and some were not buried at all. Pennsylvania's Governor, Andrew Curtin stepped in and commissioned a local attorney to purchase a suitable spot for the Union dead. Four months after the Battle of Gettysburg, reinterment began on 17 acres that became the Gettysburg National Cemetery.

On November 19, 1863, President Abraham Lincoln (and revered speaker of the day, Edward Everett) spoke at the dedication ceremonies. Lincoln's speech—just 272 words—took two minutes to deliver, and has since come to be regarded as a masterpiece of the English language.

Today, visitors to Gettysburg can visit the Gettysburg National Cemetery and the Lincoln Speech Memorial, located within the cemetery grounds.

National Park Service and the Boys Scouts of America, which is available at the bookstore in the visitor center.)

The trail starts at the High Water Mark. This is the spot where the Union forces repulsed Pickett's Charge, which came to be known as the "high-water mark" or high point of the Confederate's advances. After passing a few monuments, the trail crosses a field and you walk alongside a split-rail fence. If you can forget the paved roads and the glistening monuments, you might sense what the countryside was like in the 1860s. Out here in the fields, you get a feel of what it was like for the soldiers on both sides. The trail leads you right through the bloodstained wheat field and on to the Devil's Den, scene of some of the fiercest fighting of the battle. Devil's Den is an outcrop of boulders at the base of Little Round Top. It was from here that the Federals defended their left flank. During the battle here, the carnage was so massive that Plum Run ran red with blood, earning it the odious nickname, "Bloody Run."

When you climb Little Round Top, it's easy to see how Union sharpshooters positioned themselves behind the boulders to pick off Confederate soldiers as they attempted the uphill advance. The climb up Little Round Top is short—only about two-tenths of a mile—but it's steep, and if you're on the path, just like the Confederate soldiers were, you're frightfully exposed.

When you pass the monument to Robert E. Lee and his horse, Traveller, you're walking the very same field where Pickett's Charge took place. In fact, there's a small monument where the attack was staged. From that point it's about a half mile across an open field to where the Union troops were poised on Cemetery Ridge. It was from this ridge that Pickett and about 15,000 troops made the attack against an overwhelming barrage of Union artillery and musket fire. It was here that the battle was finally lost.

Hike Information

Trail Contacts:
Gettysburg National Military Park, Gettysburg, PA (717) 334–1124 or *www.nps.gov/gett*

Schedule:
Open year round

Fees/Permits:
No fees or permits required

Local Information:
Gettysburg Convention and Visitors Bureau, Gettysburg, PA (717) 334–6274

Local Events/Attractions:
Gettysburg Civil War Heritage Days, last weekend in June and first weekend in July, Gettysburg, PA (717) 334–6274 – *commemorates the Battle of Gettysburg with a living history encampment* • **Civil War Institute,** last weekend in June and first weekend in July, Gettysburg, PA (717) 337–6590 – *lectures and tours by prominent Civil War scholars* • **Eisenhower National Historic Site,** Gettysburg, PA (717) 338–0821

Accommodations:
The Brickhouse Inn, Gettysburg, PA 1–800–864–3464 • **Gettysburg Campground,** Gettysburg, PA (717) 334–3304

Restaurants:
Dobbin House Tavern, Gettysburg, PA (717) 334–2100

Hike Tours:
Gettysburg National Military Park, Gettysburg, PA (717) 334–1124

Other Resources:
The Gettysburg Heritage Trail Guide is available at the bookstore in the visitor center.

Local Outdoor Retailers:
Rocks & Water Mountain & River Sports, Fayetteville, PA (717) 352–3217 or 1–877–729–9286 or *www.rocksandwater.com*

Maps:
USGS maps: Gettysburg, PA; Fairfield, PA

MilesDirections

0.0 START at the overflow parking lot between the visitor center and the Cyclorama. Walk on the sidewalk around the back of the Cyclorama Center.

0.1 Arrive at the High Water Mark Trailhead. Turn right onto the paved walkway.

0.2 Bear right at the fork and walk toward Hancock Avenue.

0.3 Turn left onto Hancock Avenue.

0.5 Pass a path on your left. Walk toward the Vermont Monument.

0.7 Turn left at the fork onto Pleasanton Avenue to visit the Pennsylvania Monument. Turn right onto Humphries Avenue.

0.9 Arrive at the Minnesota Monument. Turn right at the monument and follow the footpath through the field to the split rail fence.

1.0 Turn left at the split-rail fence.

1.3 Turn right onto United States Avenue.

1.3 Cross the traffic bridge over Plum Run.

1.6 Pass the Trostle House on your right.

1.8 Turn left onto Sickles Avenue.

2.0 Turn left onto Wheatfield Road.

2.4 Arrive at the "Wheatfield" plaque. Face the plaque and walk past it to a footpath through the field.

2.5 Turn right onto Sickles Avenue. Turn left onto De Trobriand Avenue.

2.7 Pass the Pennsylvania 110th Regiment Monument. Turn left into the forest at a second sign for De Trobiand Avenue on your right. You are on an abandoned trolley grade.

2.8 Cross a footbridge over a tributary to Plum Run.

2.9 Cross a second footbridge over a tributary.

3.0 Cross Brooke Avenue.

3.3 Ford a tributary stream.

3.4 Cross a footbridge over a Plum Run tributary and turn right onto Sickles Avenue.

Population of Gettysburg

In 1863: 2,400
In 1980: 7,194
In 1990: 7,025

3.5 Turn right onto Warren Avenue and cross Plum Run on a traffic bridge.

3.6 Turn left onto a footpath to the top of Little Round Top.

3.8 Turn right at the parking lot.

4.0 Turn left at the paved path to the 20th Maine Monument.

4.1 Turn left onto Wright Avenue and turn right at the red-blazed horse trail into the forest.

4.3 Turn left onto the red-blazed Loop Trail.

4.7 Turn right on the Loop Trail.

4.8 Pass trail stanchion No. 10 on your left.

4.9 Turn left at trail stanchion No. 14 and turn left onto South Confederate Avenue. Turn right onto a footpath beside a section of split-rail fence.

5.0 Arrive at the 1st Vermont Monument. Turn right. The trail goes downhill.

5.2 Cross a wooden footbridge over Plum Run. Walk toward the white farmhouse. Notice the trail sign near the house and turn right at the sign.

5.3 Arrive at a rest area with bathroom and picnic table.

5.8 Cross Emmitsburg Avenue and turn right onto South Confederate Avenue.

5.9 Pass the horse trail on your left.

6.4 Pass the Lookout Tower on your right.

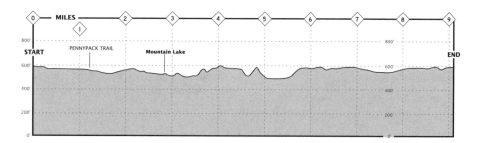

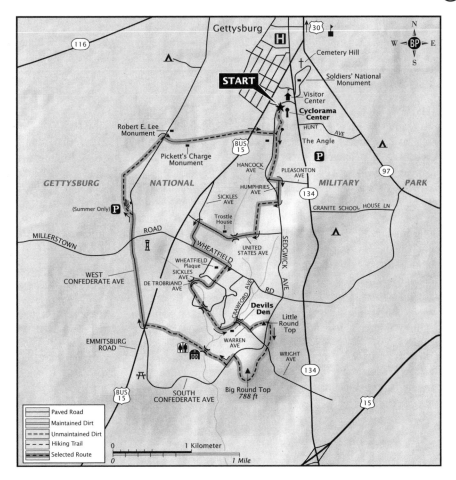

6.6 Cross Millerstown Road.

6.9 Turn left into the amphitheater parking lot. Walk to the left of the amphitheater and turn right onto the red-blazed horse trail.

7.1 Turn left at the sign for the hiking trail.

7.3 Turn right at the sign for hikers and horses.

7.6 Cross a small stream on a footbridge. Turn left at the fork.

7.9 Turn right onto a path that takes you back out to Confederate Avenue.

8.0 Arrive at the Robert E. Lee Monument. Walk to the right of the monument to get on the paved walkway.

8.1 The paved walkway ends at a small monument where Pickett's Charge began. Follow the footpath through the cornfields.

8.7 Cross Emmitsburg Road.

8.8 Arrive at the steps for "The Angle" Monument. Follow the path to the left.

9.0 Cross Hancock Avenue at Bryan House. Follow the sidewalk behind the Cyclorama.

9.1 Arrive back at your vehicle.

Sunset Rocks

Hike Specs

Start: From the parking lot for the furnace stack in Pine Grove Furnace State Park
Length: 8.3-mile lollipop
Approximate Hiking Time: 5 hours
Difficulty Rating: Moderate, due to short climbs *[Note. There is a short section of two-handed climbing over boulders.]*
Terrain: Abandoned logging roads, paved roads, and forest footpaths wind through forested mountain trails, along mountain streams, and lead to a ridge-top boulder outcrop.
Elevation Gain: 1,147 feet
Land Status: State park and state forest
Nearest Town: Shippensburg, PA
Other Trail Users: Through-hikers and hunters (in season)
Canine Compatibility: Leashed dogs permitted

Getting There

From Allentown: Drive west on I-78 and connect with I-81 toward Harrisburg. Continue south on I-81 through Harrisburg to Exit 11. Take Exit 11 and drive south on PA 233 for 8.5 miles; turn left into Pine Grove Furnace State Park and drive to the furnace stack.
DeLorme: Pennsylvania Atlas & Gazetteer: Page 77 D6

> **NOTE:** *Although the boulder outcrop section is only 0.3 miles in length, hikers should be in good physical condition to attempt this. This section is not for inexperienced hikers or small children. For hikers who want to visit Sunset Rocks and don't feel comfortable with maneuvering through the outcrop, turn left onto the Sunset Trail at mile 1.4 and climb to the mountaintop, bypassing the outcrop.*

From the Revolutionary War period to the beginning of the 20th Century, the iron industry flourished in the mountains of Pennsylvania. The iron ore was extracted from the earth, and the surrounding trees were harvested to produce charcoal to fire the furnaces, leaving behind denuded forests, abandoned quarry pits, the scarred earth of the charcoal flats, and a network of logging and mining roads. Take a trip along these abandoned roads to explore the unusual history of this area.

In 1912 the South Mountain Mining & Iron Company sold 60 square miles of clearcut forest and a 250-acre tenant farm to the state. The land was neglected and steadily deteriorated until 1933, when President Franklin Roosevelt created the Civilian Conservation Corps (CCC). The CCC, which provided forestry work for mostly unmarried young men, was one of the social programs established to alleviate the widespread unemployment during the Great Depression. Here in Pennsylvania, what came to be known as Camp Michaux was actually Camp S-51, the first CCC camp in the state. For the next nine years the young men of Camp S-51 built themselves a home, improved old forest roads, and built new ones. In 1942, with the United States involvement in World War II, young men were needed

in Europe and the Pacific, so the camp was closed and Army Intelligence chose the site to set up the Michaux Prisoner of War Camp.

Just a two-hour drive from the District of Columbia, the camp was also close to the Carlisle Army Post, and because of its remote location, the Army felt it could keep the location a secret. Staffed by 150 soldiers, the camp, which first handled only German naval officers, was expanded to include officers from Rommel's African Corps, as well as Japanese officers—for a total of 1,500 prisoners.

The POW camp was closed after the war. Then, in 1948, a church coalition signed a 10-year lease to use the site as a church camp. When the leased expired the land reverted to the state. In 1972, all the buildings were removed. Today, all that remains are the stone ruins of the barn foundation next to a giant spruce tree. Here and there along the trail, you may find posts from the barbwire fence that once surrounded the compound.

At a little over 3.5 miles into the trail you'll come to Toms Run Shelter. The shelter, which is part of the Appalachian Trail, is on the site where the tenant

Hike Information

☎ Trail Contacts:
Pine Grove Furnace State Park, Gardners, PA (717) 486–7174 • **Michaux State Forest,** Fayetteville, PA (717) 352–2211

⏱ Schedule:
Open year round

$ Fees/Permits:
No fees or permits required

❓ Local Information:
Harrisburg-Hershey-Carlisle-Perry County Tourism and Convention Bureau (includes Cumberland County), Harrisburg, PA (717) 231–7788 or 1–800–995–0969 or www.visithhc.com

♥ Local Events/Attractions:
Railways to Yesterday, Rockhill Furnace, PA (814) 447–9476

● Accommodations:
Wilmar Manor Bed & Breakfast, Shippensburg, PA (717) 597–2831 • **Pine Grove Furnace State Park,** Gardners, PA (717) 486–7174 – for camping information

🍴 Restaurants:
Gingerbread Man, Shippensburg, PA (717) 532–2049

👥 Organizations:
Potomac Appalachian Trail Club, Vienna, VA (703) 242–0965 or www.patc.net

🎒 Local Outdoor Retailers:
Rocks & Water Mountain & River Sports, Fayetteville, PA (717) 352–3217 or 1–877–729–9286 or www.rocksandwater.com

Ⓝ Maps:
USGS maps: Dickinson, PA

MilesDirections

0.0 START at the parking lot for the furnace stack. Walk across Quarry Road and turn left onto Bendersville Road. Walk past the American Youth Hostel to PA 233. Follow the white blazes.

0.1 Turn left at PA 233.

0.2 Turn right to cross PA 233 and arrive at the Appalachian Trail trailhead.

0.3 Turn right at the fork and arrive at a trail sign: "Appalachian Trail, Foot Traffic Only."

1.4 Bear to the left at the fork in the trail. Come to a trail intersection. Continue straight on the white-blazed Appalachian Trail. (The blue-blazed Sunset Trail goes off to your left.) Cross Toms Run on a footbridge and turn left on the other side.

1.6 The trail merges onto a shale road. Pass a trail sign on your left: "Halfway Springs 50 Yards."

2.1 Turn right at the double white blazes. The trail becomes a forest footpath and you pass stone ruins on your right.

2.2 The trail merges onto the paved Old Shippensburg Road.

2.5 Turn left at a trail sign for the Appalachian Trail. Notice the log gate across the trail

3.7 Arrive at Toms Run Shelter. Cross Toms Run.

3.8 Turn left at the double blue blazes onto the Sunset Rocks Trail.

4.4 Arrive at a clearing. Bear right at a fork in the trail.

4.8 *[**FYI**. Note the fence posts beside the trail. The fence was the perimeter of the Michaux POW camp during World War II.]*

4.9 Turn right onto the paved Michaux Road.

5.0 Turn left at second gravel road. Look for the blue blazes.

5.4 Arrive at the trail sign: "Little Rocky Ridge."

5.5 Enter a boulder outcropping where the trail goes over the boulders.

5.7 At the intersection with the Sunset Trail continue straight to Sunset Rocks, then retrace your steps back to the trail intersection.

6.2 Arrive back at the trail intersection and turn right.

6.7 Turn right at the intersection with the Appalachian Trail and retrace your steps back to PA 233.

8.0 Turn left at PA 233.

8.3 Arrive back at your vehicle.

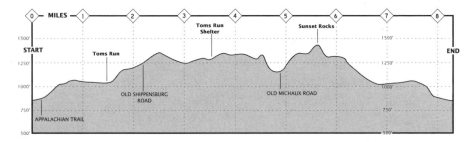

farmhouse was once located. There is a spring here and an outhouse and picnic tables. Local lore says that somewhere near the site there are the unmarked graves of three children who died of smallpox.

After you've switchbacked your way to the summit of Little Rocky Ridge, you'll need both hands to navigate over a section of precariously perched boulders. The trail

Bridge across Toms Run.

is well marked (blue blazes are painted right on the rocks); however, this section is not suitable for anyone who is not in good physical condition. And, because the ridge top is narrow, there is no way around the boulders. You either climb over them, or turn around and go back the way you came.

Your hard work pays off soon enough, though. The view at Sunset Rocks is a spectacular south-facing view of the valley and the flat ridge tops spanning the 85,000-acre Michaux State Forest.

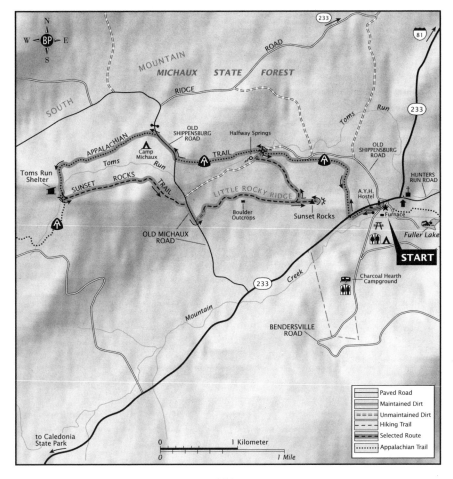

Pole Steeple

Hike Specs

Start: From the Fuller Lake day-use parking lot in Pine Grove Furnace State Park
Length: 5.4-mile lollipop
Approximate Hiking Time: 3 hours
Difficulty Rating: Moderate, due to the gradual climb and a short descent through an outcropping
Terrain: Follow a level railroad grade and make a gradual mountain ascent on an old logging road to quartzite cliffs, mountain lakes, and streams.
Elevation Gain: 779 feet
Land Status: State park and state forest
Nearest Town: Shippensburg, PA
Other Trail Users: Tourists, backpackers, and hunters (in season)
Canine Compatibility: Leashed dogs permitted

Getting There

From Carlisle: Drive south on I-81 for about 15 miles to Exit 11. Take Exit 11 and drive south on PA 233 for 8.5 miles to Pine Grove Furnace State Park. At the intersection of PA 233 North and PA 233 South, turn left onto Hunters Run Road and drive for 0.2 miles and turn right at the Fuller Lake day-use parking lot sign.
DeLorme: Pennsylvania Atlas & Gazetteer: Page 77 D6

Since the Pennsylvania section of the Appalachian Trail (AT) is 232 miles long, it's not unusual to come across a day hike that uses a portion of the famed trail. This hike, however, not only uses a section of the AT, but leads you to one its most famous spots—the halfway point. Less than a mile from the start you'll reach the stanchion and sign that mark the midpoint of the 2,138-mile trail. There's a trail register where through-hikers can leave messages, write wilderness-inspired poetry, or share their feelings about what it's like to have hiked 1,069 miles from either Springer Mountain, Georgia, or Katahdin Mountain, Maine. Either way, reading the register can be enlightening.

For those who don't know, the Appalachian National Scenic Trail—the first national scenic trail in the United States—follows the Appalachian Mountain chain through 14 eastern states. Trail construction began in 1921 and was completed over 15 years later (which isn't so bad, considering the enormity of the project). Today, a total of over 200 public agencies oversee the AT, while 12 volunteer hiking clubs totaling over 4,000 volunteers maintain the trail under the leadership of the Appalachian Trail Conference. In Pennsylvania, The Keystone Trails Association coordinates

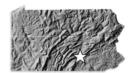

the maintenance of the trail and primitive shelters. (For more information about the Keystone Trails Association, see Trail Contacts below.)

Just south of the halfway marker, AT through-hikers have a chance to slip back into civilization for a day or two. The Appalachian Trail leaves the forest and passes through Pine Grove Furnace State Park, where the first stop for hikers is the famous Pine Grove Store. Local folklore has it that once hikers hit the establishment, most immediately head for the freezer and begin gorging on family-size containers of ice cream.

The hikers' next stop is the American Youth Hostel. Right next door to the store, it's located in the refurbished ironmaster's mansion. The original *Big House* was a two-story wooden structure built in the 1790s. Unfortunately, it burned down sometime in the early 1800s. Based on comparisons with other area structures, scholars believe the current brick house—an example of the Federal-style of architecture—was built between

MilesDirections

0.0 START at the parking lot for Fuller Lake Day Use. Walk past the bathroom and turn left onto the white-blazed gravel path.

0.1 Trail veers left at the fork in front of the food concession building. Cross Mountain Creek on a footbridge.

0.2 Cross the Fuller Lake outlet on a wooden bridge. Pass a side trail on your right.

0.4 Pass the Swamp Trail on your right.

0.7 Arrive at an access gate; the trail turns right. Come to a second access gate.

0.9 Arrive at the Appalachian Trail halfway marker.

1.9 Pass an unmarked trail on your right.

2.0 Turn left at the blue-blazed Pole Steeple Trail.

2.1 Pass an unmarked footpath on your left.

2.5 Arrive at Pole Steeple outcropping. The trail goes down through the boulders.

2.7 Arrive at the base of the outcropping and begin your descent.

3.4 Turn left onto the paved Railroad Road.

4.9 Pass the Appalachian Trail (where you started out) on your left. Retrace your steps back to the parking lot.

5.4 Arrive back at your vehicle.

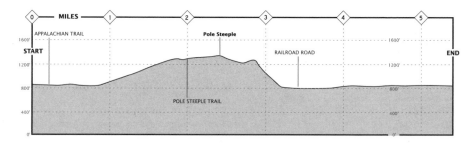

1815 and 1820. The Big House was home to a string of ironmasters and was the scene of major social events and all sorts of business excitement. Prior to the Civil War, it was a stop on the Underground Railroad, where runaway slaves could find refuge in a hiding place that is still there today.

At the hostel, worn-out hikers can avail themselves of all the amenities of home, such as showers, laundry, cooking, living areas, and dining facilities. With their appetites finally sated, they can spend the night in dormitory-style rooms, then lounge around the next day on the expansive porch, which provides a sweeping view of the activity in the park. (For information about the hostel, see the Accommodations section below.)

Boy Scouts, most likely as a part of a badge-earning expedition, used to come to Pole Steeple to stick a flag on the cliffs. The flag is long gone, but the name has stuck and the cliffs remain popular with park visitors. Most who visit Pole Steeple walk or bike the two miles from the park to the base of the cliffs, make the steep climb up, and then return the same way. Our hike route is different—it allows you to get away from the crowd, enjoy the

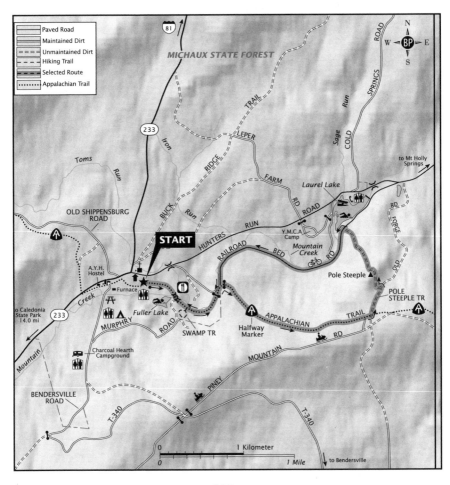

solitude of the forest, and arrive at the cliffs with plenty of energy for a climb down.

The Pole Steeple cliffs are made up of erosion-resistant quartzite from the Cambrian Period—that's nearly 600 million-year-old rock. This older quartzite is usually buried well within the rock strata, but here you'll find it right on the cliff face. A fault between Laurel Forge Pond and the cliffs moved the north side (or the pond side) upward, depositing softer rock on top of the more resistant quartzite. Millions of years of erosion have washed away the softer rock, leaving the Cambrian-era strata exposed.

On your way to the cliffs, the first stop is Fuller Lake. Everyone knows that the water in the mountain lakes of Pennsylvania is...well, cold. The waters of Fuller are colder than most—there's a sign on the beach to warn would-be swimmers. Even in the summer months the lake temperature can dip to the mid 60s. Before the lake was created, the area was the site of a 90-foot-deep iron ore quarry that supplied Pine Grove Furnace. The quarry was abandoned when it struck a spring and filled with water. Spring-fed and substantially deep, the lake remains chilly year round.

The cliffs at Pole Steeple serve a dual role: they're pretty to look at, and they provide a topnotch view of the 25-acre Laurel Lake and Mountain Creek Valley. After visiting the cliffs, descend to Laurel Lake and walk the abandoned railroad bed beside Mountain Creek back to the park. This stretch alongside the dark, clear waters of Mountain Creek, with plenty of hemlocks growing along its banks, is one of the most picturesque hikes in the state.

Enjoy.

Hike Information

◐ Trail Contacts:
Pine Grove Furnace State Park, Gardners, PA (717) 486-7174 • **Michaux State Forest,** Fayetteville, PA (717) 352-2211 • **Keystone Trails Association,** P.O. Box 251, Cogan Station, PA 17728 or *www.pennaweb.com/kta/index.htm*

◐ Schedule:
Open year round

◐ Fees/Permits:
No fees or permits required

❓ Local Information:
Harrisburg-Hershey-Carlisle-Perry County Tourism and Convention Bureau (includes Cumberland County), Harrisburg, PA (717) 231-7788 or 1-800-995-0969 or *www.visithhc.com*

◐ Local Events/Attractions:
Pennsylvania Renaissance Faire, Manheim, PA (717) 665-7021

◒ Accommodations:
Field and Pine Bed & Breakfast, Shippensburg, PA (717) 776-7179 • **American Youth Hostel,** Pine Grove Furnace State Park, PA (717) 486-7575 • **Pine Grove Furnace State Park,** Gardners, PA (717) 486-7174 – *for camping information*

◐ Restaurants:
Pine Grove Store, Pine Grove State Park, Gardners, PA (717) 486-7403 • **Black House Tavern & Inn,** Shippensburg, PA (717) 532-4141

◐ Local Outdoor Retailers:
Rocks & Water Mountain & River Sports, Fayetteville, PA (717) 352-3217 or 1-877-729-9286 or *www.rocksandwater.com*

Ⓝ Maps:
USGS maps: Dickinson, PA

Flat Rock

Hike Specs

Start: From the Colonel Denning State Park Nature Center parking lot off PA 233

Length: 7.4-mile lollipop

Approximate Hiking Time: 4 hours

Difficulty Rating: Moderate, due to uphill climbs, rocky footpaths, and steep descents

Terrain: Abandoned logging roads, improved shale roads, and some extremely rocky sections lead up a mountain to a 180-degree view of the valley below and mountain ridges beyond.

Elevation Gain: 825 feet

Land Status: State park and state forest

Nearest Town: Carlisle, PA

Other Trail Users: Tourists and backpackers

Canine Compatibility: Leashed dogs permitted

Getting There

From Harrisburg: Drive south on I-81 and take Exit 11. Drive north on PA 233 for six miles. Turn right into Colonel Denning State Park and follow the signs to the Nature Center. *DeLorme: Pennsylvania Atlas & Gazetteer:* Page 77 B5

The 273-acre Colonel Denning State Park is named after the Revolutionary War veteran William Denning—which isn't very interesting, except for the fact that Denning was never actually a colonel. Denning became famous as the manufacturer of an innovative, lightweight (at least relatively) wrought iron cannon.

The area around Colonel Denning State Park is known as Doubling Gap. Blue Mountain, one of a series of long parallel ridges that marks the beginning of Pennsylvania's Valley and Ridge Province, forms an "S," creating two gaps instead of just one. Our destination, Flat Rock viewing area, lies in the center of the southern gap.

At the one-mile mark, the trail intersects with the famous 248-mile-long Tuscarora Trail, which was built in the 1960s as a bypass of the Appalachian Trail (AT) when it was thought that development in Virginia would reroute the AT. But as a result of the National Scenic Trails Act of 1968, the AT remained intact and the Tuscarora is now a side trail. Here you'll find a primitive shelter. If you've never slept in one of these before, you can get a feel for what it would be like to spend the night in your sleeping bag snug-

View from Flat Rock.

MilesDirections

0.0 START at the Nature Center parking lot and walk to the Flat Rock Trail. Turn right and cross Doubling Gap Run on a footbridge. Climb the wooden steps. Look for double red blazes.

0.2 Turn left onto a forest road and begin your ascent.

0.3 Come to a springhouse with running water.

1.0 Arrive at a major trail intersection. Continue straight, following the Flat Rock One Mile sign. The Flat Rock Trail becomes part of the Tuscarora Trail. Follow the red and the blue blazes.

1.1 Pass a Tuscarora Trail through-hiker shelter on your left.

1.3 Stay to the right at the fork. Cross a washout stream on a footbridge.

1.9 Walk over a benchmark embedded in a boulder.

2.0 Arrive at Flat Rock. Retrace your steps.

3.0 Arrive back at the major trail inter-section and turn right onto the red-blazed Warner Trail.

3.5 Cross an open logging area. The trail becomes an improved road.

3.7 Turn right at the Warner Trail sign and begin your descent.

4.6 Turn left onto the Cider Path Trail.

5.2 Continue straight past the Cider Path Trail sign.

5.3 Arrive at the Cider Path Trail signpost and double red blazes. Turn left *precisely* beside the signpost.

6.2 Arrive at a Cider Path Trail and Shade Trail sign. Continue straight on the Cider Path Trail.

6.3 Turn left onto Doubling Gap Road.

6.7 Bear right at the fork in the road.

6.9 Bear right again at a second road fork.

7.1 Arrive at Doubling Gap Lake. Continue on the beach.

7.2 Pass through the beach parking lot and playground.

7.3 Turn left onto a wooden bridge across Doubling Gap Run at the far end of the playground. Turn right and cross a tributary on a second footbridge.

7.4 Pass through the campgrounds. Turn right onto an auto bridge across Doubling Gap Run and return to the Nature Center parking lot.

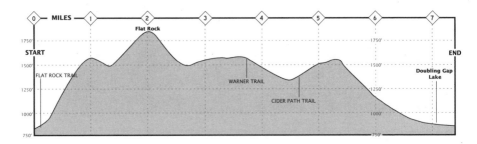

gled up on a real hardwood floor. There's no hot water or room service, but to the trail-weary through-hiker, shelters like this seem palatial.

Flat Rock Overlook is one of the highest points in Pennsylvania's Valley and Ridge Province. Just yards before the view, there's a U.S. Geological Services benchmark embedded in a flat boulder. You just might step on it, but you probably can't read it—it looks as if visitors have smashed it with a rock or a hammer in unsuccessful attempts to dislodge it.

From the edge of Flat Rock, there is a 180-degree view of the patchwork-quilt farmlands and roads of the Cumberland Valley. And, if it's a clear day, you can see South Mountain in the distance. Flat Rock is as good a place as any to eat your lunch, work on your tan, and watch the turkey buzzards swoop around searching for their next meal. And those scraggly buzzards have a sizeable area in which to search—the Tuscarora State Forest is 91,165 acres of rugged, and sometimes remote, terrain. The name Tuscarora is taken from the Tuscarora Indians, a tribe adopted by the Iroquois Nation and allowed to migrate to this area in 1714. At that time the forests con-

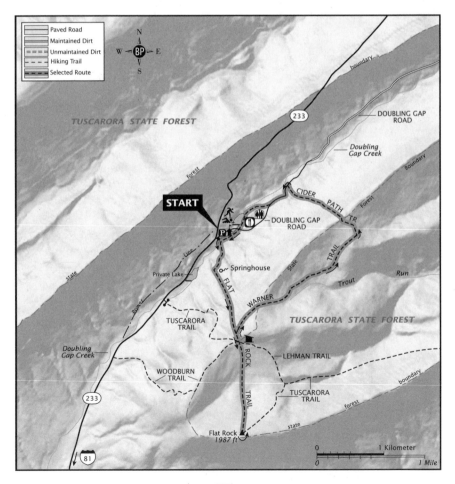

sisted of oak and chestnut, with hemlocks growing in the valleys. Like the rest of the forests in Pennsylvania these forests were logged, one could say, almost to death. Logging began here in the early 1900s and ended in 1930.

The Tuscarora State Forest is also home to a collection of undisturbed natural beauty; thousands of acres within the forest have been designated a part of either Wild or Natural Areas. Wild Area designation ensures that an area is allowed to retain its undeveloped character. The Tuscarora Wild

Area, over 5,000 acres located within the Tuscarora State Forest, was purchased by the state in 1964 and has been undisturbed since. Natural Areas are sites set aside for scientific study of natural systems, and for their natural or unusual beauty. There are three Natural Areas in the Tuscarora State Forest. The most unusual of these by far is the Hovert and Sholl Box Huckleberry Natural Area, an isolated 10-acre tract near New Bloomfield. Here you'll find a rare colony of box huckleberry—a single plant estimated to be 1,300 years old.

The box huckleberry is a member of the heath family, which includes mountain laurel, rhododendrons, azaleas, and species that produce berries, such as the blueberry and the cranberry. The box huckleberry grows about six inches a year by producing runners that fan out from the core. At the Natural Area, what looks like thousands of plants is actually just one plant that has been growing for 1,300 years.

Hike Information

🕒 Trail Contacts:
Colonel Denning State Park, Newville, PA (717) 776–5272

🕐 Schedule:
Open year round

💲 Fees/Permits:
No fees or permits required

❓ Local Information:
Harrisburg-Hershey-Carlisle-Perry County Tourism and Convention Bureau (includes Cumberland County), Harrisburg, PA (717) 231–7788 or 1–800–995–0969 or *www.visithhc.com*

📍 Local Events/Attractions:
Carlisle Fairgrounds, Carlisle, PA (717) 243–7855 or *www.cars atcarlisle.com – events begin in April; call for schedule* • **The Hovert and Sholl Box Huckleberry Natural Area –** *The area is located about seven miles north of the Colonel Denning State Park. For more information, contact the Tuscarora State Forest at* (717) 536–3191.

🛏 Accommodations:
Jacob's Resting Place: 1790 Bed & Breakfast, Carlisle, PA (717) 243–1766 or 1–888–731–1790 • **Colonel Denning State Park,** Newville, PA (717) 776–5272 – *for camping information* • **Caledonia State Park,** Fayetteville, PA (717) 352–2161 – *for camping information*

🍴 Restaurants:
Crossroads Restaurant & Bakery, Newville, PA (717) 776–5901

🚴 Organizations:
Potomac Appalachian Trail Club, Vienna, VA (703) 242–0965 or *www.patc.net*

🎒 Local Outdoor Retailers:
Keystone Country Store, Fort Loudon, PA (717) 369–2970

🗺 Maps:
USGS maps: Andersonburg, PA

Little Buffalo State Park

Hike Specs

Start: From the Little Buffalo State Park parking lot off Bloomfield Road

Length: 6.2-mile loop

Approximate Hiking Time: 3–4 hours

Difficulty Rating: Moderate, due to the series of climbs up and down hollows

Terrain: A series of abandoned railroad grades, pine needle nature trails, rocky footpaths, grassy paths, and blacktop lead you to a covered bridge, an historic gristmill, a nature trail through a hemlock forest, a creek side marsh, deep hollows, and an open meadow.

Elevation Gain: 998 feet

Land Status: State park

Nearest Town: Newport, PA

Other Trail Users: Tourists, bird watchers, and hunters (in season)

Canine Compatibility: Leashed dogs permitted

Getting There

From Harrisburg: Take U.S. 22/322 North to the Newport/PA 34 exit. Turn left onto PA 34 and drive west for three miles to the intersection with Little Buffalo Creek Road. Turn right onto Little Buffalo Creek Road and drive 1.8 miles to the intersection with New Bloomfield Road. Turn left onto New Bloomfield Road and drive 0.4 miles to a parking lot near the breast of the dam. *DeLorme: Pennsylvania Atlas & Gazetteer:* Page 77 A7

N o one *really* knows how Little Buffalo Creek or Buffalo Ridge got their names, but that doesn't seem to prevent folks from proposing theories. One theory, the one passed down and accepted by the local community, is that buffalo once inhabited the area. Of course, no buffalo bones have ever been found to support that theory...

The land on which the park is located was occupied by a succession of Native American tribes as they migrated westward, away from early settlers. In 1754, the government purchased the land from the Iroquois League of Six Nations, as part of the Albany Purchase. After the American Revolution, settlers moved onto the land and began farming. Not long after, John Koch opened the Blue Ball Tavern on the Carlisle Pike, the main road between Carlisle and Sunbury. The building, which has been restored and is open to visitors, now houses the Perry County Historical Society and an assortment of historical artifacts.

In 1808, the Juniata Iron Works commenced operations, smelting iron in charcoal-fired furnaces until 1848, when there was no more wood to burn. Evidence of charcoal making remains along the Buffalo Ridge Trail. Here

colliers stacked wood into piles, covered the piles with leaves, and then covered it all by packing soil on it. The piles were then burned for eight to 10 days, turning the wood into charcoal. Look for the 20-foot diameter flat areas along the trail; this is all that remains of the process.

Little Buffalo State Park opened in 1972, the result of an initiative that began in 1955, when the Department of Forests (now the Department of Conservation and Natural Resources) set a goal to provide a state park within 25 miles of every Pennsylvania resident. From 1955 to 1970, the state park system grew from 45 to 87 parks. Today, over 37 million people visit 114 Pennsylvania state parks annually.

Your first stop on this hike is Clay's Covered Bridge, an 82-foot-long covered bridge across Little Buffalo Creek. This bridge was designed and patented by Theodore Burr. Its innovative design involves one long arch extending from one side of the bridge to the other. The floor and the roof are attached to this arch by a series of king posts. Tied together, the struc-

Clay's Covered Bridge spans 82 feet.

Volksmarching

The hike through Little Buffalo State Park has been chosen by the American Volksport Association (AVA) as one of its 10-kilometer Volksmarching hikes. The AVA, which has over 500 walking clubs nationwide, is allied with the International Volkssport Federation based in Europe, which has thousands of clubs worldwide. AVA hikes are located throughout the United States.

The AVA selects a trail based on its safety, scenic interest, historic areas, natural beauty, and walkability. The chosen hikes are noncompetitive 10-kilometer walks designed for anybody and everybody, children and pets included. The hikes are mapped out and there are Volksmarch signs and white arrows placed along their chosen trails. As you hike the Little Buffalo hike outlined in this book, you'll notice the club's brown hiker signs and white arrows along the trail. However, the hike in this book is slightly different from the Volksmarch Hike.

Some hikes, like the one at Little Buffalo, are year-round events. This means the hike is self-guided: hikers sign in at the registration site, do the hike at their own pace, and then contact the group to get credit for the walk. Members can receive awards and special recognition for milestone events such as 10 events or 500 kilometers.

For more information, contact the group's website at www.ava.org/vmfaq.htm or call 1–800–830–WALK.

ture provides superior strength. Because of his unique arch, Burr was able to build the longest single-arch, wooden bridge in the world at nearby McCall's Ferry. Clay's Covered Bridge is one of 14 covered bridges that can still be found in Perry County.

Schoaf's Mill has been grinding away since the early 1800s, churning out wheat and buckwheat flour, cornmeal, and livestock feed. Although the mill closed as a business in 1940, it has been completely restored, and today visitors can watch as its gigantic waterwheel grinds cornmeal and cracked corn—occasionally apples for apple cider—as part of the park's educational programs.

After crossing Clay's Covered Bridge and visiting Schoaf's Mill, the trail follows the grade of the defunct Newport & Sherman's Valley Railroad. The Newport was one of many narrow-gauge railroads built throughout the state in the 19th Century to haul logs and freight for the logging industry. These narrow-gauge railroads were smaller than standard-size railroads—standard track width is 56.5 inches; a narrow gauge is 36 inches wide, with its engines and cars proportionally smaller as well. The Newport operated here from 1890 to 1937, when it went bankrupt, losing out to a standard-size railroad.

For the self-guided nature trail section of this hike, you need a pamphlet (available at the park office), which guides you past a series of numbered stanchions along the trail. This section is less than a mile long and passes through a magnificent hemlock forest. After the nature walk, the trail reconnects with the railroad bed to the west end of Holman Lake.

The 88-acre Holman Lake is a fisherman's delight—fish year round for largemouth bass, catfish, panfish, and adult brook, brown, and rainbow trout. Holman has been designated a big bass lake. Bass must be at least 15 inches to keep, and there is a daily limit of four. Electric and nonpowered boats are permitted, and a boat rental operates from Memorial Day to Labor Day, 11 A.M. to 7 P.M.

The trail parallels the Holman Lake inlet and Little Buffalo Creek. This section of the trail is a flat walk on a grass path that leads you through the marsh-like area. Here is where you'll almost certainly see a little green heron, a great blue heron, or wood ducks. During migration, many waterfowl use the lake as a rest stop. There have been sightings of Canadian geese, mallards, blue-winged teal, mergansers, buffleheads, common loons, and ring-necked ducks.

Once you cross Little Buffalo Creek Road, your real workout begins. Simply put: You go up one ravine then down the next, ad infinitum. In this section of the hike, you cross a total of seven wooden bridges, over seven washout streams, over five major ridges. There are also about a million short switchbacks. Yes it's repetitive and grueling—even tortuous, but it's totally worth it because, hey, that's what hiking is, right?

If your legs can carry you back to the road, you'll find yourself, ironically, on the Exercise Trail. There are 18 permanent stations along this short stretch, offering such delights as a balance beam, a pull-up bar, and bar vaults. If you've got anything left, give it a whirl. If, however, you need a little rest, you can slow down and check out the bluebird nestboxes. Little Buffalo, along with 50 other state parks, is part of a bluebird rescue program

Hike Information

❶ Trail Contacts:
Little Buffalo State Park: (717) 567-9255

◷ Schedule:
Open year round

❺ Fees/Permits:
No fees or permits required

❓ Local Information:
Perry County Tourism and Recreation Bureau, New Bloomfield, PA (717) 582-2131

❾ Local Events/Attractions:
Old Sled Works Museum, Duncannon, PA (717) 834-9333 – open Wednesday through Sunday 10 A.M. to 5 P.M.

❤ Accommodations:
The Tressler House Bed & Breakfast, New Bloomfield, PA (717) 582-2914 • Little Buffalo Family Campground, Newport, PA (717) 567-7370

🍴 Restaurants:
Pat's Restaurant, Newport, PA (717) 567-3352

🏪 Local Outdoor Retailers:
Ray Straining Sporting Goods, Harrisburg, PA (717) 652-9346

Ⓝ Maps:
USGS maps: Newport, PA

that began in 1981. One of the problems for bluebirds, as well as other nesting birds, is that they need to nest in open cavities in trees. As civilization continues to encroach on the bluebird's habitat, nests are eliminated. Nestboxes are provided to replace tree cavity nests. More than 25,000 bluebirds have fledged since the program began.

From the bluebird trail, it's a short walk to the Blue Ball Tavern and back to the parking lot.

MilesDirections

0.0 START from the bulletin board in the parking lot near the bathrooms. Turn left onto the sidewalk and walk past the bathrooms toward the playground. Turn left again at the sign "Mill & Covered Bridge."

0.1 Turn right at the sign for Schoaff's Mill. Cross Clay's Covered Bridge and turn left at the sign for Schoaf's Mill. After visiting the mill, return to the trail and turn left.

0.2 Pass the visitor center on your right.

0.3 Pass the Mill Race Trail on your left.

0.4 Turn left at the brown hiker sign. Go up the wooden steps and turn left onto the Self-Guiding Nature Trail.

1.2 Arrive at a trail intersection with the Buffalo Ridge Trail. Turn right at the "Short Cut to Main Area" sign.

1.3 Pass a water tank on your left.

1.4 Pass a forest road with a white arrow and continue straight toward the picnic area.

1.5 Come to an access gate and turn left onto the abandoned railroad bed.

1.8 Cross a park service road. Pass the new bathrooms on your left and an access gate on your right. Cross a tributary on a wooden footbridge and enter the forest.

1.9 Pass the older bathrooms on your right. Pass the Buffalo Ridge Trail on your left and continue straight onto the Little Buffalo Creek Trail.

2.0 Turn right onto the mowed path.

2.1 Arrive at the marsh of Holman Lake and turn left.

2.2 Pass two mowed paths on your left. Continue straight, following the white arrow.

2.4 Cross a tributary to Little Buffalo Creek on a wooden footbridge.

2.6 A trail merges from your right. Continue to walk upstream alongside Little Buffalo Creek.

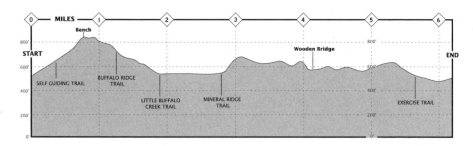

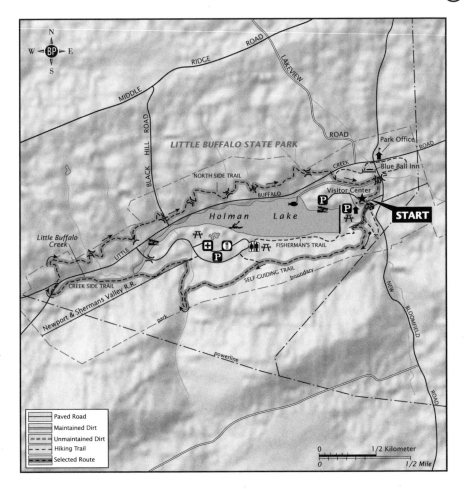

2.7 Pass under the power line. Turn right onto the wooden steps and arrive at Little Buffalo State Park Road. Turn right at the brown hiker sign and walk alongside the road.

2.8 Come to a brown hiker sign and turn left to cross the road. Then turn right at the Mineral Ridge Trail sign. Follow the red blazes and white arrows.

2.9 Continue straight where the trail forks.

3.1 The trail turns left on a dirt road.

3.7 Stay to the left at the fork in the trail.

3.9 Cross Black Hill Road.

5.6 Stay to the right at the fork.

5.7 Cross Little Buffalo State Park Road and turn right at the brown hiker sign. The trail becomes part of the Exercise Trail.

5.8 Cross a tributary stream on a wooden bridge and turn right onto the hikers' bridge over Little Buffalo Creek. The trail is now blacktop.

6.2 Cross the paved park road and arrive at the parking lot and your vehicle.

Trough Creek State Park

Hike Specs

Start: From Trough Creek State Park picnic area No. 5 on Trough Creek Drive
Length: 8.2-mile loop
Approximate Hiking Time: 5 hours
Difficulty Rating: Moderate, due to a long, steep climb
Terrain: Abandoned jeep roads, rocky footpaths, stone steps, and laurel streamside paths wind through mixed hardwood forests, mountain stream valleys, and to a ridge-top view of Raystown Lake.
Elevation Gain: 1,465 feet
Land Status: State park and state forest
Nearest Town: Huntingdon, PA
Other Trail Users: Tourists and hunters (in season)
Canine Compatibility: Leashed dogs permitted

Getting There

From Altoona: Drive south on U.S. 220/I-99 to the East Freedom exit. In East Freedom, get on PA 164 and drive east about 15 miles through Martinsburg to PA 26. Turn left onto PA 26 and drive about seven miles to Entriken and PA 994. Turn right onto PA 994 and cross Raystown Dam. Drive about two miles to Farm Hill Road. Turn left onto Farm Hill Road and drive about two miles and turn left at the Trough Creek State Park sign. Drive all the way to the north end of the park to picnic area No. 5 on your left. *DeLorme: Pennsylvania Atlas & Gazetteer:* Page 75 B6

H iking the trails of Trough Creek State Park gives you first-hand knowledge of the ridge and valley system of Pennsylvania's mountains. One early traveler of Pennsylvania wrote in his journal: "Pennsylvania's mountains are old and ornery, and equally inaccessible in all directions." When you begin the steep ascent out of Great Trough Creek Gorge, you learn right off that what makes the mountains so ornery is that they're just plain steep.

The Brumbaugh Trail, which begins at the boundary between the state park and the state forest, leads directly to the ridge top. It may have been a well-maintained trail at one time, but these days, it's clogged with dead trees toppled every which way across the trail. The dead trees are the victims of the gypsy moth that has devastated Pennsylvania's forest for four decades.

The gypsy moth is native to China, but in 1863 a French scientist brought some to his laboratory in Massachusetts in an attempt to crossbreed them with silkworms. Some moths escaped and began infesting New England and eastern seaboard states, arriving in Pennsylvania in the 1960s. But it's the gypsy moth caterpillar, which eats the leaves, that is the real culprit. The most affected trees are oaks, sugar maples, beech, and aspen.

This bridge across Trough Creek is a path from the pavilion to Old Forge Road and offers a great view of the dam.

When 30 percent of a tree's foliage is destroyed, the tree is sufficiently weakened and becomes susceptible to disease and attack from other insects, and can eventually die.

In 1999, over 280,000 acres were defoliated by the gypsy moth. Without a natural predator to control the population, alien species like the gypsy moth can cause virtually unlimited devastation. Fortunately, they do have a natural enemy—an infectious disease caused by a fungus that essentially *eats* the caterpillar. The fungus thrives on the moisture, so when there's a dry season, the fungus is curtailed and more gypsy moths survive. Leaving little to chance, the Department of Conservation & Natural Resources sprays a biological insecticide from helicopters and small airplanes, flying 50 feet above the treetops. The insecticide is bacillus thuringiensis, variety kurstaki, or Btk.

At the top of the ridge, you're rewarded with a spectacular view of Raystown Lake. The lake, which was created when the Army Corps of Engineers built a dam across the Juniata River, is 30 miles long and covers

MilesDirections

0.0 START from the pavilion at picnic area No. 5. Walk across the footbridge over Trough Creek.

0.2 Turn right onto the Old Forge Road. Look for blue blazes. Notice the sign: "TMT" (Terrace Mountain Trail).

0.4 Turn left onto the orange-blazed Brumbaugh Trail.

3.0 Cross Old Forge Road. Notice the springhouse.

3.1 Pass a water spigot coming out of the ground beside a cabin.

3.2 Turn right and walk between the boulders on the Raven Rock Trail. Then turn right again to Balanced Rock.

3.3 Walk to the Rhododendron Trail. Follow white blazes down the steps to Rainbow Falls viewing area.

3.5 Cross a bridge to Rainbow Falls.

4.7 Turn left onto the Copperas Rock Trail.

4.8 Turn left onto Trough Creek Drive and cross the traffic bridge.

5.1 Turn right onto the Laurel Run Trail.

7.2 Cross Terrace Mountain Road.

7.7 Turn right onto the Ice Mine Trail.

8.1 Reach Ice Mine. Cross Trough Creek Drive.

8.2 Arrive back at picnic area No. 5.

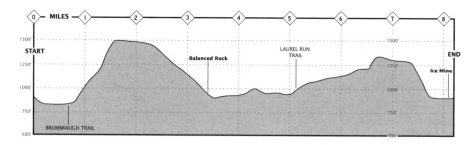

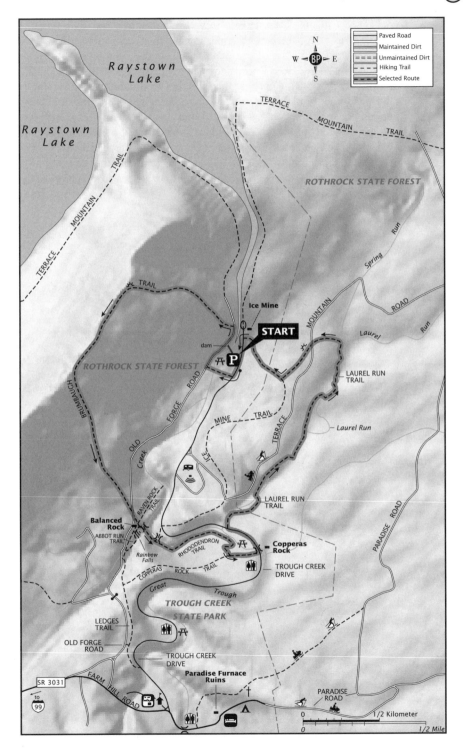

8,300 acres, making it the largest body of water in the state. With 13 public-use areas, boat launches, a marina, a swimming beach, and plenty of fishing, Raystown is the top recreational spot in central Pennsylvania.

You'll reach Balanced Rock at the halfway point. You can read all about it at the educational plaque viewing area, but to anyone in his right mind, it looks like a giant boulder that is about ready to topple into the gorge below. But the truth is, Balanced Rock (a.k.a. an *erosion element*) has been hanging on for thousands of years. It was once part of a much higher cliff comprised of hard rock and softer rock, which has eroded away. In the process, the precariously perched rock was eased into its current position.

You begin your descent into the gorge and pick up the appropriately named Rhododendron Trail, which intersects the Copperas Rock Trail.

This trail is named for the coppery-yellow stain on the cliff surface. The stain is actually ferrous sulfate, which is yellow precipitate that leaches out from a small pocket of coal in the cliff.

As you might guess, the Ice Mine Trail leads to the Ice Mine, a hole in the slope that functions as a natural refrigerator. There is an interpretive station that explains this phenomenon. In short, winter air enters the mine opening and diffuses up the hillside. In spring and summer, cold air flows down the slope and into the hole; this keeps the mine cold. When melting snow water runoff gets inside the hole, the cold air inside freezes the water into ice.

Perhaps all state parks have at least one unique feature—Trough Creek certainly has a few, but it also has its own legend. The story goes that after visiting the park and seeing the ravens that nested on the cliffs of Raven Trail, renowned American author Edgar Allen Poe wrote his famous poem, "The Raven."

Hike Information

🕐 Trail Contacts:
Trough Creek State Park, James Creek, PA (814) 658–3847

🕐 Schedule:
Open year round. This trail and others at the park are closed during the winter months for safety reasons, generally mid December through March, so call before planning this hike.

💲 Fees/Permits:
No fees or permits required

❓ Local Information:
Huntington Country Visitors Bureau, Hesston, PA 1–888–RAYSTOWN or *www.raystown.org*

📍 Local Events/Attractions:
Swigart Antique Auto Museum, Huntington, PA (814) 643–0885 – *open Memorial Day through October, $4 per person*

🛏 Accommodations:
Weaver's Ridge Bed & Breakfast, Saxton, PA (814) 635–3730 • **Trough Creek State Park Reservations,** James Creek, PA 1–888–PA–PARKS – *32 campsites, electric hookup. No showers. Camping season is from the second Friday in April though the last day of doe season in mid December. Fees vary for camping.*

🍴 Restaurants:
The Eatery at Seven Points Marina, Hesston, PA (814) 658–2955 • **The Marina Café at Raystown Resort,** Hesston, PA (814) 658–2955 – *at the marina* • **Boxer's Café,** Huntingdon, PA (814) 643–5013

🎒 Local Outdoor Retailers:
Rothrock Market, James Creek, PA (814) 658–3290 • QBS Sports, Huntingdon, PA (814) 643–1120

🆑 Maps:
USGS maps: Cassville, PA; Entriken, PA **Trough Creek State Park map**

Canoe Creek State Park

Hike Specs

Start: From the visitor center parking lot

Length: 4.6-mile loop

Approximate Hiking Time: 2 hours

Difficulty Rating: Easy, due to mostly short climbs over knolls

Terrain: Shale walkways, forest footpaths, abandoned dirt roads, and a boardwalk lead the hiker to limestone kilns, an abandoned limestone quarry, and alongside a creek to a fishing and swimming lake.

Elevation Gain: 969 feet

Land Status: State park

Nearest Town: Altoona, PA

Other Trail Users: Tourists, anglers, and equestrians

Canine Compatibility: Leashed dogs permitted

Getting There

From Altoona: Drive south on PA 36 for approximately four miles to the intersection with U.S. 22. Turn left onto U.S. 22 and drive past the first sign for Canoe Creek State Park (0.9 miles from the intersection with PA 36). Drive 3.5 miles from the first park sign to the second park sign. Turn left at the second park sign onto Turkey Valley Road and into Canoe Creek State Park. *DeLorme: Pennsylvania Atlas & Gazetteer:* Page 75 A5

Canoe Creek State Park is a jewel in the crown of the state park system. At 958 acres, it's small, but it's loaded with features. There are modern rental cabins, a food concession, and hot showers in the beach changing bathhouse.

Canoe Lake is a 155-acre lake that provides crystal clear, icy cold water for swimming, canoeing, and fishing. It's stocked with walleye, muskellunge, bass, trout, chain pickerel, catfish, crappies, and other panfish. There is also ice fishing when there is an extended trout season. All Pennsylvania Fish & Boat Commission laws apply. Visitors wishing to fish need to get a Pennsylvania fishing license. The lake is open to non-powered and registered electric boats. Non-powered boats must display a State Park Launching Permit or a State Park Mooring Permit or a current Pennsylvania registration. Boats registered in other states must display a Pennsylvania State Park Launch Permit, as well as current registration.

This hike, which includes a visit to the historic Blair Limestone Company Kilns, is part of the "Path of Progress," a 500-mile automobile route that passes through nine southwestern Pennsylvania counties. It leads the traveler on a journey through the area's industrial past, and in doing so, teaches visitors how major industries, such as coal mining and steel production, helped create a cultural heritage.

As you begin this hike, you pass a number of educational kiosks, which explain limestone mining and the role of limestone in the production of steel. Leaving the kilns, a spur leads to a quarry. At the quarry, you notice a number of what appear to be small caves. These are not caves; these are entrances to limestone mines. These openings lead to a 1.5-mile-long network of tunnels. Miners went into the mine on a 45-degree tramway that led to four different levels, the deepest of which is 300 feet below the surface.

Nowadays, these abandoned mines are home to six species of bat, including the Indiana Bat, which is on the endangered species list. The bats hibernate in the mines over the winter. In June, the females roost in the attic of the abandoned church on Turkey Road, across from the park office. The young are born and the cycle begins again.

If you want to learn more about bats, attend one of the park's bat walks held at 8 P.M. (during the summer months). Park employees or guest lecturers will tell you everything you've always wanted to know about bats. And they'll lead you to the church building across from the park office where you'll see the largest colony of brown bats in the state—18,000 bats, just hanging around.

Lime stone kilns at Canoe Creek State Park.

MilesDirections

0.0 START from the parking lot near the visitor center. Walk to a small footbridge and sign for the visitor center. Walk through a small picnic area and turn right at the Limestone Trail trailhead sign.

0.1 Pass a water fountain and an amphitheater on your right. At the first trail fork, stay to the right. At the second trail fork, stay to the left.

0.2 Come to the Limestone Trail sign. Turn right onto the paved park road and take a quick left to the Limestone Trail kiosk.

0.3 Turn right onto the footbridge over Mary Ann's Creek, then turn left at the Limestone Kilns sign.

0.4 Arrive at the Limestone Kilns and kiosk. Turn right and walk uphill behind the kilns. Pass the Moore's Hill Trail on your right.

0.5 The horse trail goes off to your right; veer left onto the Limestone Trail.

0.6 Come to Kiosk No. 3. Take the right fork to the stone quarry.

0.7 Arrive at an open area and the quarry.

0.8 Come to a lookout bench, then retrace your steps downhill to the Limestone Trail.

0.9 Arrive back at Kiosk No. 3. Turn right onto Limestone Trail and look for the blue blazes.

1.1 Turn right onto Moore's Hill Trail.

1.2 Turn right at the fork in the trail and begin an uphill climb.

1.7 Arrive at right switchback.

1.8 Come to a bench.

2.1 Arrive at a plateau.

2.4 Trail turns left at a blue arrow.

2.8 Pass a kiln on your right.

3.0 Pass an intersection with the horse trail, then turn right. Follow the blue blazes. Canoe Creek is on your left.

3.2 Turn right onto the boardwalk.

3.4 Pass another intersection with the horse trail. Continue straight.

3.5 Pass through a meadow on your left.

3.6 The trail turns right. Look for the blue blaze and a yellow arrow. Pass a jeep trail on your left and continue straight into forest.

3.8 Pass an intersection with unnamed trail. Continue straight.

3.9 Cross the paved access road to the water tower.

4.1 The trail turns right.

4.2 Arrive back at the limestone kilns and kiosk. Turn left onto the Limestone Trail. Retrace your steps back to the visitor center parking lot.

4.6 Arrive back at your vehicle.

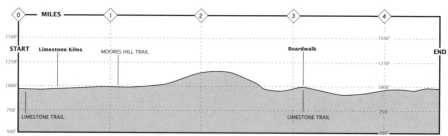

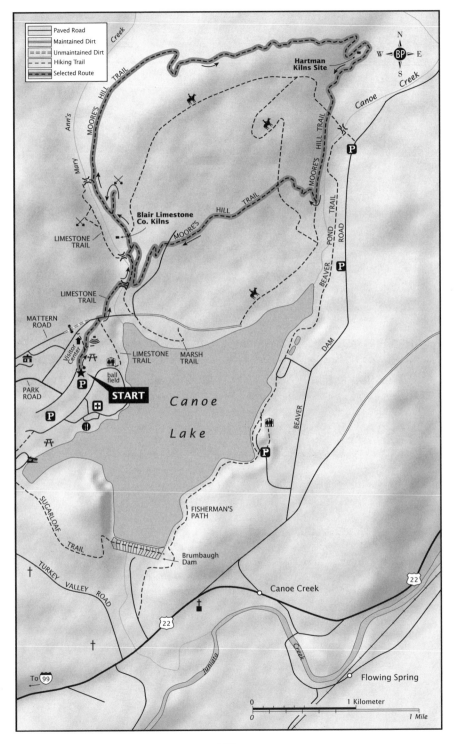

Legend
- Paved Road
- Maintained Dirt
- Unmaintained Dirt
- Hiking Trail
- Selected Route

Hartman Kilns Site

MOORE'S HILL TRAIL

Ann's Creek

Mary

MOORE'S HILL TRAIL

Blair Limestone Co. Kilns

LIMESTONE TRAIL

MOORE'S HILL TRAIL

BEAVER POND TRAIL ROAD

Canoe Creek

LIMESTONE TRAIL

MATTERN ROAD

Visitor Center

LIMESTONE TRAIL

MARSH TRAIL

PARK ROAD

START

ball field

Canoe Lake

BEAVER DAM

SUGARLOAF TRAIL

FISHERMAN'S PATH

TURKEY VALLEY ROAD

Brumbaugh Dam

Canoe Creek

22

To 99

Flowing Spring

Juniata Creek

0   1 Kilometer
0   1 Mile

A healthy patch of poison ivy.

Hike Information

☎ Trail Contacts:
Canoe Creek State Park, Hollidaysburg, PA (814) 695–6807

🕐 Schedule:
Open year round

💲 Fees/Permits:
No fees or permits required

❓ Local Information:
Allegheny Mountain Convention & Visitors Bureau, Altoona, PA (814) 943–4183 or 1–800–84–ALTOONA

📍 Local Events/Attractions:
Altoona Railroaders Memorial Museum, Altoona, PA (814) 946–0834 or 1–888–425–8666 or *www.railroadcity.com* • Horseshoe Curve National Historic Landmark, Altoona, PA (814) 946–0834

🛏 Accommodations:
Hoenstines Bed & Breakfast, 414 North Montgomery Street, Hollidaysburg, PA 16648 • Wrights Orchard Station Campground, Duncansville, PA (814) 695–2628

🍴 Restaurants:
The Dream Family Restaurant, Hollidaysburg, PA (814) 696–3384

🚴 Local Outdoor Retailers:
Campbells Sporting Goods, Hollidaysburg, PA (814) 695–8552 • Locker Room, Hollidaysburg, PA (814) 695–8515 • Dunham's Discount Sports, Altoona, PA (814) 942–3311

🗺 Maps:
USGS maps: Frankstown, PA

If you want to get a head start on your bat knowledge, below are the questions and correct answers to Pennsylvania's Department of Conservation and Natural Resources true or false bat test.

1. Bats really are blind.

False. Though they don't see in color, they see better than we do at night! And, many bats can "see" by sonar.

2. The world's smallest bat weighs less than a penny.

True. It's the bumblebee bat of Thailand, the world's smallest mammal.

3. Some bat's hearing is so keen they can hear the footsteps of an insect walking on sand more than six feet away.

True. Many bats find their way and locate prey using the sound of echoes.

4. Bats are cruel by nature.

False. Some bats are so kind they adopt orphans and will risk their lives to share food with less-fortunate bats.

5. Vampire bats are the only mammals that feed on nothing but blood.

True. By the way, vampire bats live only in Latin America, where most people will never even see one.

6. Bats hang by their nose.

False. They hang by their toes, counter-balanced by their upside-down weight.

7. Bats get tangled in your hair.

False. People may have thought this because bats fly over our heads hunting bugs. If a bat flies by you, it's probably chasing a mosquito.

8. All bats live in attics and caves.

False. Some choose trees or other sites; tropical bats make homes everywhere from banana leaves to spider webs.

9. Bats are vicious.

False. Bats pose little threat to people who leave them alone; they will bite in self-defense if mishandled.

Greenwood Furnace State Park

Hike Specs

Start: From the Greenwood Furnace State Park office parking lot

Length: 5.5-mile loop

Approximate Hiking Time: 3 hours

Difficulty Rating: Moderate, due to a long gradual climb, followed by a rocky footpath, then a very steep descent

Terrain: Abandoned wagon trails, forest footpaths, rocky outcroppings, and shale roads lead you through an historic tour of the park. Begin at an old church, follow a wagon road up the mountainside for a magnificent view, then descend to an historic cemetery, a dam, and a restored village.

Elevation Gain: 1,007 feet

Land Status: State park

Nearest Town: State College, PA

Other Trail Users: Tourists and backpackers

Canine Compatibility: Leashed dogs permitted

Getting There

From State College: Drive south on PA 26 to the flashing yellow stoplight in Pine Grove Mills. From the stoplight, drive 9.6 miles south on PA 26 and turn left onto PA 305. Drive 4.5 miles to the Greenwood Furnace State Park office parking lot on your left. *DeLorme: Pennsylvania Atlas & Gazetteer:* Page 62 C2

T his hike has a lot going for it. It's located in a National Historic District, the trails are well maintained, there's an excellent view, and the area is just plain beautiful. If you were interested in introducing someone to hiking, this hike would be an excellent choice. It's one of the few hikes in the state where just about anyone—experienced hiker or not—can get to a breathtaking vista without an exhaustive uphill climb.

Greenwood Furnace State Park offers a number of hikes with an historical flavor. (In this National Historic District, I suppose it would be difficult to avoid.) Once upon a time, teams of mules pulled small rail cars loaded with iron ore along a wooden-railed tramway from the Brush Ridge Ore Banks to the furnaces. Today, hikers can walk this same tramway and its connected roadways. Another short hike (it'll take about an hour) guides visitors through the historic village, past the company meat house, furnace stacks, wagon and blacksmith shop, and the six-acre lake created to supply power for the company gristmill and water for the iron furnaces.

Greenwood Lake swimming area.

Our hike begins on the old wagon road that linked Greenwood Furnace to Belleville. Pig iron ingots were hauled over this road to the steel works in Burnham, which is today Standard Steel. It's a little less than three miles from the trailhead to the Stone Valley Vista, where the first mile and a half is a gentle climb on a grassy wagon road. The trail gets a little rocky in the last mile, but the view from the vista, which stretches 10 to 20 miles on a clear day, is more than worth the effort.

Standing on the rocks of Stone Valley Vista and surveying the valley and mountains, it's hard to believe that a thick black smoke filled this valley during the seven decades the Greenwood Furnace Iron Works operated

MilesDirections

0.0 START from the park office parking lot and walk east alongside PA 305.

0.1 Arrive at the historic Greenwood Furnace Church. Turn right to cross PA 305 and walk to the Link Trail trailhead. Follow the orange blazes.

0.2 Come to a gate across the trail.

0.3 Notice the deer exclusion fenced area on your right. Enter forest the canopy.

0.5 Arrive at an open area.

0.8 The trail runs along the ridge.

1.1 Notice the outcropping on your right.

1.2 The trail switchbacks to the right.

1.5 The trail turns left and becomes a footpath.

2.1 Trail turns right. Begin an uphill climb.

2.9 Arrive at Stone Valley Vista.

3.1 Arrive at an intersection with the Turkey Trail. Turn right and follow the blue blazes, beginning your descent.

3.5 Pass the trail marker for the Link Trail and Turkey Trail and arrive at the base of the mountain.

3.8 Arrive at a clearcut area where the trail turns right onto an access road.

4.0 Turn right onto Turkey Hill Road.

4.4 Pass the Greenwood Furnace State Park boundary sign.

5.0 Pass the campground contact station.

5.1 Arrive at the historic Greenwood Furnace Cemetery.

5.2 Cross PA 305 and follow the walkway through the picnic area.

5.4 Come to the wooden steps to the park office parking lot.

5.5 Arrive back at your vehicle.

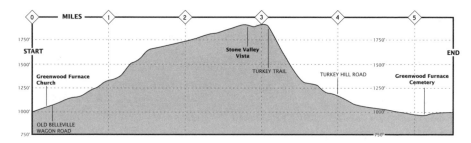

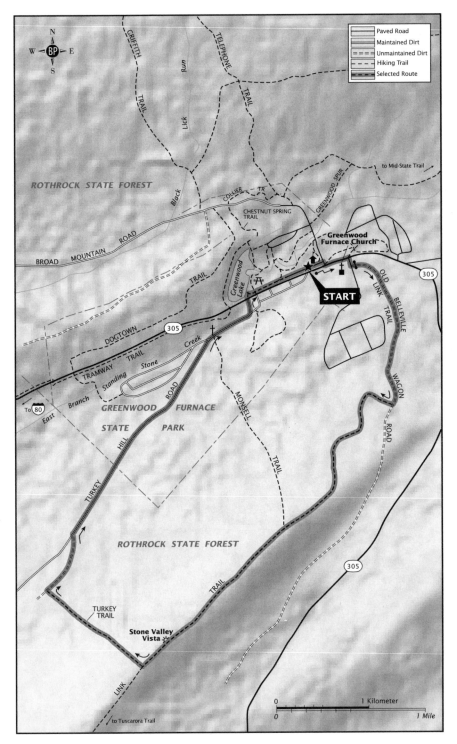

(from 1834 to 1904). Greenwood Furnace State Park was once the site of a booming 19th-century industrial village. Three hundred employees and their families lived and worked here in this company town that produced iron for the burgeoning national railroad system.

The main fuel of the iron maker's furnace was charcoal. During its heyday, the Greenwood Furnace Company owned nearly 40,000 acres of forest, which it harvested for the charcoal furnaces. These furnaces consumed timber at the remarkable rate of an acre of forest per day. And though the area was clearcut, not all trees were harvested for charcoal. The preferred trees were hickory and oak. The other timber was used in constructing the village.

Aside from its historical grandeur and its picturesque setting, there's another reason Greenwood Furnace is popular with hikers and backpackers: It's an access point for two major backpacking trails. This particular trail is the northern terminus of the 72-mile Link Trail, which continues south to Cowans Gap State Park where it links to the Tuscarora Trail. Going in the opposite direction, hikers use the Greenwood Spur to connect with the Mid State Trail, a 189-mile trail that runs from the Little Juniata Natural Area in Bedford County to just past the town of Blackwell.

This dam was built to provide power for the company gristmill.

Hike Information

📞 Trail Contacts:
Greenwood Furnace State Park, Huntingdon, PA (814) 667–1800

🕐 Schedule:
Open year round

💲 Fees/Permits:
No fees or permits required

❓ Local Information:
Centre County Convention & Visitors Bureau, State College, PA (814) 231–1400 or 1–800–358–5466 or www.visitpennstate.org • **Huntingdon Country Visitors Bureau,** Hesston, PA 1–888–RAYSTOWN or *www.raystown. org*

📍 Local Events/Attractions:
Old Home Days, first weekend in August, Greenwood Furnace State Park, Huntingdon, PA (814) 667–1800 • **Centre County Historical Society,** State College, PA (814) 234–4779

🛏 Accommodations:
Edgewater Acres Bed & Breakfast, Alexandria, PA (814) 669–4144 or www.edgewateracres.com • **Greenwood Furnace State Park,** Huntingdon, PA (814) 667–1800 – *for camping information*

🍴 Restaurants:
Faccia Luna, State College, PA (814) 234–9000

🖇 Organizations:
Mid State Trail Association, P.O. Box 167, Boalsburg, PA 16827 • **Penn State Outing Club,** State College, PA (814) 865–2472 or *www.clubs.psu. edu/outing*

♿ Local Outdoor Retailers:
Appalachia Ski & Outdoors, State College, PA (814) 234–3000 or *www.theadventuresource.com*

🗺 Maps:
USGS maps: McAlveys Fort, PA; Barrville, PA

In Addition

How to Grow a State Forest

Dr. Joseph Trimble Rothrock may not have been one of Pennsylvania's most notable residents on a national or international level, but within the state—and especially within the state forest and conservation community—he was *the* major force. His efforts earned him the title *The Father of Pennsylvania Forestry*.

Rothrock was accomplished in a number of disciplines: He was a medical doctor and surgeon, an explorer, a botanist, and a university professor. Rothrock's father was also a physician, the son of a German immigrant who had settled his family in Berks County, Pennsylvania. Rothrock was born in Mifflin County in 1839 and went on to graduate from Harvard in 1862 with a degree in botany. The next year, he enlisted in the Union Army and saw action at Antietam and Fredericksburg, where he was wounded. By the end of the Civil War, he was a captain in the 20th Pennsylvania Cavalry.

In 1867 he received his medical degree from the University of Pennsylvania, and became one of the founders of the Wilkes-Barre Hospital. From 1867 to 1869 he was professor of botany and human anatomy and physiology at the Agricultural College of Pennsylvania (now Penn State).

In 1880 Dr. Rothrock left Pennsylvania to study botany at the University of Strassburg in Germany, where he had a chance to study the managed forests of Europe. Obviously affected by what he had seen in Germany, Rothrock returned to Pennsylvania and began his campaign to save the state's forest. In 1895 he became the first commissioner of forestry, setting in motion the purchase of lands for State Forestry Reservations (now called State Forests). He also initiated programs for the training of state foresters, the establishment of forest nurseries for reforestation, and the establishment of an agency to detect and extinguish forest fires.

During Rothrock's lifetime, he witnessed the clearcutting of Pennsylvania's forests. In a 1915 speech he stated, "Sixty years ago I walked from Clearfield to St. Marys; thence on to Smethport—60 miles; most of the way through glorious white pine and hemlock forests. Now these forests are gone. [Today] 6,400 square miles; more than 4 million acres of the state are desolated, cut and unprotected from fire."

Rothrock's namesake, the 94,287-acre Rothrock State Forest, located in Huntingdon, Mifflin, and Centre counties, began its existence in 1903. At that time the forests in the area had been stripped bare to provide charcoal for the furnaces at the Greenwood Furnace & Iron Works. When two furnaces were shut down, Rothrock was instrumental in helping the Bureau of Forestry purchase 35,000 acres. From there, other land purchases followed, and in 1953, after various forest districts were combined or eliminated, Rothrock State Forest was named.

Indian Steps

Hike Specs

Start: From the designated parking area on Harrys Valley Road

Length: 4.1-mile loop

Approximate Hiking Time: 3 hours

Difficulty Rating: Moderate, due to a rugged descent over a rocky trail

Terrain: A series of improved shale and forest jeep roads gradually climb a mountain for great views. Walk along a rocky trail across the narrow mountaintop ridge for more views, then make a steep descent on mysterious stone steps.

Elevation Gain: 1,480 feet

Land Status: State forest

Nearest Town: State College, PA

Other Trail Users: Backpackers and hunters (in season)

Canine Compatibility: Leashed dogs permitted

Getting There

From State College: Drive south on PA 26 to the flashing yellow stoplight in Pine Grove Mills. From the stoplight, drive 3.1 miles south on PA 26 and turn right onto Harrys Valley Road. From this point, drive exactly 2.0 miles and park on the jeep road on your left that is blocked with boulders. *DeLorme: Pennsylvania Atlas & Gazetteer:* Page 62 C1

The highlight of this hike is undoubtedly the mystery of the Indian Steps. Someone, no ones knows just who for sure, built these steps using enormous flat rocks found alongside the trail. One theory holds that Native Americans, probably the Kishacoquillas, built the steps. Dissenters argue that most Native American trails were chosen because they were the easiest routes, and these steps are not the easiest way to cross this mountain.

Regardless, there are clearly man-made steps crossing Tussey Mountain. Our hike will only cover one half of the steps. To see the steps on the other side, which are purportedly in better condition, leave Pennsylvania 26 and drive in on Kepler Road to where the Indian Steps Trail crosses it. From there it's a short out-and-back. Walk up the steps and then back down to your car.

This hike has been designed so you can walk down, as opposed to walking up, the steps. The ravine on which the steps are located is extremely steep, and even though the steps are a little more than one-tenth of a mile long, going down them is a challenge. Be sure to wear good hiking boots with good tread. Small rocks and pebbles on the steps can create kind of a

walking-on-marbles hazard. If you're carrying a camera or other gear, stow it in your pack before beginning this section. It's only a little over a half mile, but it's going to seem longer.

The trail runs through a steep washout ravine that is at times muddy, and always rocky. As for the steps themselves, the rocks are thick and wide, too wide for one person to have maneuvered. Placing these steps was the work of two or three (or perhaps more) workers. And, no matter how long ago the steps were built, in the places where they have held up, they do help the hiker on his way.

There are a number of spectacular views all along this trail. The first one is at about the one-mile mark, on the Pump House Road Trail—an aban-

doned dirt road that is now a grassy footpath. The ridgeline hike along the paved Pennsylvania Furnace Road is startlingly open. As with many forest roads, there are no guardrails; consequently, you can walk to the very edge of a number of steep talus slopes, with nothing in front of you but sky.

When you reach the top of the mountain and turn right onto the Mid-State Trail, there's a large, flat boulder—a good place to stop and eat your

MilesDirections

0.0 START To get to the starting point of this hike, check your odometer when you turn off PA 26 onto Harrys Valley Road. From PA 26 drive exactly 2.0 miles to a blocked-off jeep road on your left, where you will park. To begin the hike from your car, turn left onto Harrys Valley Road.

0.2 Pass a blocked jeep road on your left.

0.4 Bear right onto the Pump House Road Trail. Look for two large boulders blocking vehicle traffic and unused chain stanchions on both sides of the trail. Begin your ascent.

0.5 Pass through a rock outcropping.

0.8 *[FYI. Notice the steep, rock-covered ridge on your right.]*

1.0 Come to a rocky area on your right and your first view on your left.

1.1 *[FYI. Notice the talus slope and views on your left.]*

1.3 Connect with the Pennsylvania Furnace Road. Note more views.

1.5 Arrive at the mountaintop. Turn right

onto the orange-blazed Mid State Trail.

1.7 Pass a camping site fire ring.

1.8 Arrive at the Tussey Fire Tower ruins. *[FYI. Notice the elevation plaque (2,238 feet) and the Mid State Trail sign.]*

1.9 The trail gets rocky. Pass an open area on flat boulders. Look for the orange blazes in the forest ahead.

2.0 Pass a sign on your left that reads "H20".

2.9 Arrive at the Schalls Gap Overlook.

3.4 Come to the sign "Indian Steps Trail to Kepler Road" on the left. Do not take this trail. Continue straight.

3.5 Come to the trail post: "Harrys Valley Road 1 Mile" and "Indian Steps Trail" (on the other side of the post). Turn right and begin your descent through a steep ravine.

3.6 Arrive at an open area. Steps begin.

3.7 Steps discontinue.

4.0 Turn right onto Harrys Valley Road.

4.1 Arrive at you vehicle.

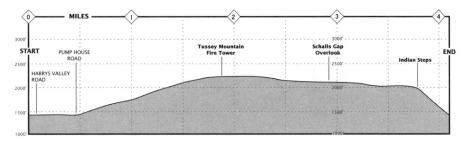

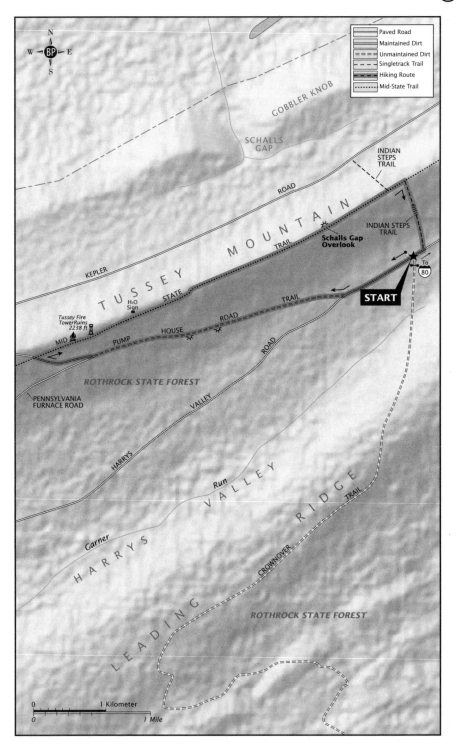

lunch. Your next stop is a visit to the Tussey Mountain Fire Tower ruins and vista; from there, it's onto the Schalls Gap Overlook. Both of these views are on your left.

It's easy to see why the 189-mile-long Mid-State Trail is a popular backpacking trail. It's well marked and well maintained. At this point on the Mid State Trail, you're near the southern terminus, which is in the Little Juniata Natural Area off U.S. Route 22. The northern terminus is in Pine Creek Gorge off Pennsylvania 44 near the village of Blackwell, where the

Mid-State Trail connects with the West Rim Trail, which continues along the west rim of the Grand Canyon of Pennsylvania.

On the two-mile stretch of the Mid-State Trail between Pennsylvania Furnace Road and the Indian Steps turn-off, the trail runs along a ridge flank on the mountaintop. At points the trail runs over large boulder outcroppings, the ridge is narrow, and there is no forest canopy overhead. Walking along these open areas, you get a feeling of freedom—like it's just you and the mountain and the sky.

Hike Information

🕑 Trail Contacts:
Rothrock State Forest, Huntingdon, PA (814) 643–2340

🕐 Schedule:
Open year round

💲 Fees/Permits:
No fees or permits required

❓ Local Information:
Huntingdon County Visitors Bureau, Hesston, PA (814) 643–3577 or 1-800-269-4684 or www.raystown.org

🌄 Local Events/Attractions:
Indian Caverns, Spruce Creek, PA (814) 632–7578 – open April through October, $8.50 per person • Swigart Antique Auto Museum, Huntingdon, PA (814) 643–0885 – open Memorial Day through October, $4 per person

🛏 Accommodations:
The Inn at Solvang, Huntingdon, PA (814) 643–3035 or www.solvang.com
• Greenwood Furnace State Park Campgrounds, Huntingdon, PA (814) 667–1807 – open second weekend of April through mid December

🍴 Restaurants:
Miller's Diner, Mill Creek, PA (814) 643–3418

👥 Organizations:
Mid State Trail Association, P.O. Box 167, Boalsburg, PA 16827

🎿 Local Outdoor Retailers:
Appalachia Ski & Outdoors, State College, PA (814) 234–3000 or www.theadventuresource.com • QBS Sports, Huntingdon, PA (814) 643–1120

🅽 Maps:
USGS maps: Pine Grove Mills, PA

Alan Seeger Natural Area to Greenwood Fire Tower

Hike Specs

Start: From the new Alan Seeger Natural Area picnic area parking lot

Length: 5.1-mile out-and-back

Approximate Hiking Time: 4 hours

Difficulty Rating: Moderate, due to a steep, strenuous climb

Terrain: A pine needle nature trail leads through giant hemlock trees, tunnels of huge rhododendron, shaded slopes and across mountain streams. You'll also follow a steep, rocky footpath through boulders and a high plateau path through huckleberries.

Elevation Gain: 1,018 feet

Land Status: State forest

Nearest Town: State College, PA

Other Trail Users: Backpackers and picnickers

Canine Compatibility: Leashed dogs permitted

Getting There

From State College: Drive south on PA 26 to the flashing yellow stoplight in Pine Grove Mills. Continue south 8.5 miles on PA 26 and turn left at the sign for Alan Seeger Road. Drive 5.9 miles to the new Alan Seeger Natural Area picnic and parking area. *DeLorme: Pennsylvania Atlas & Gazetteer:* Page 62 C3

L ike unsolved mysteries? On this hike there are two. The first concerns the area's namesake, Alan Seeger. Seeger was an American who moved to Paris to become a poet. When World War I broke out, he joined the French Foreign Legion, and received a number of medals for his courage. His claim to fame came about as a result of his poem, "I Have a Rendezvous with Death," which eerily came true when he was killed in battle on July 4, 1916. Today, no one knows why his name was attached to the Natural Area. There are no available records to show if or when Seeger ever visited this part of the state.

The second mystery revolves around the very existence of the Alan Seeger Natural Area. From 1834 to 1903, the entire area surrounding Alan Seeger was clearcut to produce charcoal for the furnaces at nearby Greenwood Furnace & Iron Works. For some reason—no one knows why— 118 acres of old-growth forest were spared the axe. This tract served as the foundation for the 368-acre park. As a result, you can see some of the oldest trees in Pennsylvania along the Natural Area's short interpretive trail.

At one point, you come face to face with a 500-year-old eastern hemlock that was struck by lightning in 1982 and lies across the trail. Also in this first section of your hike, you'll see some of the largest rhododendron in the state. With trunks thicker than your arm, these shrubs have intertwined themselves and created tunnels that are in some places 20 feet high.

After the interpretive trail, begin a 1,000-foot climb up a ravine to the top of Broad Mountain. Along the way, you pass through a second-growth

MilesDirections

0.0 START from the new picnic area parking lot and turn left onto the paved road.

0.4 Cross the bridge over Detweiler Run and enter the original picnic area parking lot. Walk to the Alan Seeger Trail sign beside the trail bulletin board.

0.6 Arrive at the intersection with the Mid-State Trail North. Turn left and veer right onto the Greenwood Spur South. Cross the first wooden bridge over Standing Stone Creek and enter an area of dense rhododendron.

0.7 Cross a second bridge over Standing Stone Creek and come to a sign for the giant eastern hemlock. Cross a third bridge over Standing Stone Creek.

0.8 Turn left onto a wooden truss bridge over Standing Stone Creek and enter a hemlock forest.

1.2 Cross Alan Seeger Road and arrive at the trailhead for the Mid State Trail and Greenwood Spur and the Johnson Trail. Turn left onto the Johnson Trail and follow the blue blazes.

1.7 Begin a serious uphill climb.

1.8 Pass a sign for a spring on your left.

1.9 Notice the striped maple at edge of boulder outcropping. The trail becomes rocky.

2.0 Cross Alan Seeger Road.

2.1 Come to a series of switchbacks.

2.6 Trail levels off as you reach the mountaintop.

2.9 Arrive at the Greenwood Fire Tower. Retrace your steps. Cross Alan Seeger Road.

4.6 Arrive at Alan Seeger Road a second time. This time turn left onto the bridge over Standing Stone Creek.

4.7 Cross the bridge over Detweiler Run and retrace your steps to the new parking lot.

5.1 Arrive back at the new picnic area parking lot.

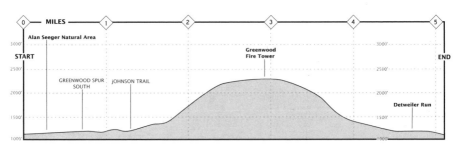

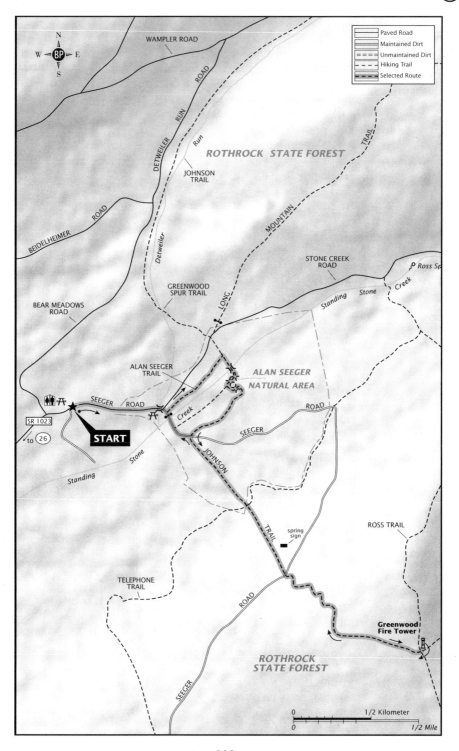

forest of oak, hemlock, pine, black birch, and white birch. Striped maples can also be seen growing along boulder outcroppings. This species, with its distinctive vertical stripes, is right at home here. It thrives on shaded slopes and deep ravines.

Near the top of the mountain you'll work your way through a series of short switchbacks. The reason for these closely spaced switchbacks is simple: The trail is *very, very* steep at this point, as opposed to lower down the ravine, where the trail is just *very* steep. But no matter how many times you do it, it's always exhilarating to reach the top of a climb. Broad Mountain is no exception. As soon as the trail levels off, a high-mountain breeze—welcome in the warmer months—cools you. (If you make this hike in the cooler months, be sure to layer clothing so you can add and remove them as necessary.) Walking through the dense huckleberry patches in the sunlight, you can almost forget that you just climbed up a rocky ravine that, in short order, you must hike back down.

Enjoy yourself while you can. The flat area around the Greenwood Fire Tower is grassy, a natural spot for lunch and a little R&R. If you want to see why this section of Pennsylvania is known as the Valley and Ridge Province, climb the fire tower. On a clear day, you can see a number of ridges separated by broad valleys. In this area, however, you may notice the pattern is irregular. Some ridges do not run parallel and some of the valleys are deep and narrow as opposed to being wide, which is the norm.

Much of the area you are viewing from the tower lies within the 94,264-acre Rothrock State Forest, named after Dr. Joseph Rothrock, a professor at the University of Pennsylvania. As early as the late 1800s, Rothrock championed two ideas: He warned of the problems that would occur as a result of clearcutting, and he believed in Pennsylvania's public ownership of forests. For his efforts, Rothrock was elected the first president of the Pennsylvania Forestry Association, forerunner of the Bureau of Forestry.

Hike Information

ⓒ Trail Contacts:
Rothrock State Forest, Huntingdon, PA (814) 643–2340

⊙ Schedule:
Open year round

Ⓢ Fees/Permits:
No fees or permits required

❓ Local Information:
Centre County Convention and Visitors Bureau, State College, PA (814) 231–1400 or 1–800–358–5466 or *www.visitpennstate.org*

ⓞ Local Events/Attractions:
Central Pennsylvania Festival of the Arts, second week in July, Downtown State College, PA (814) 237–3682 • **Downtown State College Partnership Inc.,** State College, PA (814) 238–7004 or *www.downtownstate college.com*

ⓘ Accommodations:
Spruce Creek Bed & Breakfast, Spruce Creek, PA (814) 632–3777 • **Greenwood Furnace State Park Campgrounds,** Huntingdon, PA (814) 667–1807 – *open from the second weekend in April through the middle of December*

ⓘ Restaurants:
Duffy's Tavern, Boalsburg, PA (814) 466–6241

ⓞ Organizations:
Mid State Trail Association, P.O. Box 167, Boalsburg, PA 16827

ⓢ Local Outdoor Retailers:
Appalachia Ski & Outdoors, State College, PA (814) 234–3000

Ⓝ Maps:
USGS maps: McAlveys Fort, PA; Barrville, PA

Southcentral Pennsylvania

Compiled here is an index of great hikes in the Southcentral region that didn't make the A-list this time around but deserve recognition. Check them out and let us know what you think. You may decide that one or more of these hikes deserves higher status in future editions or, perhaps, you may have a hike of your own that merits some attention.

(0) Caledonia State Park

Located in Adams and Franklin counties, midway between Chambersburg and Gettysburg on U.S. 30, Caledonia is the second oldest park in the state system and one of the most popular. I'm sure Thaddeus Stevens didn't consider the beauty of his location when he built an iron furnace here in 1837, but, as you'll discover even before you get into the park, the hemlock forests, historical buildings, and creeks with man-made spillways make the area picture-postcard perfect. There are over 10 miles of trails in the park, plus a short section of the Appalachian Trail.

To get there from Chambersburg, drive east on U.S. 30 for 11 miles and turn left at the park sign on PA 233. For more information, call Caledonia State Park at (717) 352–2161. *DeLorme: Pennsylvania Atlas & Gazetteer:* Page 91 5A

(P) Blue Knob State Park

Situated in the northwestern tip of Bedford County, west of I-99. The park boasts the second-highest peak in the state. Its namesake, a majestic quartzite peak called Blue Knob, is 3,146 feet above sea level, just 67 feet below the highest point in the state, Mount Davis. Blue Knob is situated on a spur of the Allegheny Front, providing spectacular views and abundant photo opportunities—plus some premiere downhill skiing.

To get there from Altoona, drive south on I-99 and take the Roaring Springs exit. Follow Old Route 220 south to PA 164 west. Turn right onto PA 164 west and drive about five miles to the town of Blue Knob. In Blue Knob, turn left on Blue Knob Road and drive five miles to the park entrance. For more information, call Blue Knob State Park at (814) 276-3576. *DeLorme: Pennsylvania Atlas & Gazetteer:* Page 74 B3

Southwest
PENNSYLVANIA

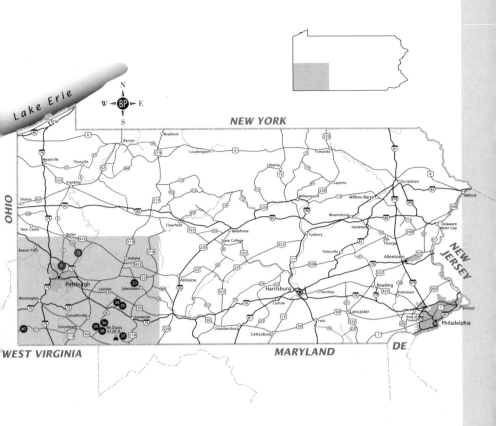

The Rides

Conemaugh Gorge **33.**
Linn Run State Park **34.**
Wolf Rocks Trail **35.**
Bear Run Nature Reserve **36.**
Mount Davis Natural Area **37.**
Ferncliff Peninsula Natural Area **38.**
Youghiogheny River to Jonathan Run Falls **39.**
Ryerson Station State Park **40.**

Honorable Mentions

Q. Todd Sanctuary
R. The Beechwood Farms Nature
Reserve

Southwest Pennsylvania

For sheer beauty, it would be hard to beat the Laurel Highlands of Southwestern Pennsylvania. Here, hikers can walk to the edge of the 1,000-foot-deep Conemaugh Gorge, or if that's too tame, they can peer into the 1,700-foot-deep Youghiogheny River gorge. Or, for the backpacker in the family, there's the 70-mile-long Laurel Highlands Hiking Trail that begins in the Youghiogheny Gorge, traverses the Laurel Ridge, and ends at the Conemaugh Gorge.

[*Tip: Do this or any part of the Laurel Ridge Trail when the mountain laurel are in bloom (usually from the middle of June to the end of the month) and you'll be awestruck by the spectacularly beautiful blooms. Mountain Laurel didn't get to be the state flower for nothing. (See Hike 30)*]

If the gorges don't get your blood moving, you could join the 100,000 people who raft the Youghiogheny River every year. Or if you just want to be lazy and try an easy hike, you can walk across the flat rocks leading over the river and get right up close to the famous Ohiopyle Falls. *(See Hike 35)*

Before leaving the subject of the Ohiopyle area, it should be said that Ohiopyle State Park may just be the nicest state park in the system. (With over two million visitors a year, it's certainly one of the busiest.) It should also be pointed out, however, that if you are towing a big camper you'll need to call the park first to determine the best way to get to the campground. The drive out of the gorge bottom is so steep and so long, there may be some vehicles that just can't make it up.

There are two hikes in the southwest where you'll be able to leave the crowds behind. Mount Davis, the highest point in the state, confirms the old saw that it's lonely at the top. It's not the easiest drive and the weather can change rapidly, but what hiker in his right mind would pass up a chance to get to the state's pinnacle?

Ryerson Station State Park sits all alone on the western fringes of the state, proving once again that it's location, location, location. It was precisely the remote location that prompted the government to build a fort to protect early settlers. Now you can get away from the crowds and commune with bluebirds and the great blue heron, or climb one of the steepest slopes around to an old family cemetery.

Finally, there is nowhere else in the country where you can hike one day and visit what scholars have declared "the only real piece of art created in America." If you live anywhere near the Laurel Highlands (or anywhere in Pennsylvania, for that matter) and you've never been to Fallingwater, take a hike up to Frank Lloyd Wright's masterpiece. *(See Hike 36)* Actually, there are two of his works here; Kentuck Knob is out of the gorge not five minutes from the Ohiopyle Campgrounds.

Overview

Conemaugh Gorge

The highlights of this hike are a visit to Big Spring Reservoir and the views of Conemaugh River Gorge. Pass through a dense understory of rhododendron and mountain laurel to get to the gorge's edge, where outcroppings provide excellent places to relax and take in the deep gorge panorama. *(See page 220)*

Linn Run State Park

There are some strenuous climbs as the trail makes its way alongside a stream, past a waterfall, and out of the first valley. Above the falls, there are smaller feeder streams that wash over mossy rock outcroppings, creating grotto-like falls. *(See page 224)*

Wolf Rocks Trail

This hike is in the heart of the Laurel Highlands region of the Allegheny Mountains. There are two highlights: the blooming mountain laurel and Wolf Rocks, an outcropping of boulders along the edge of Laurel Summit that provides an impressive view of Linn Run Valley and Chestnut Ridge. If you choose, there is also a short side trip—after the hike—to Spruce Flats Bog. *(See page 230)*

Bear Run Nature Reserve

There are a number of highlights on this hike. The trail begins in a pristine stand of pines, continues on gently rolling grassy roads, and finally leads to a heart-stopping view into the 1,700-foot deep Youghiogheny River Gorge. Returning from the gorge, you pass Fallingwater, Frank Lloyd Wright's masterpiece. *(See page 236)*

Mount Davis Natural Area

Here's your chance to rise above it all, to the highest point in all of Pennsylvania, Mount Davis (3,213 feet). Because of its altitude, the area surrounding this hike is different than the typical

mountain trails at lower elevations. You'll see trees charred from lightning fires, peculiar rock circles, and stunted trees. The immediate area around the "highest point" monument and tower is tourist-friendly: flat and paved. But the majority of this hike is ideal for those who want to rough it a bit and explore the unusual high-mountain ecosystem. *(See page 242)*

Ferncliff Peninsula Natural Area

This easy hike loops the 100-acre Ferncliff Peninsula, giving hikers the best views of the Youghiogheny River rapids and Ohiopyle Falls. The trail leads you right to the river's edge onto flat sandstone boulders, where you can examine tree fossils embedded in the rock. At points, a canopy of rhododendron shades the trail. At marked sites along the way, learn about the peninsula's unique environment, which includes Southern wildflowers and umbrella magnolia trees. *(See page 248)*

Youghiogheny River Trail to Jonathan Run Falls

For an easy, Sunday-stroll-type hike, this one can't be beat. It starts at the refurbished train depot and traces an abandoned railroad grade. The path is, quite literally, flat the whole way. There are excellent river views en route, and at the end there's a deep forest waterfall. *(See page 256)*

Ryerson Station State Park

Ryerson is a pleasant hike in a small park. If you're looking to get away from the crowds and want to spend a day exploring nature and soaking up local history, this is the hike for you. The hike consists of a series of short climbs up extremely steep hollows. A 300-year-old *wolf tree* greets you on your first ascent to an overlook 400 feet above the park. Follow a mowed pathway alongside a lake inlet and into a meadow, where the vegetation is over six feet high. Scan the inlet for the great blue heron, explore a bluebird box trail, and visit an old family cemetery. *(See page 260)*

Conemaugh Gorge

Hike Specs

Start: From the Seward Trailhead parking area off PA 56

Length: 7.2-mile out-and-back

Approximate Hiking Time: 4 hours

Difficulty Rating: Moderate, due to the steady uphill climb to the edge of the gorge

Terrain: Walk along a rocky footpath and dirt road through mountain laurel to the edge of a 1,000-foot gorge.

Elevation Gain: 1,281 feet

Land Status: State park

Nearest Town: Johnstown, PA

Other Trail Users: Hikers only

Canine Compatibility: Leashed dogs permitted

Getting There

From Altoona: Drive west on U.S. 22. Take the PA 56 Exit and drive south to Seward. Drive one mile past the intersection with PA 711 to an access road on the right. Turn right onto the access road and drive 0.4 miles to the trailhead parking area where the road ends.
DeLorme: Pennsylvania Atlas & Gazetteer: Page 73 A6

Looking into this great gorge, it's difficult not to be awestruck by the forces that have steadily worked for millennia to create this giant gash in the earth. For all its serenity, it's equally difficult to imagine that you're looking down on the site of one of the most disastrous events in United States history—the Johnstown Flood.

For residents of central Pennsylvania, the summer of 1889 will forever be memorable for its unprecedented flooding and natural disasters. While the flooding was devastating on both sides of the Alleghenys, it was staggering in the Conemaugh Valley. On May 31, 1889 over 2,200 people lost their lives when the South Fork Dam on the Conemaugh River burst, sending a 35-foot wall of water 14 miles downstream to the city of Johnstown. By the time it reached the unsuspecting city, it struck with enough force to carry a 48-ton locomotive over a mile. Tens of thousands of people lost their homes and three square miles of the city were destroyed.

Newspaper reports and eyewitness accounts describe a level of destruction so complete that the town seems never to have existed. Buildings, bridges, utility infrastructure, streetcar lines, and stone sidewalks were destroyed and so thoroughly buried that residents could no longer even trace the lines of the once busy and crowded downtown streets.

Remarkably, the city began rebuilding. With supplies sent in from all over the country, the mills that were left standing were opened, and those men who could went back to work. Clara Barton, who had founded the

American Red Cross just seven years earlier, set up hospitals throughout the city. There is a flood museum in Johnstown, as well as a national monument at the sight of the dam. Surprisingly, the dam, with the exception of the center part that gave way, is still standing, and visitors can walk out on it

This hike begins at the northern terminus of the 70-mile-long Laurel Highlands Hiking Trail. (You can find the southern trailhead in the Youghiogheny River Gorge in Ohiopyle.) The trail is well maintained and popular with backpackers. It has mile markers and eight overnight camping areas (each with potable water, restrooms, tent pads, and shelters). Whether you do the entire 70 miles of the trail, or just the seven miles of this hike, you soon learn that the Laurel Highlands section of the Allegheny Mountains is just what the name implies: a high plateau covered with wall-to-wall mountain laurel.

But there's more to this hike than just views from the ridge. Your first treat is the pristine Big Spring Reservoir and its emerald water. Also, if you take this hike in mid June, you'll be rewarded with a wonderland of mountain laurel in full bloom. Sassafras, tulip poplar, beech, oak, and maple trees provide plenty of shade, while the tenacious hemlocks cling to the ravines. Exposed limestone and sandstone boulders provide plenty of natural viewing areas, so sit back and enjoy.

Big Spring Reservoir.

MilesDirections

0.0 START at the trailhead in parking area. Look for the yellow blazes.

0.1 Come to a concrete 70-mile marker, a trailhead bulletin board, and a sign-in register.

0.2 Pass the Big Spring Reservoir on your right.

0.6 Cross a power line swath.

0.7 Cross a dirt road. Come to milepost 69. Begin a climb.

0.9 Cross the dirt road second time.

1.1 Reach a rock outcropping for a view of the gorge.

1.2 *[FYI. Notice the abandoned quarry ruins.]*

1.5 Cross a dirt road the third time.

1.7 Come to milepost 68.

2.7 Come to milepost 67.

3.0 Come to a view of Johnstown.

3.6 Arrive at a dirt road. Turn around and retrace your steps back to the trailhead.

7.2 Arrive back at the trailhead.

Hike Information

🕐 **Trail Contacts:**
Highlands Hiking Trail, Sierra Club of Pittsburgh, Pittsburgh, PA (724) 455–3744 • **Laurel Ridge State Park,** Rockwood, PA (724) 455–3744

🕐 **Schedule:**
Open year round

💲 **Fees/Permits:**
There is a fee to use the overnight camping areas. Call (724) 455–3744 for more information.

❓ **Local Information:**
Johnstown Area Heritage Association, Johnstown, PA (814) 539–1889

🚌 **Bus Service:**
Westmoreland County Transit, Route 12 (Johnstown to New Florence) will stop on PA 56 at the access road weekdays only. Call (724) 834–9282 or visit *www.geocities.com/ CapitolHill/Lobby/5240/westmor* for more information.

💡 **Local Events/Attractions:**
Johnstown National Flood Museum, St. Michaels, PA (814) 495–4643 • **The Johnstown Inclined Plane, Inc.,** Johnstown, PA (814) 536–4328 or *www.InclinedPlane.com*

🛏 **Accommodations:**
Windmill Bed & Breakfast, Johnstown, PA (814) 269–4625 • **Blue Knob State Park,** Imler, PA (814) 276–3576 – *for camping information*

🔄 **Other Resources:**
Western Pennsylvania Conservancy, Pittsburgh, PA (412) 288–2777

🔦 **Local Outdoor Retailers:**
Hornick's Sporting Goods, Johnstown, PA (814) 535–7724

🗺 **Maps:**
USGS maps: New Florence, PA; Vintondale, PA

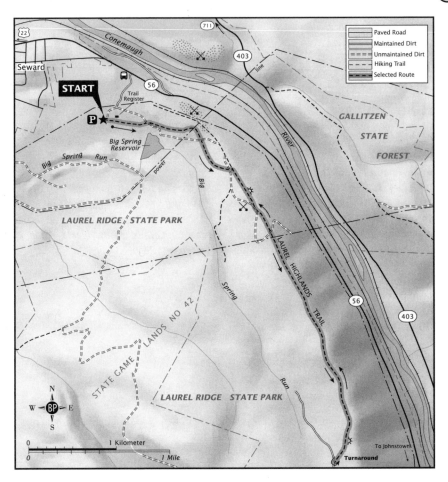

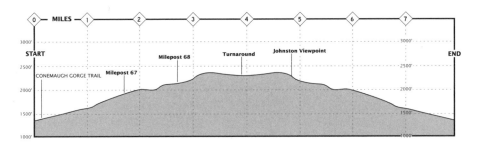

Linn Run State Park

Hike Specs

Start: From the Grove Run Picnic Area parking lot

Length: 4.2-mile loop

Approximate Hiking Time: 3 hours

Difficulty Rating: Moderate, due to a strenuous climb out of the stream valley

Terrain: Using a rocky footpath and encountering washouts, climb out of a deep valley to a waterfall, cross the ridge, and descend the other side of the valley.

Elevation Gain: 919 feet

Land Status: State park

Nearest Town: Ligonier, PA

Other Trail Users: Hunters (in season)

Canine Compatibility: Leashed dogs permitted

Getting There

From Pittsburgh: Drive east on U.S. 30 to Ligonier. Continue two miles past Ligonier and turn right on PA 381. Continue four miles to the village of Rector and turn left onto Linn Run Road. Drive four miles and enter Linn Run State Park. Turn right into the Grove Run picnic area. *DeLorme: Pennsylvania Atlas & Gazetteer:* Page 73 C5

I f you've never been to this area of the Laurel Highlands, you're in for a treat. Driving the last few miles on Pennsylvania 381 to the tiny village of Rector makes the whole trip worthwhile—and you don't even have to get out of your car. In this remote area, it's hard to know where the countryside ends and the state parks begin.

As Linn Run makes its way down the gorge from the Laurel Highlands to the Ligonier Valley, it widens substantially and takes on a more serene feel. Eastern hemlocks line both banks, creating a deep green shade. Mature maples and oaks create a canopy across the road as you drive by hundreds of acres of rustic-fenced horse property. It feels as though you're driving on a movie set that was designed to give the impression of wealth. What you're passing is Rolling Rock Farms, the private enclave of the Mellon family, owners of (among other things) the Pittsburgh-based Mellon National Bank and Rolling Rock Beer.

The founder of this dynasty was Andrew William Mellon, financier, industrialist, and statesman. Like most other magnates of the early 20th Century, Mellon made his money in the coal, oil, and iron industries. Eventually he crossed over into politics and served as Secretary of the Treasury under three consecutive presidents: Warren Harding, Calvin Coolidge, and Herbert Hoover. In 1932 and 1933 he enjoyed a position as American ambassador to Britain.

Water cascades over mossy boulders, creating a grotto-like effect.

Mellon is also remembered as a philanthropist. He was instrumental in the establishment of the Mellon Institute in Pittsburgh, which merged with the Carnegie Institute in 1967 to become Carnegie Mellon University. But perhaps his most important philanthropic act came about in 1937, when he decided to donate his vast art collection to the people of the United States. The result: the establishment of the National Gallery of Art in Washington, D.C.

But, alas, we leave all this behind when we exit the world of the rich and famous and reenter the real world of Linn Run State Park. Not far from the park entrance you'll find the Grove Run Picnic Area on your right. The highlight of this picnic area is a large stone fountain of free-flowing water from Grove Run Spring. It's ice cold and sparkling clear, and by the look of the traffic to the fountain, it may be the most popular attraction in the park. There is a steady stream of water-gatherers with dozens of containers.

Fill up your water bottle and start your climb up the ravine. On your way up the gorge, there are a number of cool places to rest. You'll find cave-like pockets in the outcropping along the trail, where a steady stream of water trickles from one mossy ledge to the next. You'll find that you can hear the waterfall at Grove Run long before you can see it. Like the smaller washout falls along the trail, it's set in a deep pocket of outcropping.

This causes the sound of the falls to echo off the walls, making it sound much larger than it is.

This hike is sure to provide a good workout. There is a steep, unrelenting, two-mile climb out of the valley before you reach the grassy plateau where the trail levels off. From there, cut across another ridge overlooking Linn Run Valley. In sections along this ridge, wild grapevines are the predominate vegetation. There is also an abundance of catbrier, a prickly vine that you wouldn't think would be much good for anything except snagging your clothes; however, its bluish to black seeds, greenish leaves, and flowers provide food for deer, grouse, and smaller animals.

The trail skirts along a slope high above Linn Run and Linn Run Road before you dip back into the valley, ford Grove Run on the exposed rocks, and come out at the picnic area where you can refill your water bottle.

Hike Information

● Trail Contacts:
Linn Run State Park, Rector, PA (724) 238–6623 • **Forbes State Forest,** Laughlintown, PA (724) 238–1200

● Schedule:
Open year round

● Fees/Permits:
No fees or permits required

● Local Information:
Laurel Highlands Visitors Bureau, Ligonier, PA (724) 238–5661 or *www.laurelhighlands.org*

● Local Events/Attractions:
Pennsylvania Arts & Crafts Country Festival, last weekend in May, Fayetteville County Fairgrounds, Irwin, PA (724) 863–4577 • **Rolling Rock 5- Mile Run,** part of the July 4th weekend celebration, Latrobe, PA (724) 537–0597

● Accommodations:
Ligonier Country Inn B&B, Laughlintown, PA (724) 238–3651 or *www.ligoniercountryinn.com* • **Linn Run State Park,** Rector, PA (724) 238–6623 – *rustic cabins available year round* • **Laurel Hill State Park,** Somerset, PA (814) 445–7725 – *for camping reservations call 1–888–PA–PARKS*

● Restaurants:
Ligonier Tavern, Ligonier, PA (724) 238–4831

● Organizations:
Laurel Highlands Hiking Trail, Laurel Ridge State Park, Rockwood, PA (724) 455–3744

● Local Outdoor Retailers:
All Around Athletes, Ligonier, PA (724) 238–8544 or *www.tshirtsand uniforms.com* • **Loyalhanna Fishing Post,** Ligonier, PA (724) 238–5551

● Maps:
USGS maps: Ligonier, PA

MilesDirections

0.0 START at the Grove Run Picnic Area parking lot. Walk to the Grove Run Trail sign at the west end of the lot. Pick up the blue blazes.

0.1 Cross two small runs that drain into Grove Run.

0.3 Grove Run is on your right.

0.4 Bear right and begin an uphill climb.

0.7 The trail levels off a bit. *[FYI. Notice the wild grapevines.]*

0.9 Come to a wooden bridge across Grove Run and a waterfall. Cross the stream and turn left.

1.0 Pass through two washout areas.

1.1 Ford a tributary of Grove Run. *[FYI. Notice the water cascading over the mossy boulders.]*

1.2 Ford a second tributary. Begin a serious uphill climb.

1.3 Come to you first switchback.

1.4 *[Note. Watch for the thick greenbriar in this area.]*

1.5 Come to an abandoned trail register.

1.6 Arrive at your second switchback.

1.8 Cross Quarry Trail snowmobile road. Come to a sign "Fish Run Trail." Stay on the Grove Run Trail, continuing straight ahead.

1.9 Pass through a rocky area. Cross a pine covered plateau and a small washout.

2.1 Cross over two more washouts.

2.8 Pass through an area of boulders. *[FYI. Notice the extensive wild grapevines.]*

2.9 Come to open, blow-down area. You can hear Linn Run below.

3.1 Cross the Quarry Trail a second time. Come to a sign for the Grove Run Trail.

3.2 Come to a sign that says Grove Run Picnic area to the left and Linn Run Road to the right. Go left to picnic area.

3.3 Cross several washouts. Enter an area of large boulders.

3.6 Cross a wide, rocky washout.

3.8 Linn Run Road is on your right. Pass through more rocky washouts.

3.9 The trail turns left onto a raised area.

4.0 Ford Grove Run on the exposed rocks.

4.2 Arrive at the picnic area and parking lot.

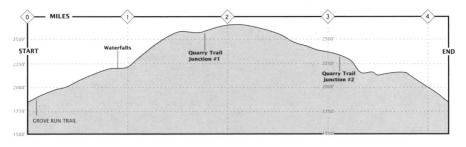

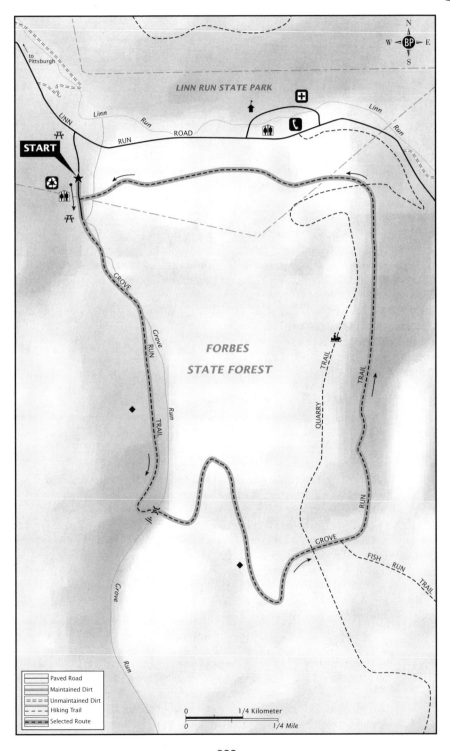

Wolf Rocks Trail

Hike Specs

Start: From the Laurel Summit State Park picnic area parking lot
Length: 4.5-mile circuit
Approximate Hiking Time: 2.5 hours
Difficulty Rating: Moderate, due to an extremely rocky section
Terrain: Using a rock- and root-covered footpath and cross-country ski trails, you'll walk a ridge-top path through acres of mountain laurel to an outcropping of boulders for a breathtaking view.
Elevation Gain: 311 feet
Land Status: State park
Nearest Town: Ligonier, PA
Other Trail Users: Cross-country skiers and hunters (in season)
Canine Compatibility: Leashed dogs permitted

Getting There

From Pittsburgh: Drive east on U.S. 30 to Ligonier. Continue two miles past Ligonier and turn right on PA 381. Continue four miles to Rector and turn left onto Linn Run Road. After four miles, enter Linn Run State Park. Continue on Linn Run Road for five miles to Laurel Summit State Park and turn left into the park and picnic area. *DeLorme: Pennsylvania Atlas & Gazetteer:* Page 73 C5

Laurel Summit State Park lies within the 58,000-acre Forbes State Forest. With a mere 15 acres, Laurel Summit State Park basically constitutes the area surrounding Wolf Rocks Trail. Nearby are three other Laurel state parks: Laurel Mountain, Laurel Hill, and Laurel Ridge. The other Laurel parks are considerably larger, and it's easy to get these parks confused. Your best bet is to get a Pennsylvania State Parks and Forests Map, and highlight or circle the parks in different colors.

Gnarly comes to mind when describing this trail. Plenty of trails have roots and rocks underfoot, but this trail, for the most part, has you stepping from root to rock, without pause for dirt. But before long, you'll get into the rhythm of stepping from one rock to the next. In fact, once you pass through the delicate white and pink mountain laurel blossoms, it's possible to forget the trail completely.

The show-stopping highlight (and the turnaround point) on this hike is the Wolf Rocks overlook. These sandstone and limestone boulders were heaved to the mountaintop during one of the more recent (and that's a *very* relative term) tectonic events. Along most mountain ridges, boulders like those at Wolf Rocks remain underground; however, in rare instances they may erupt to the surface. Evidence of this eruption lies all about. The smaller rocks, which are farther inland from the edge, have ragged edges and are

scattered every which way. The larger rocks that sit right on (and at some points over) the edge are flat rocks split apart by horizontal cracks. In some places, the larger rocks look as if they were crudely stacked one on top of the other. The rocks are a great place for lunch. If you come at the right time of day, they're an absolutely fabulous spot to stretch out, listen to the wind whistle up out of the valley, and tan yourself.

On your return to the picnic area, you'll pass the mysterious 28-acre Spruce Flats Bog, part of the 305-acre Spruce Flats Wildlife Management Area. When loggers arrived in the area, they found a stand of hemlock in the swampy woodland—which, incidentally, they mistook for spruce, forever mislabeling the bog. And once they had harvested the trees, the swampy woodland reverted to a bog, which scientists believe it was originally. It has remained a bog ever since. The existence of a bog is by no means mysterious; the existence of one this far south, however, is curious. Here's the problem: Nearly all bogs are formed as the result of glaciation,

The view from Wolf Rocks. At 2,700 feet above sea level, this is one of the highest peaks in the state.

which occurs when a glacier melts or retreats, and in doing so, alters the underlying topography and environment. When scientists mapped the southern reach of the glaciers during the last ice age, none extended this far south—hence the confusion. Some experts suggest, with rather obvious logic, that the bog is simply the result of an earlier ice age, but until this is proven, the bog's presence here remains a mystery.

Regardless of its convoluted history, there are a number of interesting plants growing in Spruce Flats Bog's acidic and nutrient-poor ecosystem today. Representing the heath family of evergreen bushes is the cranberry, cousin to the ubiquitous mountain laurel and rhododendron. But don't pick the red berries and expect them to taste like the stuff you eat at Thanksgiving: Cranberries are bitter and need to be processed before humans can eat them. Wildlife, on the other hand, love the wild berry.

Two of the region's most common insect-eating plants can be found in the bog as well: the sundew and the pitcher plant. The sundew usually has

MilesDirections

0.0 START at the parking area of the Laurel Summit State Park picnic area. Look for the red blazes.

0.2 Cross over a pipeline swath.

0.4 Come to a culvert over a small run.

0.6 Turn left at the sign for Wolfs Rocks Loop.

1.1 Careful of the steep ravine on your left.

1.2 Pass through a fern-covered open area.

1.5 Turn right at the double red blazes.

1.8 Cross over a deep wash.

2.0 Come to a flat area covered with waist-high fern.

2.1 Turn left onto the Old Wolfs Rocks Trail.

2.4 Arrive at the Wolfs Rocks overlook. Retrace your steps.

2.7 Come to a fork, where a grassy path goes off to the left. Stay to the right on the red-blazed footpath. Come to a trail intersection and the sign, "Wolfs Rocks Loop Trail Turn Right." Do not turn right; continue on the Old Wolfs Rocks Trail.

3.6 *[FYI. Notice the bog on your left.]*

3.9 Arrive back the Wolf Rocks Loop Trail intersection. Continue straight.

4.0 Cross the pipeline swath.

4.3 Arrive back at parking area.

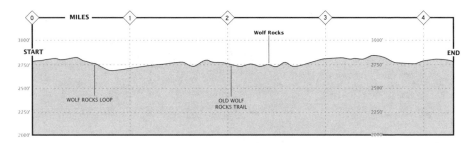

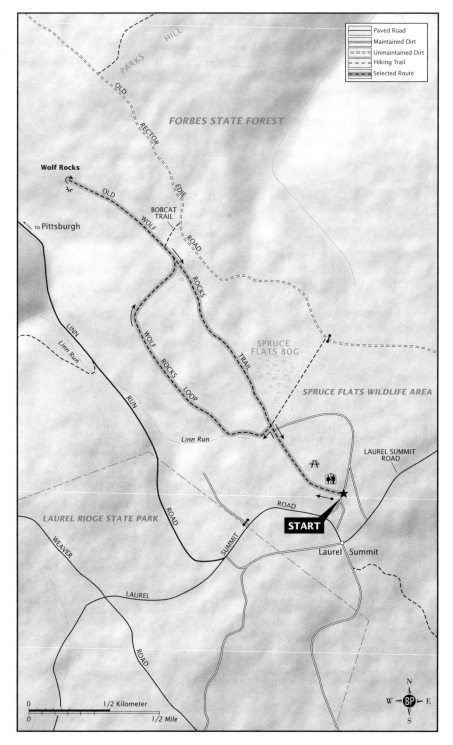

The Whiskey Rebellion

As you hike along the trails of the Laurel Highlands, the last thing you'd think of is a riot—you know, the kind of thing where people are angry and shots are fired and federal troops are sent out. Believe it or not, that's exactly what took place in Southwestern Pennsylvania in the 1790s.

The farmers who settled this corner of the state, many of whom were of Irish and Scottish descent, were famous for their rye whiskey. Rye is a cereal grass that, once ground into flour, is used to make bread and other baked items. It's also used as livestock feed. But despite its many uses, it was not a terrific cash crop. That is, unless it was sold as alcohol. And so the majority of these grain farmers received the bulk of their incomes from the sale of whiskey.

In 1791 Federalist leader and Secretary of the Treasury Alexander Hamilton imposed an excise tax on whiskey sales. The farmers felt this tax was unwarranted and organized a resistance, which included the tarring and feathering of federal revenue officials.

It all came to a head in the spring of 1794 when arrest warrants were issued for the farmers who refused to pay the tax. In the riot that ensued, one federal official was killed and the home of the regional excise tax inspector was burned. In August of that year, President George Washington stepped in, first by sending negotiators to the area, and then, when that failed, by mobilizing the militia.

His troops marched to the area and set up camp on the hilltop where Laurel Hill State Park is today. There was no bloodshed, and the rebellion ended with Washington making a deal with the farmers. If they would grow only corn, he said, they would be given free land in Virginia (what is now Kentucky). The farmers agreed...and soon began making corn whiskey—better known as Kentucky bourbon.

an eight-inch stalk that supports a pink rosette covered with sticky hairs. These hairs trap insects and the plant devours them. The pitcher plant is appreciably larger. It has a 20-inch stalk with red vase-like leaves filled with water and sticky hairs. Insects, attracted to the plant's bright color, venture inside the leaves and are trapped by the plant's hair. They're subsequently drowned and consumed.

The best way to visit Spruce Flats Bog is to return to the picnic area parking lot and get on the short trail that leads to it. If you visit the bog, keep your eyes open for wildlife and birds. This special management area has been set up specifically to improve wildlife habitat, and all the trails within the area are used as viewing trails. Look for small clearings where the trees have been recently been removed. These areas were created to provide the appropriate environment for grouse and songbirds.

Foresters from the Forbes State Forest monitor the wildlife activity here and conduct mammal track counts after January and February snowstorms to see if their efforts are paying off. In addition, the Audubon Society of Western Pennsylvania conducts annual bird surveys here in the late spring.

Hike Information

● Trail Contacts:
Laurel Summit State Park, c/o Linn Run State Park, Rector, PA (724) 238–6623 • Forbes State Forest, Laughlintown, PA (724) 238–1200

● Schedule:
Open year round

● Fees/Permits:
No fees or permits required

● Local Information:
Laurel Highlands Visitors Bureau, Ligonier, PA (724) 238–5661 or www.laurelhighlands.org

● Local Events/Attractions:
Mountain Craft Days, second weekend in September, Somerset Historical Center, Somerset, PA (814) 445–6077 • **Fort Ligonier,** Ligonier, PA (724) 238–9701

● Accommodations:
Ligonier Country Inn, Laughlintown, PA (724) 238–3651 or www.ligonier countryinn.com • **Laurel Hill State Park,** Somerset, PA (814) 445–7725 – cabins available for rent year round

● Restaurants:
Ligonier Tavern, Ligonier, PA (724) 238–4831

● Organizations:
Laurel Highlands Hiking Trail, Laurel Ridge State Park, Rockwood, PA (724) 455–3744

● Local Outdoor Retailers:
All Around Athletes, Ligonier, PA (724) 238–8544 or www.tshirtsand uniforms.com • **Loyalhanna Fishing Post,** Ligonier, PA (724) 238–5551

● Maps:
USGS maps: Bakersville, PA; Ligonier, PA

Bear Run Nature Reserve

Hike Specs

Start: From the Bear Run Nature Reserve parking lot off PA 381

Length: 8.0-mile loop

Approximate Hiking Time: 5 hours

Difficulty Rating: Moderate, due to a section of strenuous climbing

Terrain: Pass through stands of pine and patches of rhododendron along a gently rolling trail through oak and hemlock forests; follow a mountain stream; and then climb a ridge for views of the river gorge. Surfaces include grassy jeep roads, a forest footpath, and a rocky ridge path.

Elevation Gain: 1,038 feet

Land Status: Western Pennsylvania Conservancy property

Nearest Town: Ohiopyle, PA

Other Trail Users: Cross-country skiers and hunters (in season)

Canine Compatibility: Dogs not permitted

Getting There

From Pittsburgh: Drive east on I-70/76 and take Exit 9 at Donegal. Drive east on PA 31 to Jones Mills. Turn right onto PA 381 and drive south to Normalville. Continue south on PA 381 to Mill Run. Drive 3.5 miles past the village of Mill Run and turn left into the Bear Run Nature Reserve. The parking lot is behind the buildings. *DeLorme: Pennsylvania Atlas & Gazetteer:* Page 86 B3

The Bear Run Nature Reserve is a 5,000-acre natural area owned and maintained by the Western Pennsylvania Conservancy. On the east side of the reserve, you'll find gently rolling grassy terrain, the visitor center, and a bulletin board of information about the trails. Across Pennsylvania 381, on the western side of the reserve, is rugged, rocky terrain that ends at the Youghiogheny River Gorge. Here you'll also find an unusual treat for a woodland hike: The Conservancy also owns and operates Frank Lloyd Wright's famous structure Fallingwater, built of local sandstone and cantilevered over a waterfall on Bear Run.

The Conservancy buildings are rustic. Near the trailhead there's an old-fashioned hand pump where you can fill your water bottle and rest in the shade of the gently swaying pines. The informative bulletin board, which holds maps and brochures, can be found at the southeast corner of the parking lot.

Though the trails are well marked, it's a good idea to get one of the Conservancy's trail maps. Some of the trails are blazed with the same color and shape; others have the same color blaze with either a rectangular- or circular-shaped blaze to set them apart.

The hikes on the east side of Pennsylvania 381 are quite hiker-friendly. These are short, easy nature trails that showcase their namesakes: the Tulip Tree Trail, the Aspen Trail, etc. You might even see a warbler on the

Your first view of the Youghiogheny River from Laurel Ridge.

237

Warbler Trail, or you might be moved to write a verse or two on the Poetry Trail. Dotted along the trails are group camping sites where naturalists from the Conservancy have set up youth programs to study the surrounding wildlife, flora, ecosystems, and geology.

Once you cross Pennsylvania 381, it's a whole different matter. You won't have time to write poetry over here. After following Laurel Run into the valley bottom, taking in the beauty of the rhododendron and hemlocks, you begin a strenuous, rocky climb to the top of Laurel Ridge and a view of the 1,700-deep Youghiogheny River Gorge.

As you near the summit, the trail passes beneath the telephone lines that run one side of the ridge and down the other. Along the ridge the trail gets close to the edge, where natural overlooks provide the best views of the gorge. Paradise Overlook is a great spot to eat your lunch and rest.

The Peninsula Trail takes you on a loop around one of the many peninsulas on the Youghiogheny River. These peninsulas were created as the river ran through the valley bottom, cutting its snake-line design into the soft sandstone that lined the river's edge.

Leaving the forest, you pass through a meadow and connect with a farm road, which takes you back to Pennsylvania 381 and the parking lot.

MilesDirections

0.0 START at the parking area behind buildings. Walk to north end of parking lot to the signs "Tree Trail" and "Skiing Area." Follow the arrows to a stand of pines. Look for yellow circle-blazes. Pass by an unmarked trail on your left. Veer right. Begin an uphill climb.

0.1 Pass Pine Trail intersection on your right. Continue through the pine trees.

0.2 Come to an intersection with the Aspen Trail on your right. Look for yellow rectangle-blazes. Continue straight.

0.3 The trail veers to the right.

0.4 Cross Beaver Run on a wooden bridge. The Tree Trail ends in an intersection with Rhododendron Trail. Turn left onto the Rhododendron Trail. Look for white circle-blazes.

0.5 Pass the Teaberry Trail on your right. Continue straight.

0.7 Arrive at an intersection where the Rhododendron Trail turns right. Continue straight onto the Snow Bunny Trail. Follow the orange rectangle-blazes.

0.9 Cross Beaver Run on wooden bridge a second time.

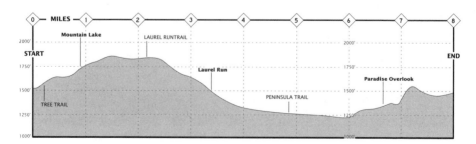

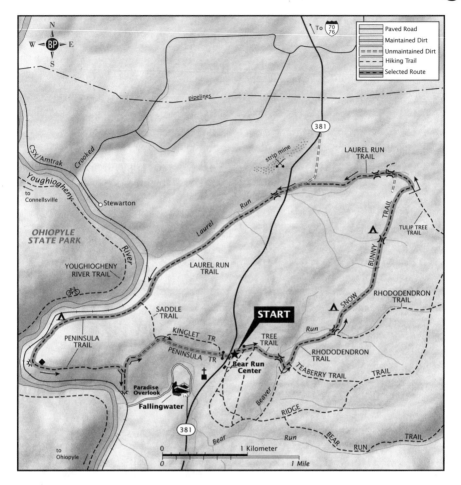

1.0 Pass a group camping site on your left.

1.6 Begin your descent.

1.7 Cross a wooden bridge over a Laurel Run tributary stream. Pass a second group camping area on your left.

2.1 Snow Bunny Trail ends at the intersection with Tulip Tree Trail and Laurel Run Trail. Turn left onto Laurel Run Trail. Look for white rectangle-blazes. Start downhill.

2.4 Pass an unmarked jeep road on your left. Come to a bridge over Laurel Run. Pass an unmarked trail on your right and continue straight.

2.5 Cross a small tributary on a plank bridge. At this point, the trail becomes rocky. There's a small outcropping and second plank bridge.

2.6 Look for the double white blazes. The trail turns right.

2.7 Turn right at the double white blazes onto jeep road.

2.8 Come to a marker for Laurel Run Trail. Turn left and go downhill. *[FYI. In season, you can pick a handful of blackberries along this section of trail.]*

3.1 Cross PA 381. Look for the signpost "Laurel Run Trail."

3.2 Cross a tributary on a plank bridge.

3.3 Come to double white blazes. Turn downhill.

3.4 Cross Laurel Run on stone pathway.

3.7 Cross a washout. Turn downhill at the double white blazes.

3.9 Pass an unmarked trail on your left. Continue straight.

4.0 The trail turns right. Look for double white blazes. Descend to a flat area beside Laurel Run. Cross a washout.

4.2 Trail veers left. Begin ascent through rocks. Come to a signpost. Laurel Run is to the right.

4.4 Pass a signpost for Laurel Glen on your right. Continue straight.

4.6 Cross a washout.

4.8 Arrive at an intersection with Saddle Trail. Continue straight onto the

Peninsula Trail. Look for white rectangle-blazes.

5.0 Pass campsite No. 4 on your right.

5.1 Cross a washout. Note the first glimpse of the railroad down the cliff on your right.

5.4 Reach the ridge top. Walk under the telephone lines. This is the first view of river gorge.

5.5 The trail turns left into the forest.

5.6 Pass through an area of earthen mounds.

5.8 Arrive at the telephone line swath. Turn left onto the swath. Look for a white blaze on a telephone pole.

6.1 Come to first the overlook. Begin steep climb.

6.8 Arrive at Paradise Overlook. Turn right. Retrace your steps.

7.1 Trail becomes a jeep road. Turn left at the Peninsula Trail sign. *[**FYI.** The Fallingwater service parking lot is on your right.]*

7.4 Arrive at the Peninsula Trail stanchion. Turn right and pass through a meadow. Stay to the right on the Peninsula Trail.

7.5 Arrive at a second Peninsula Trail stanchion at a jeep road. Continue straight. Tall pines line the road on your left.

7.9 Arrive at a wooden farm gate. Cross PA 381.

8.0 Arrive at parking area and your vehicle.

Hike Information

◐ Trail Contacts:
Western Pennsylvania Conservancy, Pittsburgh, PA (412) 288–2777

◷ Schedule:
Open year round

ⓢ Fees/Permits:
No fees or permits required

❓ Local Information:
Laurel Highlands Visitor Bureau, Ligonier, PA (724) 238–5661 or *www.laurelhighlands.org*

◉ Local Events/Attractions:
Frank Llloyd Wright's Fallingwater, Mill Run, PA (724) 329–8501 or *www.paconserve.org* • **Fort Necessity Battlefield,** National Park Service, Farmington, PA (724) 329–5512 or *www.nps.gov/fone*

⬤ Accommodations:
Rafferty Manor Bed & Breakfast, Ohiopyle, PA (724) 329–1732 • **Laurel Hill State Park,** Somerset, PA (814) 445–7725 – *for camping reservations call 1–888–PA–PARKS* • **Ohiopyle State Park,** Ohiopyle, PA (724) 329–8591 – *for camping information*

🍴 Restaurants:
Country Cottage Restaurant, Rockwood, PA (814) 926–4078

🎒 Local Outdoor Retailers:
Falls Market, Ohiopyle, PA (724) 329–4973 • **Caney Valley Sports Shop,** Markleysburg, PA (724) 329–8700 • **Z's Sports World,** Chalk Hill, PA (724) 438–5210

Ⓝ Maps:
USGS maps: Mill Run, PA

37

Mount Davis Natural Area

Hike Specs

Start: From the Mount Davis Picnic Area
Length: 3.4-mile loop
Approximate Hiking Time: 2.5 hours
Difficulty Rating: Easy, due to a level terrain
Terrain: Grassy road, rocky, rugged footpaths, and improved shale road. Highest point in Pennsylvania. Unique mountaintop area, stunted trees, earth mounds, stone rings, and a lookout tower.
Elevation Gain: 384 feet
Land Status: State forest
Nearest Town: Somerset, PA
Other Trail Users: Tourists and hunters (in season)
Canine Compatibility: Leashed dogs permitted

Getting There

From Pittsburgh: Drive east on I-70/76 and take Exit 10 at Somerset. Get on U.S. 219 and drive south 22 miles to Meyersdale. In Meyersdale, turn right on Broadway Street and follow the signs for Mount Davis. It is 8.5 miles from the right turn on Broadway to the Mount Davis Monument sign. Drive 0.5 miles past the sign (you will be hiking back to the monument) and turn right into the Mount Davis Picnic Area. *DeLorme: Pennsylvania Atlas & Gazetteer:* Page 87 B5

A t 3,213 feet above sea level, Mount Davis is the highest point in Pennsylvania. There are plenty of geological features unique to this lonely spot to lure the undecided hiker, but it's probably enough to say that you're going to the top of it all.

Mount Davis Natural Area lies within the 30-mile-long Negro Mountain Range of the Allegheny Plateau. The 581-acre natural area surrounds a seven-acre tract where you'll find the observation tower, monument, and tourist parking lot.

The climate on Mount Davis can be summed up in one word: *awful.* Annual temperatures range from -30°F to 95°F. There are plenty of high winds, more than three feet of both rain and snow a year, and a frost in every month. The best time to visit is in the late spring or early summer. At other times of the year, the weather can be miserable with cold rainy winds—and of course snowstorms in the winter.

This miserable climate, however, has created a number of geological and natural features worth noting. The natural area is home to the pitch pine, a stubby-looking tree with limbs that reach out like gnarled fingers. Early settlers to the region extracted the pitch from the pine, also known as pine tar, by burning pine knots and catching the residual tar. At the Tar Kiln

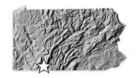

Site, visitors can see how a tar kiln was built on top of a huge boulder and a trough was hollowed out to guide the tar to containers. The pitch was used as a lubricant for wagon axles, to mark sheep, and as a cure for distemper in horses.

On the geologic end, the continual freezing and thawing during the Pleistocene Age (some 70,000 years ago) caused the Pottsville sandstone of the mountaintop to break up into stone circles. There are educational plaques embedded on the rocks around the tower to explain this phenomenon, but the best way to see the extent of these circles is to view them from the 40-foot tower. And it's from atop this tower that you'll have a chance to experience another local phenomenon. From the observation tower, a number of the surrounding peaks appear to be higher than Mount Davis. Plaques on the tower platform assure that, while there are nearby peaks over 3,000-feet high, none of the surrounding mountains are taller than Mount Davis. It's merely an optical illusion.

The tip of the triangular boulder is considered
the highest point in Pennsylvania.

A pitch pine rises out of the mountain
laurel and rhododendron.

The area is also rich in history and folklore. Mount Davis is named after the former landowner John Davis, one of the last surviving veterans of the Civil War. Davis was a land surveyor and a naturalist adept at identifying all the plants and animals in the area. It was he who surveyed the area and determined that this one particular rock was the highest point in the state.

And, according to the folklore, even George Washington slept here. In 1753, during the French & Indian War, the 21-year-old lieutenant passed through here and along Negro Mountain as part of a supply train aiding troops in Pittsburgh. (Incidentally, Negro Mountain, though at risk of being politically incorrect, was named after an African-American soldier who distinguished himself before dying in battle. He was buried on the mountain.)

Just as the name implies, the natural area has been left to nature—for the most part. As you walk the Shelter Rock Road on the return loop, you'll notice a white-tailed deer exclusion area. Just as you'd fence out a rabbit from your garden, the U.S. Forest Service has erected this fenced barrier to keep the pesky whitetail from devouring the newly planted trees.

Hike Information

● Trail Contacts:
Forbes State Forest, Laughlintown, PA (724) 238-1200

◔ Schedule:
Open year round

$ Fees/Permits:
No fees or permits required

❷ Local Information:
Somerset County Chamber of Commerce, Somerset, PA (814) 445-6431 or www.somersetcntypa chamber.org

♀ Local Events/Attractions:
Somerset Historical Center, Somerset, PA (814) 445-6077 – closed Mondays • Windber Coal

Heritage Center, Windber, PA (814) 467-6680 or 1-877-826-3933 or www.allegheny.org/windber

● Accommodations:
The Bayberry Inn, Somerset, PA (814) 445-8471 • Laurel Hill State Park, Somerset, PA (814) 445-7725 – for camping information

◍ Restaurants:
The Italian Oven, Somerset, PA (814) 445-4141

❀ Local Outdoor Retailers:
Mountain Sports, Inc., Somerset, PA (814) 445-2115

Ⓝ Maps:
USGS maps: Markleton, PA

MilesDirections

0.0 START by walking uphill in the parking lot to northwest corner of the picnic area. Look for the trail sign. Turn left onto the High Point Trail and follow the blue blazes.

0.1 Pass the Tub Mill Run Trail on your left. Continue straight.

0.6 The trail gets rocky. *[**FYI.** Notice the huckleberries along the trail.]*

0.7 Pass the Mount Davis Trail on your left. Continue straight.

0.8 Arrive at the rock monument and the tower. Retrace your steps to the circular paved road. Turn right onto the paved road then turn left on the Shelter Rock Trail at the trail sign.

1.0 Pass the Mount Davis Trail on your left. Continue straight. The trail gets rocky. *[**FYI.** Notice the pitch pine tree on the trail.]*

1.2 Pass a large, flat area of dead trees.

1.3 Begin a descent down a small ridge.

2.0 Cross Tub Mill Run.

2.1 Turn left onto Shelter Rock Road.

2.2 Pass a fenced-in deer exclusion area on your right.

2.4 The exclusion area ends. There are small boulders placed on the road at culverts. Count four culverts.

2.9 Arrive at the Tub Mill Trail sign just before fifth culvert on your left. The Tub Mill Trail sign is vertical and nailed to a tree set back from road. Turn left onto the Tub Mill Trail.

3.3 Come to an intersection with the High Point Trail. Turn right onto the High Point Trail.

3.4 Arrive back at the trailhead and retrace your steps to the parking lot.

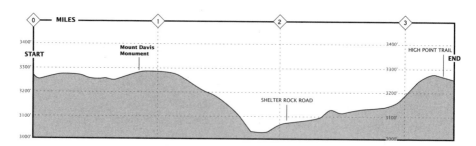

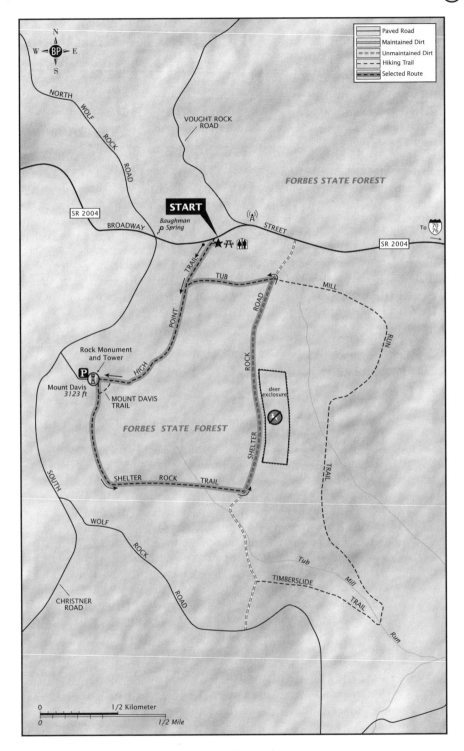

Ferncliff Peninsula Natural Area

Hike Specs

Start: From the parking area off PA 381 near the railroad tracks

Length: 2.4-mile loop

Approximate Hiking Time: 2 hours

Difficulty Rating: Easy, due to the level terrain

Terrain: Typical rocky footpath and flat boulders at the river's edge. Gain a close up view of Ohiopyle Falls, the river, and the white water rapids; southern wildflowers; and umbrella magnolia trees.

Elevation Gain: 172 feet

Land Status: State park

Nearest Town: Ohiopyle, PA

Other Trail Users: Naturalists, tourists, swimmers, and anglers

Canine Compatibility: Leashed dogs permitted

Getting There

From Pittsburgh: Drive east on I-70/76 and take Exit 9 at Donegal. Drive east on PA 31 to Jones Mills. Turn right onto PA 381 and drive 21.0 miles south to the city of Ohiopyle. As soon as you cross the two railroad tracks of the Baltimore & Ohio Railroad, turn right into the parking lot. Drive to where boulders block a shale road. Start hiking between the boulders on the shale road. *DeLorme: Pennsylvania Atlas & Gazetteer:* Page 86 A3

Simply stated, this hike gives you an unparalleled view of Ohiopyle Falls. You're led right to the edge of the Ohiopyle River and onto a series of flat boulders, which at points jut into the river. You're as close to the falls as anyone is going to get. That is reason enough to lace up your boots.

Ohiopyle Falls is truly a showstopper—it even stopped a young George Washington. The year was 1754. While scouting for a route to get his British troops and supplies to Pittsburgh to capture Fort Duquesne from the French, he traced the Youghiogheny (pronounced YAWK-a-gay-nee) River as a supply route. Everything was fine until he came to Ohiopyle Falls, where he had to abandon his plans and go the rest of the way over land. Unfortunately, his bad luck continued, and his troops lost the Battle of Fort Duquesne—one of the early battles of the French & Indian War. Ultimately, the British would defeat the French, in 1763, to maintain control of the American Colonies. And the hard-luck officer would go on to lead those colonies to independence.

In the 1800s, renowned Scottish geologist Charles Lyell visited the area. Lyell, a major force in modern geology, was the founder of stratigraphy—the study of the earth's layers. But more important to the area, Lyell was also an inspiring artist. As a result of one of his sketches of the falls, Ohiopyle became a popular summer resort area, catering to over 10,000

MilesDirections

0.0 START at the parking area off PA 381, beside the railroad tracks. This parking area is also for the Great Gorge Trail and the American Youth Hostel.

0.1 Pass under the old railroad bridge, now part of the Rails-to-Trails bicycle trail. Come to the Ferncliff Trail sign. Pick up the black blazes and veer left along the river out of the forest canopy and onto the boulders.

0.2 Arrive at the fossil education plaque on a flat boulder. The trail is on the boulders.

0.3 Come to a lifesaving ring stanchion. *[FYI. Notice the thick rhododendron.]*

0.4 Turn left onto the steps at the Falls Overlook sign. After viewing the falls, retrace your steps to the trail, which begins a climb up the cliff edge.

0.5 Pass wooden guardrails.

0.6 Arrive at an intersection with the Butternut Trail. You'll see the Natural Overlook sign and an information plaque. Continue straight.

0.8 Arrive at an intersection with the Oakwoods Trail. Continue straight.

0.9 Come to unmarked river trail. Turn left for a view of rapids.

1.0 Arrive at the rapids viewing area. Retrace steps back to trail. Turn left onto the trail.

1.3 Come to an intersection with Fern Wood Trail. Veer left on the Ferncliff Trail.

1.4 *[FYI. Notice the beech tree with initials carved all around it.]*

1.5 The trail veers left down the gorge toward river. Come to an educational plaque about the Eastern hemlock.

1.7 Come to stepping stones across a huge washout.

1.8 Turn left onto an unmarked side trail for a view of the river. Retrace your steps.

1.9 Arrive back at the trail. Turn left.

2.0 The trail turns away from river. Look for black blazes.

2.1 Pass through a small meadow.

2.2 Arrive at the Ferncliff Peninsula Natural Area National Landmark plaque and trail intersection. Continue straight. The trail veers to the left.

2.3 Come to the intersection with the Fern Wood Trail and the Oakwoods Trail to the right. Continue straight through the intersection. The trail veers to the left. Turn left onto the Ferncliff Trail and retrace your steps back to the parking area.

2.4 Arrive back at the parking area.

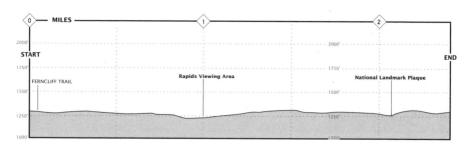

visitors each summer. The Baltimore & Ohio Railroad even ran Sunday excursion trips from Pittsburgh. Wealthy visitors preferred to stay at the one luxury hotel on Ferncliff Peninsula, which had all the amenities of its day, including a tennis court, a bowling alley, and a dance hall.

Today, nothing remains of that time and place on the peninsula. In fact, because of Ferncliff's unusual ecosystem, the area has been designated a National Natural Landmark by the U.S. Department of the Interior, as well as a Natural Area by the Pennsylvania Bureau of State Parks. These natural area designations ban new construction, and the entire peninsula has been allowed to return to its natural state.

The peninsula's ecosystem is unusual because of a horseshoe bend in the river. While this may not seem overly significant, it causes the flow of the river to slow as it makes the turn. This allows the seeds that have been suspended in the water to be deposited along the shore. And, because the gorge provides a natural shelter from the weather, the climate is warmer on the peninsula. For those reasons, some species of Southern wildflowers

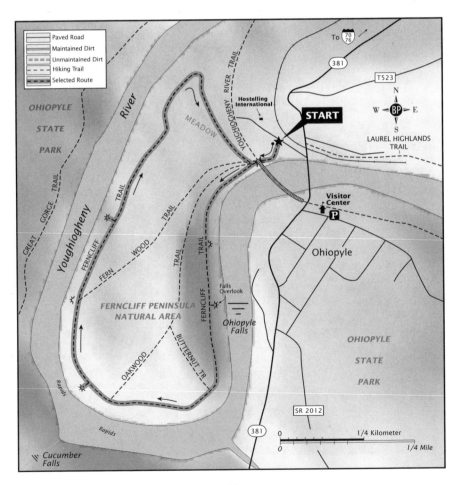

Ohiopyle Falls.

have flourished here. If you slow your pace, and know what you're look-ing for, you can find the Carolina tassle-rue, also called false bugbane, and the large-flowered marshallia, also known as Barbara's buttons. The Carolina tassel-rue blooms in midsummer with a white composite flower on a separate flower stem. Barbara's buttons blooms in late June or early July with a pink flower the size and shape of a dandelion, three-ribbed leaves, and a one- to three-foot stem.

And of course, as its name suggests, you'll find a number of fern species growing on the peninsula. Christmas, marginal wood, and spinulose grow in the forest, while royal and cinnamon ferns grow along the river. There's also an abundance of rhododendron here, as well as old-growth hemlock, white pine, oak, hickory, tulips, and maples, and there is even a tradi-tionally Southern tree, the Southern magnolia. Along the trail, there are a number of interpretive plaques that not only educate, but also force you to slow down and smell the forest.

Hike Information

❶ Trail Contacts:
Ohiopyle State Park, Ohiopyle, PA (724) 329–8591

🕐 Schedule:
Open year round

⑤ Fees/Permits:
No fees or permits required

❓ Local Information:
Fay-Penn Economic Development Council, Uniontown, PA (724) 437–7913

♀ Local Events/Attractions:
Kentuck Knob (a Frank Lloyd Wright house), Chalk Hill, PA (724) 329–1901 – *open year round; however, you'll need to call for a reservation January through March* • **Fort Necessity National Battlefield,** Farmington, PA (724) 329–5512

🛏 Accommodations:
Lodge at Chalk Hill, Chalk Hill, PA (724) 438–8880 or 1–800–833–4283 or *www.dc1.net/~thelodge* • **Ohiopyle State Park,** Ohiopyle, PA (724) 329–8591 – *camping information*

🍴 Restaurants:
The Smokehouse, Ohiopyle, PA (724) 329–1810 – *spring to fall, weekends only* • **The Stone House,** Farmington, PA (724) 329–8876

✪ Other Resources:
Western Pennsylvania Conservancy, Pittsburgh, PA (412) 288–2777

🎒 Local Outdoor Retailers:
Falls Market, Ohiopyle, PA (724) 329–4973 • **Youghiogheny Outfitters,** Ohiopyle, PA: 1–800–967–2387

Ⓝ Maps:
USGS maps: Ohiopyle, PA; Fort Necessity, PA

The mission of the Rails-to-Trails Conservancy is to "enhance America's communities and countryside by converting thousands of miles of abandoned rail corridors and connecting open spaces into a nationwide network of public trails."

Every large city and small town in America, by the early 20th century, was connected by steel and railroad ties. In 1916, the United States had laid nearly 300,000 miles of track across the country, giving it the distinction as having the world's largest rail system. Since then, other forms of transportation, such as cars, trucks, and airplanes, have diminished the importance of the railroad and that impressive network of rail lines has shrunk to less than 150,000 miles. Railroad companies abandon more than 2,000 miles of track each year, leaving unused rail corridors overgrown and idle.

It wasn't until the mid 1960s that the idea to refurbish these abandoned rail corridors into useable footpaths and trails was introduced. And in 1963, work began in Chicago and its suburbs on a 55-mile stretch of abandoned right-of-way to create the Illinois Prairie Path.

It took nearly two decades for the idea of converting old railways into useable footpaths to catch on. Then in 1986 the Rails-to-Trails Conservancy was founded, its mission specifically to help communities see their dreams of having a useable rail corridor for recreation and non-motorized travel a reality. At the time the Conservancy began operations, only 100 open rail-trails existed. Today, more than 500 trails are open to the public, totaling more than 5,000 miles of converted pathways. The Rails-to-Trails Conservancy is currently working on more than 500 additional rails-to-trails projects.

Ultimately, their goal is to see a completely interconnected system of trails throughout the entire United States. If you're interested in learning more about rails-to-trails and wish to support the Conservancy, please write to:

Rails-to-Trails Conservancy
1400 16th Street, NW, Suite 300
Washington, DC 20036-2222
or call (202) 797–5400

Youghiogheny River Trail to Jonathan Run Falls

Hike Specs

Start: From the visitor information center in Ohiopyle
Length: 6.4-mile out-and-back
Approximate Hiking Time: 2 hours
Difficulty Rating: Easy, due to the level trail
Terrain: Hike alongside a river over Rails-to-Trails bridges on forest footpath and a crushed limestone bicycle trail along an abandoned railroad grade.
Elevation Gain: 855 feet
Land Status: State park
Nearest Town: Ohiopyle, PA
Other Trail Users: Cyclists, tourists, swimmers, and kayakers
Canine Compatibility: Leashed dogs permitted

Getting There

From Pittsburgh: Drive east on I-70/76 and take Exit 9 at Donegal. Drive east on PA 31 to Jones Mills. Turn right onto PA 381 and drive 21.0 miles south to the city of Ohiopyle. Pass under the railroad bridge and turn right into the public parking lot. *DeLorme: Pennsylvania Atlas & Gazetteer:* Page 86 A3

After you've spent a day or two watching bicyclists weave their way across the 600-foot-long Rails-to-Trails bridge, you'll want to get up there yourself. And it'll be worth it when you do. Two old railroad bridges span the river, each over 100 feet above the water. From the first bridge, you can watch swimmers wading in the wide, shallow waters to the east. But look the other way and the river narrows dramatically into the famous Ohiopyle Falls. It's here, to the west, that the river snakes around the Ferncliff Peninsula, so that when you are on the second bridge, you're just above the rafter put-in area on the peninsula. This provides a ringside seat to listen to the adrenaline screams and watch the kayakers and rafters as they are sent careening down the river.

Over 100,000 people ride the Youghiogheny River rapids every year. Half of these people opt to take a professionally guided tour, while the other 50,000 brave it alone or with friends. This is not an insignificant fact: From 1976 to 2000, 17 rafters have died on the river—three just last year (2000). But before shying away from the river forever, you should know that research compiled in a five-year study by American Whitewater shows the risk of dying in a river is 15 times lower than dying behind the wheel of a car. Easterners can rest easy; findings show that the Arkansas River—with 17 deaths in five years—is the country's most dangerous river for riding rapids.

This hike itself covers a short section of the 67-mile Rails-to-Trails route from near McKeesport to Confluence. Expect a well-groomed trail (a level, crunchy surface) with all the amenities—a bathroom and drinking fountain at the start and a bathroom along the route—and plenty of shade and views of the river. And, you get to wander into the forest for a short distance to see the gently cascading Jonathan Run Falls.

On the return trip, you don't even have to think. Just follow the bicyclists, joggers, and other walkers back to Ohiopyle. Some trail users may want to see the trail all the way to its southern terminus in Confluence, about 10 miles beyond Ohiopyle. Or you can just stop in Ohiopyle and reward yourself with some ice cream, found less than a block from the visitor information center.

Hike Information

📞 Trail Contacts:
Ohiopyle State Park, Ohiopyle, PA (724) 329–8591 • **Allegheny Trail Association:** www.atatrail.org

🕐 Schedule:
Open year round

💲 Fees/Permits:
No fees or permits required

❓ Local Information:
Fay-Penn Economic Development Council, Uniontown, PA (724) 437-7913

🔊 Local Events/Attractions:
Laurel Caverns Geological Park, Farmington, PA (724) 438-3003 or 1-800-515-4150 or www.laurel caverns.com • **Mountain Pike Heritage Center,** The Plough House, Farmington, PA (724) 329-8573

🛏 Accommodations:
Ohiopyle State Park, Ohiopyle, PA (724) 329–8591 – *for camping information* • **Fayette Springs Guesthouse,** Chalk Hill, PA (724) 437-2051

🍴 Restaurants:
Historic Summit Inn, Farmington, PA (724) 438-8594 or 1–800–433–8594 or *www.hhs.net/summit*

🔵 Other Resources:
Western Pennsylvania Conservancy, Pittsburgh, PA (412) 288-2777

🎒 Local Outdoor Retailers:
Pechin Sports World, Dunbar, PA (724) 277–4251 or *www.pechin.com* • **Zac's Sporting Goods,** Dunbar, PA (724) 628-2313

🗺 Maps:
USGS maps: Ohiopyle, PA; Fort Necessity, PA

This retired train bridge is now a beautiful passageway for bicyclists and pedestrians.

MilesDirections

0.0 START at the public parking lot. Cross PA 381 and walk to the elevated Visitor Information Center, a renovated railroad depot; the hike begins at the center. Walk across the first bridge.

0.1 Reach the other side of the bridge.

0.3 *[Note. Outdoor bathrooms.]* Arrive at a sign for Bike Trail Rules.

0.4 Arrive at the second bridge.

0.5 Reach the other side of the bridge. Pass the Great Gorge Trail on your left. Continue straight.

0.6 Pass a sign for the Campground Trail and the Beech Trail on your left.

0.7 Note a washout on your left.

0.8 Pass mile marker 11.

1.5 *[FYI. Notice the waterfalls on Stulls Run to your left.]*

1.7 Pass mile marker 12.

2.0 Pass a rescue stanchion and bench.

2.3 There's a major rock outcropping on your left.

2.6 Note a pullout area with sign "Unauthorized Rapids Swimming Prohibited." Pass mile marker 13.

3.1 Turn left onto the Jonathan Run Trail, entering the forest. (There's a sign for Kentuck Trail.)

3.2 Turn right onto a short access path to Jonathan Run Falls. Turn around and retrace your steps to the visitor information center.

6.4 Arrive back at the visitor information center.

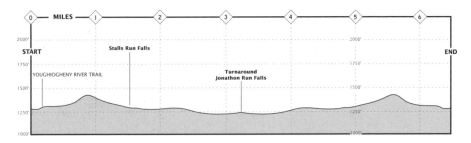

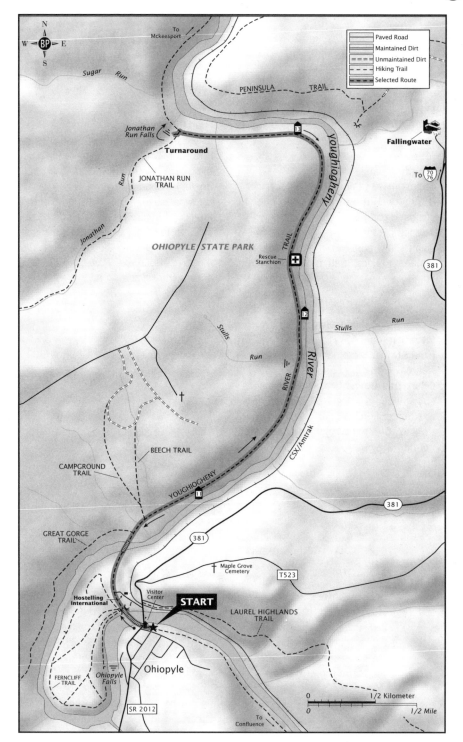

Ryerson Station State Park

Hike Specs

Start: From the third parking lot at the end of Fordway Road, near the large picnic area

Length: 5.4-mile circuit

Approximate Hiking Time: 3 hours

Difficulty Rating: Moderate, due to climbs in and out of steep hollows

Terrain: Smooth, well-groomed cross-country ski trails, snowmobile roads, and mowed walking paths. Expect steep ridges, a spectacular view of R.J. Duke Lake, tall meadows along an inlet, a leisurely stroll along a bluebird trail, and a climb to an old family cemetery.

Elevation Gain: 1,421 feet

Land Status: State park

Nearest Town: Waynesburg, PA

Other Trail Users: Cross-country skiers, snowmobilers, anglers, birdwatchers, and hunters (in season)

Canine Compatibility: Leashed dogs permitted

Getting There

From Pittsburgh: Drive south on I-79 and take Exit 3 at Morrisville. Drive west on PA 21 for 22 miles to Bristonia Road and the park entrance. Turn left onto Bristonia Road and drive 0.8 miles to Fordway Road. Turn right on Fordway Road, just before the dam, and drive 0.7 miles to the large picnic area parking lot on your left. Drive to the last row, nearest the lake. *DeLorme: Pennsylvania Atlas & Gazetteer:* Page 84 A2

Ryerson Station State Park opened to the public in 1967, taking its name from nearby Fort Ryerson, a small refuge built in 1792 to defend then-frontier settlers against Native American raids. In this 1,100-acre park, you'll find a 10-mile network of trails available to hikers from spring to fall—cross-country skiers and snowmobilers take over the trail in the winter.

One of the main attractions along this hike is the 300-year-old oak tree often referred to as the *Wolf Tree*. This is an expression used by foresters to describe a tree that has flourished for hundreds of years by *wolfing down* all the available sunlight in an area, essentially eliminating the possibility of any other tree growing near it.

At the top of the first ravine, you're treated to a view of the valley and 62-acre R.J. Duke Lake. The North Fork of Dunkard Fork was dammed in 1960 to create the lake, and though it may be somewhat unnatural, the lake inlets are home to an immensely diverse wildlife population. Watch for

osprey during their spring migration. You're treated year round to great blue herons, which have a rookery in a nearby grove of sycamore trees. In the open areas, look for the Carolina chickadee, Acadian flycatchers, and the willow flycatcher. The wetlands are home to beaver, muskrat, deer, rabbit,

squirrel, and skunk, as well as box and snapping turtles and the Eastern spiny soft-shell turtle.

The trail passes an old iron bridge that you'll cross on your return. At the bridge, start the Pine Box Trail through thick meadow vegetation—look for Queen Ann's Lace, nettles, flebane, and spy lily. Along the way, you'll pass a bluebird nestbox trail. Ryerson Station, along with 50 other state parks, is part of a bluebird rescue program that began in 1981. From its inception, the program has fledged more than 25,000 bluebirds. (For more information on the Bluebird Trails Program in Pennsylvania state parks, see Other Resources below.)

The Pine Box Trail leads you to a traffic bridge and then up a steep ravine to Stahl Cemetery. The *pine box* in the trail name, you now understand, refers to the coffins that, for some reason, the families felt compelled to trudge up this unmercifully steep grade to their final resting place.

It's all downhill from the cemetery, as you make your way into the steep Applegate Hollow, across the hollow bottom, and on to Bristoria Road. Then, it's across the iron bridge and back to the land of the living.

MilesDirections

0.0 START at the third and largest parking lot at the end of Fordway Road. Park in the row nearest the lake and walk to the trail bulletin board and map. Follow the arrows for the Lazear Trail and Fox Feather Trail.

0.1 Turn right onto the Lazear Trail.

0.3 *[FYI. Come to a bench and a plaque that describes the 300-year-old oak Wolf Tree.]*

0.4 Note the poison ivy stanchion on your left.

0.5 Arrive at an intersection with the Orchard Trail. Turn right onto the Lazear Trail.

0.6 Leave the forest canopy as you pass through an open area. *[FYI. Notice the blackberry bushes and wild grapevines.]*

0.8 Come to the overlook sign and walk to the overlook.

0.9 Begin your descent. Re-enter the forest canopy.

1.2 Note a huge sycamore tree on the right.

1.4 Come to an intersection with the Tiffany Ridge Trail. Continue straight on the Lazear Trail and descend into Munnell Hollow.

1.7 Arrive at the cliff edge above Munnell Hollow.

1.8 Pass the Tiffany Ridge Trail on your left and continue straight. Pass the Fox Feather Trail on your left and continue straight.

1.9 Turn right onto the Iron Bridge Trail. There is a trail sign: "To Campground."

2.1 Reach the marshy area alongside R.J. Duke Lake inlet.

2.3 Pass the Iron Bridge on your left. Continue straight onto the Pine Box Trail. *[FYI. Notice the short paths to the bluebird boxes.]*

2.7 Begin a climb up the stream bank, away from stream.

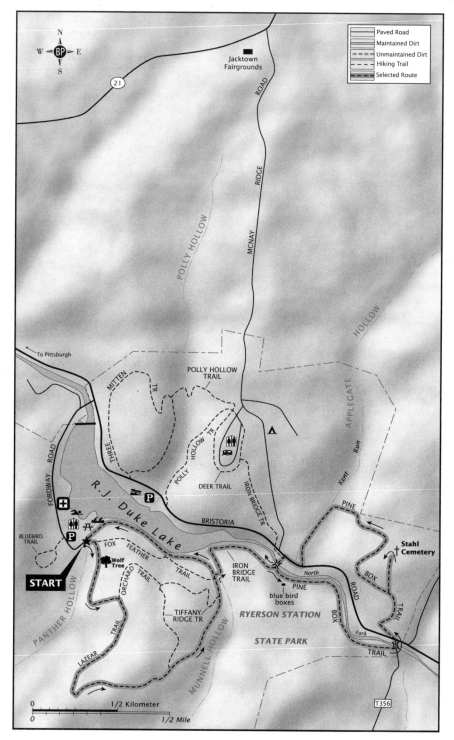

2.8 Cross a small wooden bridge.

2.9 Cross under the telephone lines into a meadow. Turn left onto a traffic bridge across the North Fork of Dunkard Fork and cross Bristoria Road.

3.1 Turn left onto the Pine Box Trail. Sign reads "Chess Cemetery." Begin a serious uphill climb.

3.2 Come to the trail sign for Pine Box Trail and the cemetery to your right.

3.3 Come to a switchback and trail signs for the Pine Box Trail and cemetery; turn left.

3.4 Come to a signpost that reads Cemetery straight ahead. Continue straight.

A great blue heron flies across this lake inlet.

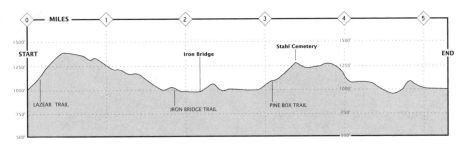

3.5 Arrive at the cemetery. Retrace your steps back to the Pine Box Trail.

3.6 Turn right onto the Pine Box Trail and walk along a very steep ridge.

3.8 Begin your descent into Applegate Hollow.

4.0 Cross over a deep washout.

4.2 Turn left at the yellow arrow sign at the hollow bottom.

4.5 Turn right at Bristoria Road.

4.6 Turn left to cross the Iron Bridge and then turn right onto the Iron Bridge Trail. Retrace your steps through the meadow and along the inlet.

5.0 Come to the intersection of the Fox Feather Trail and the Lazear Trail. Turn right onto the Lazear Trail, heading toward the lake.

5.1 Cross a small wooden bridge.

5.2 Come to a trail intersection with signs for the Fox Feather Trail, the Long Loop, the Short Loop, To Campground, and the Lazear Trail. Turn right toward the lake.

5.3 Pass behind the boat rental building and take the path through the picnic area.

5.4 Arrive at the parking lot.

Hike Information

◐ Trail Contacts:
Ryerson Station State Park, Wind Ridge, PA (724) 428–4254

◑ Schedule:
Open year round

⑤ Fees/Permits:
No fees or permits required

❓ Local Information:
Waynesburg Area Chamber of Commerce, Waynesburg, PA (724) 627–5926 or *www.greenepa.net/~wbgchamb*

◍ Local Events/Attractions:
Greene County Fair, second week of August, Waynesburg, PA (724) 852–2175 • **Greene County Historical Society and Museum,** Waynesburg, PA (724) 627–3204

● Accommodations:
Castle Victoria, Waynesburg, PA (724) 627–5545 • **Ryerson Station State Park,** Wind Ridge, PA (724) 428–4254 – *camping information*

⑪ Restaurants:
Willow Inn, Waynesburg, PA (724) 627–9151

◐ Other Resources:
Bureau of State Parks Bluebird Program, c/o Environmental Education & Interpretive Division, Harrisburg, PA 1-888-PA-PARKS • **Western Pennsylvania Conservancy,** Pittsburgh, PA (412) 288–2777

◍ Local Outdoor Retailers:
Pat's Sporting Goods, Waynesburg, PA (724) 627–8201

Ⓝ Maps:
USGS maps: Wind Ridge, PA

Honorable Mentions

Southwest Pennsylvania

Compiled here is an index of great hikes in the Southwest region that didn't make the A-list this time around but deserve recognition. Check them out and let us know what you think. You may decide that one or more of these hikes deserves higher status in future editions or, perhaps, you may have a hike of your own that merits some attention.

Ⓠ Todd Sanctuary

Located in the southeast corner of Butler County, Todd Sanctuary has five miles of trails running over its 162 acres. The Audobon Society of Western Pennsylvania owns the sanctuary and welcomes public use. Started in 1942 by the late E.W. Clyde Todd, curator for the Carnegie Museum of Natural History, the sanctuary is one of the first natural areas to be preserved in the Pittsburgh area. This is an easy walk suitable for both children and seniors.

To get there from Pittsburgh, drive north on PA 28 about 25 miles to Exit 17. Drive west on PA 356 for 1.0 miles to Monroe Road. Turn right onto Monroe Road and drive 1.3 miles to Kepple Road. Turn right on Kepple Road and drive 1.9 miles to the sanctuary on the right. For more information call the Audubon Society of Western Pennsylvania (412) 963–6100. *DeLorme: Pennsylvania Atlas & Gazetteer:* Page 58 C1

Ⓡ The Beechwood Farms Nature Reserve

This reserve is located in Fox Chapel, eight miles northeast from downtown Pittsburgh. There are five miles of interlocking trails on this 134-acre reserve. The Audubon Society of Western Pennsylvania leases the land from the Western Pennsylvania Conservancy. There are no dogs, bikes, or picnicking allowed. Great spot for bird watching, walk through wildflowers, and, in season, view migratory birds.

To get there from Butler, drive south on PA 8 to 3.1 miles past I-76 and turn left on Harts Run Road and continue 3.5 miles to Dorseyville Road. Turn right on Dorseyville Road and drive 0.2 miles to the reserve on you right. For more information call Beechwood Farms (412) 963-6100. *DeLorme: Pennsylvania Atlas & Gazetteer:* Page 57 D7

Northwest
PENNSYLVANIA

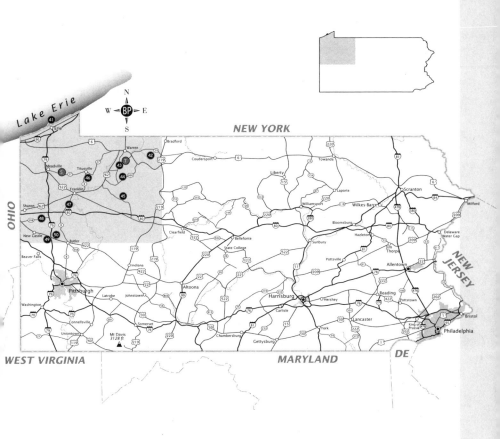

The Rides	Honorable Mentions
Presque Isle **41.**	**S.** The Erie National Wildlife Refuge
Hemlock Run **42.**	**T.** Chapman State Park
Tom's Run **43.**	
Minister Creek **44.**	
Cook Forest State Park **45.**	
Oil Creek State Park **46.**	
Allegheny Gorge **47.**	
Schollard's Wetlands **48.**	
McConnell's Mill State Park **49.**	
Moraine State Park **50.**	

Northwest Pennsylvania

The Northwest Section dips below Interstate 80 to include Moraine and McConnell's Mill State Parks. Aside from Presque Isle, which is (pardon the pun) an island unto itself, the far northwestern corner of Pennsylvania is dominated by the Allegheny National Forest.

The 750,000-acre Allegheny National Forest is situated at the western end of the Allegheny Plateau. The ravines and peaks are not as deep and dramatic as those in the central and eastern part of the state, because the western end of the state was farther removed from the tectonic event that shaped the mountains we have today. The event took place along what is now the Eastern Seaboard; consequently, the eastern half of the state got the Bigger Bang.

Here's something to ponder: The Allegheny National Forest is, relatively speaking, lightly used, yet it's within a day's drive of one-third of the nation's population and half of Canada's. Despite the proximity, you'll find spots in the forest remarkably remote and unused. There are 170 miles of hiking trails, and if you get too tired to take another step, there are over 500 miles of forest roads on which you can drive. There are also a number of paved state roads that traverse the park. Believe it or not, some park visitors just drive around in their cars, from one area of interest to the next.

If you're too tired to hike and don't want to drive, consider renting a canoe and getting a friend to paddle you along the Allegheny River. While you've got the canoe, you could even try canoe camping along the shores of the 12,000-acre Allegheny Reservoir.

Speaking of water: Over four million people visit Erie's Presque Isle every year. The reason for that is very simple: It's the only place in the state where you can visit a great beach without having to fight the dreaded beach traffic. When you look at the ocean-like waves off Presque Isle, you'd swear you were at "The Shore" somewhere on the Atlantic Ocean.

The hiking trails on the isle are flat, except for an occasional shifting sand dune. The level terrain makes the one multi-use trail a popular place for in-line skaters, cyclists, and joggers. In season and on weekends, this trail gets crowded; but if you're smart, you'll hike it on a weekday and do your weekend hiking on the network of trails that are more toward the isle's interior.

The land around McConnell's Mills and Moraine State Parks has a little more relief than the rest of the northwestern corner—most folks are surprised when they visit McConnell's Mill and see the deep gash. During the last ice age, a moraine was formed when a glacier retreated; this moraine not only stopped the natural flow of water, it actually reversed the flow—creating the unusual topography of Moraine State Park and Slippery Rock Gorge.

Overview

Presque Isle

Walk the same rough-poured sidewalk that the old lighthouse keeper walked when he went from his home in the Presque Isle Lighthouse to his boat at the U.S. Lighthouse Service boathouse on Misery Bay. Along the way, you pass a marsh with thriving vegetation and vernal ponds. *(See page 274)*

Hemlock Run

There are two highlights to this hike that make it a must-do: the view of the sparkling green waters of Chappel Bay and a world-class beaver dam the size of a football field. This hike is mostly downhill, but it's not easy. The multiple stream crossings and the effort it takes to pick your way across the rocks make this a challenging—but rewarding—hike. *(See page 280)*

Tom's Run

This is an easy hike that leads you through a forest of giant hemlocks—some 60 to 75 feet in height—to an old railroad logging grade that parallels the white-capped waters of Tom's Run. The west branch of Tionesta Creek snakes its way down the slope and joins with Tom's Run at the point where you begin your final ascent. Along the way you'll see sandstone boulders the size of small houses perched above. Let the rushing waters of the streams and the hemlock-scented breeze carry you away from the cares of the outside world. *(See page 286)*

Minister Creek

Minister Creek Trail is one of the most popular trails in the Allegheny National Forest. After a half mile climb from the parking lot to the trailhead, you begin the rock and root-covered trail by

271

heading into the valley for your first encounter with the bubbling waters of Minister Creek. As you ascend from the valley, you are in the midst of mammoth sandstone boulders, some 100 feet wide and 50 feet high. At one point the trail even passes right through a fissure in one of these giants. *(See page 292)*

Cook Forest State Park

This hike takes you into the Clarion River Valley and alongside the dark waters of the Clarion River. This descent is followed by a climb out of the gorge to River Valley and a heart-stopping view from an 80-foot fire tower. (There is also a natural overlook for the faint of heart.) As you loop back to where you began, you'll pass through the Forest Cathedral, a virgin stand of white pine that loggers—for some reason—left behind. Be sure and look for the plaque that proclaims the area a national natural landmark. *(See page 298)*

Oil Creek State Park

This hike makes a loop around the Drake Well Museum and oil field, site of the first commercial oil well in the world. It begins with a strenuous uphill climb for a view of the majestic Oil Creek Gorge, followed by a descent into the valley wetlands, where it passes over the tracks of an excursion railroad. The trail then crosses Oil Creek on a cable bridge—also called a *swinging bridge* because of the way it sways in the breeze. Along the trail you can stop and inspect oilfield ruins and the relics that remain frozen in time. *(See page 304)*

Allegheny Gorge

The highlight of this hike is standing on a viewing platform 480 feet above the Allegheny River. The trail follows an old wagon road to the ruins of a 19th-century iron ore furnace, then leads you across a plateau to the viewing platform. From there it descends another gorge to a stream with four cable bridges. *(See page 310)*

Schollard's Wetlands

Springfield Falls is one of the highlights of this hike; the other is the absolutely pristine surroundings along the first stretch. The vast majority of this hike is along remarkably flat terrain, so it's suitable for all types of hikers, including children and the elderly. Be sure to carry your lunch in with you so that you can take advantage of the park-like setting beneath the falls. *(See page 316)*

McConnell's Mill State Park

After a steep descent into a 400-foot gorge, the trail continues downstream alongside a gushing stream, where giant sandstone boulders have created whitewater rapids. The trail passes through boulders on the slopes—where runoff waters create miniature waterfalls. It then passes a restored mill and a covered bridge. At the turnaround point, it crosses the creek on a traffic bridge. On this side of the creek it is a typical forest footpath, running about 100 feet above the stream. *(See page 320)*

Moraine State Park

This hike provides a good workout as you climb and descend four deep ravines. The trail also makes its way along a glacial lake, into its coves covered with lily pads, and past marshes stuffed full of cattails and wild grapes. At the halfway point you can rest, use the bathrooms, and take on water at a full-service marina. There is even a restaurant on the water's edge. *(See page 326)*

Presque Isle

Hike Specs

Start: From the Perry Monument parking lot
Length: 5.0-mile loop
Approximate Hiking Time: 2 hours
Difficulty Rating: Easy, due to the flat terrain
Terrain: Walk across a peninsula, from a bay to a lighthouse, past a marsh and ponds, using rough sidewalk, beach, and sandy forest footpath.
Elevation Gain: 41 feet
Land Status: State park
Nearest Town: Erie, PA
Other Trail Users: Tourists
Canine Compatibility: Leashed dogs permitted

Getting There

From Downtown Erie: Drive west on PA 5 (which is also 12th Street) and turn right onto Peninsula Drive (also PA 832). Pass the main gate and drive 5.4 miles to the Perry Monument parking area on East Fisher Drive. • **Summer Shuttle Bus:** From the Waterworks ferry dock, take the EMTA shuttle to the Presque Isle Lighthouse and pick up the hike at mile 1.8. *DeLorme: Pennsylvania Atlas & Gazetteer:* Page 27 C5

There's a reason over four million people visit Presque Isle every year. The phrase "something for everybody" has been bandied around, and though it's worn thin from overuse, nothing could be truer. There really *is* something for everyone, whether you're an outdoor lover, a history buff, a natural history student, a birdwatcher, or, of course, a hiker.

Thirteen miles of roads transport visitors from one end of this 3,200-acre park to the other. A 9.6-mile multi-purpose trail runs along the bay, loops the far peninsula, and returns on the lakeside to its beginning point. You can hike the trail, but it is predominantly a bicyclist and in-line skater path.

Our hike, which combines the Sidewalk Trail and the Dead Pond Trail, gives you the opportunity to visit both the Presque Isle Lighthouse and the Perry Monument—the two centerpieces of the park. The 57-foot, red brick Presque Isle Lighthouse, situated on the shores of Lake Erie, was built in 1872 and is today a private residence—visitors, however, can use a nearby beachside path to access a photo site. Visit the educational gazebo at the lighthouse parking area for more information on this and other area lighthouses.

The Perry Monument, built in 1926, commemorates Commodore Perry and his men for their bravery during the War of 1812. Perry commanded the U.S. fleet that defeated British forces in the Battle of Lake Erie in 1813. His report of the battle to General Harrison has become famous: "We have met

The Presque Isle Lighthouse was first lit in July 1873.

This view from Lighthouse Beach shows one of the regularly spaced white-rock breakers set 100 feet from the shore.

MilesDirections

0.0 START from the Perry Monument parking area. Walk out the main entrance, cross East Fisher Drive and turn right. Cross bridge over Misery Bay.

0.5 Turn left onto the Sidewalk Trail. The marsh is on your right.

1.6 Arrive at an intersection with the Marsh Trail, the Fox Trail, and the Dead Pond Trail. Continue straight.

1.7 Cross Peninsula Drive (PA 832). Walk to the educational gazebo. Walk to sign: "Beach View and Photo Opportunity" and turn right toward the beach.

1.8 Turn left at a white stanchion with green arrow. View the lighthouse. Retrace your steps back to the educational gazebo.

2.0 Cross Peninsula Drive (PA 832) to Sidewalk Trail bulletin board. Continue

straight on Sidewalk Trail. Retrace your steps.

2.1 Turn left onto the Dead Pond Trail.

2.4 Pass intersection with A Trail on your left.

2.9 Pass intersection with B Trail on your left.

3.5 Veer right at trail fork.

3.7 Arrive at East Fisher Drive. Turn right. Walk on right shoulder.

3.8 Pass intersection with North Pier Road on your left.

4.5 Pass Sidewalk Trailhead on your right.

5.0 Turn left into Perry Monument parking lot.

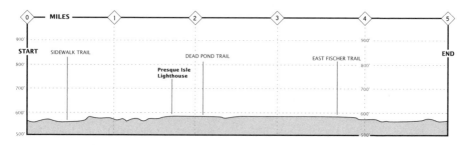

the enemy and they are ours." Locals have another connection to Perry, in that six of his 11 vessels were built in Erie with timber from Presque Isle.

After visiting the monument and the lighthouse, make your way onto the Dead Pond Trail for a decidedly different hike experience. Though the Dead Pond Trail is only a little over two miles long, it manages to span a number of distinct ecological zones. The terrain will go from sandy to grassy to a typical forest path, and then it's sandy again. In the forested areas are red and silver maples, pin oaks, and pine plantations, as well as stands of poplar and sassafras. Everywhere else, you'll find chokecherry and

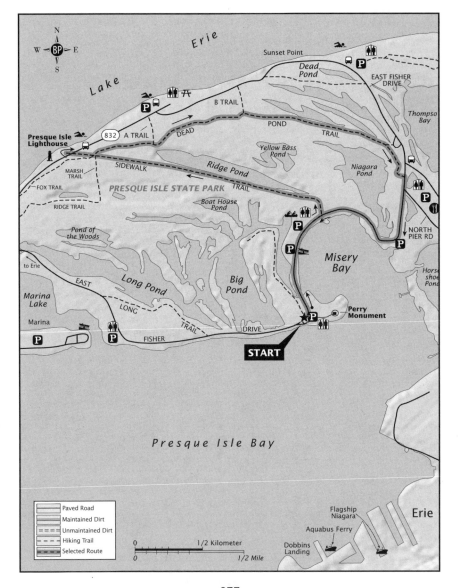

serviceberry lining the path. There's also an assortment of honeysuckle along the trail: elderberry, hobblebush viburnum, and arrowwood. But by far the most abundant (and least desirable) vegetation is the phragmite known as the common reed. It's still not known how this peevish plant, native to Europe and the Orient, made it into the United States, but as with most invasive species, the reed has thrived and taken over much of the landscape—or would if allowed to do so. On Presque Isle, it's a full-time

project trying to eradicate the plant. Park workers are routinely dispatched to cut the invader, which can reach heights over 12 feet, back away from the roadways and paths.

Before summarily dismissing this plant as an out-an-out pest, it should be said that the reed enjoys a better reputation in the Orient, where it has traditionally been used for thatch to build roofs. Today, it's often used as a packing material. Try to keep this in mind when you're surrounded by this *plague*. The best place to see how this reed has taken over along this hike is while you're walking beside East Fisher Drive, from the Dead Pond Trail trailhead to the Perry Monument parking lot.

Presque Isle is a hiker's utopia. You can experience all that the Erie area has to offer: excellent restaurants, a planetarium, and museums; and yet, in a matter of minutes, you can leave all this behind and enter another world of sand dunes, exotic flora, American history, and, best of all, solitude.

Hike Information

● Trail Contacts:
Presque Isle State Park, Erie, PA (814) 833-7424

● Schedule:
Open year round

● Fees/Permits:
No fees or permits required

● Local Information:
Erie Area Chamber of Commerce, Erie, PA (814) 454-7191 or www.eriepa.com

● Local Events/Attractions:
Flagship Niagara, Erie Maritime Museum, Erie, PA (814) 452-2744 • **Erie Art Museum at Discovery Square**, Erie, PA (814) 459-5477 or www.erieartmuseum.org

● Bus and Ferry Service
Erie Metro Transit Authority (EMTA): (814) 452-2801 • **Presque Isle Aquabus:** (814) 881-2502 or www.erie.net/~chamber/aquabus.html – ferry service between Downtown Erie and the Waterworks ferry dock

● Intercity Rail Service:
Amtrak, Erie, PA 1-800-872-7245 or www.amtrak.com

● Accommodations:
Spencer House Bed and Breakfast, Erie, PA (814) 454-5984 or www.erie.net/~spencer • **Sara Coyne Campgrounds**, Erie, PA (814) 833-4560 – open from April through the end of October

● Restaurants:
Pie In The Sky, Erie, PA (814) 459-8638

● Organizations:
Erie Outing Club, P.O. Box 1163, Erie, PA 16512

● Local Outdoor Retailers:
Calypso, Erie, PA (814) 833-9016 • **Erie Sports Store**, Erie, PA (814) 833-4042 or www.eriesportstore.com

● Maps:
USGS maps: Erie North, PA

Hemlock Run

Hike Specs

Start: North Country Trail parking area off PA 59

Length: 6.8-mile point-to-point

Approximate Hiking Time: 4 hours

Difficulty Rating: Moderate, with short, difficult climbs

Terrain: Abandoned logging roads, railroad grade, forest trails pass through an old-growth forest of towering hemlocks and huge sandstone boulders. Hike in and out of a deep ravine and alongside a stream (and be prepared for multiple stream crossings).

Elevation Gain: 331 feet

Land Status: National forest

Nearest Town: Warren, PA

Other Trail Users: North Country Trail through-hikers, backpackers, and campers

Canine Compatibility: Leashed dogs permitted

Getting There

To Shuttle Point: From Dubois, drive north on U.S. 219 through Ridgway. Continue north to the intersection with PA 59. Turn left onto PA 59 and drive 8.1 miles to the intersection with PA 321. Turn left on onto PA 321 and drive 4.5 miles south to the North Country Trail sign and the parking area on your right. • **To Start:** Leave one vehicle at the parking area on PA 321. Drive north on PA 321 to the intersection of PA 59. Turn left and drive 2.3 miles to the North Country Trail sign and FS 265 on your left. Turn left on FS 265 and drive 300 feet to the parking area and trailhead. *DeLorme: Pennsylvania Atlas & Gazetteer:* Page 31 B7

T he North Country National Scenic Trail is one of the more ambitious trail-construction projects currently underway in our park system. When completed, the trail will stretch 4,400 miles through seven northern states, from the Adirondack Mountains in New York all the way to the vast plains of west-central North Dakota. Hemlock Run Trail is your opportunity to hike a part of this massive trail system—and an immensely popular one among folks who should know. Much of the 96-mile section of the North Country Trail in Pennsylvania was built and is maintained by the Allegheny Outdoor Club, headquartered 20 miles to the west in Warren. One member of this hiking club likes this trail so much that if he can't find a partner to do a car shuttle with him, he drops his bicycle off at the first parking area, does the hike, then bikes the six miles back to his vehicle.

One thing you learn when you hike this part of the state is that early settlers came here to harvest the timber. This region boasted giant white pines and hemlocks. The white pines were used to build houses and ships. The

This abandoned oil field shed is over 125 years old, preserved by oil.

hemlock tree was also valuable, but not for its wood, which, incredibly, was left discarded in the forest. Instead, the bark of the hemlock tree was harvested and made into tannin, the substance used to tan leather.

Though the giant white pines and hemlocks are no longer pervasive, hikers can still find one of the most valuable stands of hardwood in the world in the Allegheny National Forest. The most prized of these trees is the black cherry, which is used throughout the world to produce fine furniture and veneer. You'll also find yellow poplar, white ash, red maple, and sugar maple mixed in. Today, the white ash is used to produce Louisville Slugger baseball bats.

MilesDirections

0.0 START from the North Country Trail sign. Two flat boulders flank the trail. Look for blue blazes.

0.2 Turn right at the blue blaze with directional arrow.

0.4 Turn right onto the original trail. Look for the directional arrow on the blue blaze.

0.6 Continue straight as another road cuts off to the left.

0.7 Come to a grassy meadow.

1.3 Turn left onto FR 517. Turn right at Hemlock Run and trail sign.

1.5 Come to a small beaver dam.

2.1 Cross a clearing. Look for "House Rock." Veer left into the ravine. Look for blue blazes.

2.3 Cross Hemlock Run for the first time. Come up out of the ravine.

2.7 Cross Hemlock Run again. Cross back and forth three more times.

3.5 Pick up an abandoned railroad grade.

4.3 Cross Hemlock Run back and forth two times.

4.6 Turn left. You can see the waters of Chappel Bay.

4.8 The road veers off to the left. Continue straight. Look for blue blazes.

5.2 Pick up the railroad grade through the bog.

5.7 Cross Briggs Run. Turn left and begin an uphill climb.

5.8 Turn right onto a pipeline swath. Continue through a stand of saplings onto an old road.

6.7 Come to a power line swath, beaver dam, and two footbridges.

6.8 Arrive at the parking area and your shuttle.

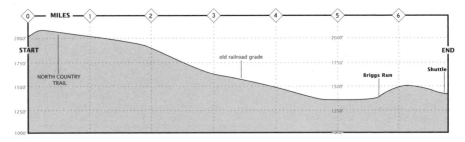

Logging companies built networks of roads to get around in the forest and narrow-gage railroads to haul the logs out to nearby sawmills or to a river, where the logs were floated downstream to cities like Pittsburgh. When the logging companies pulled out, their roads and railroads remained. In 1859, when the first commercial oil well in the world was drilled in near-

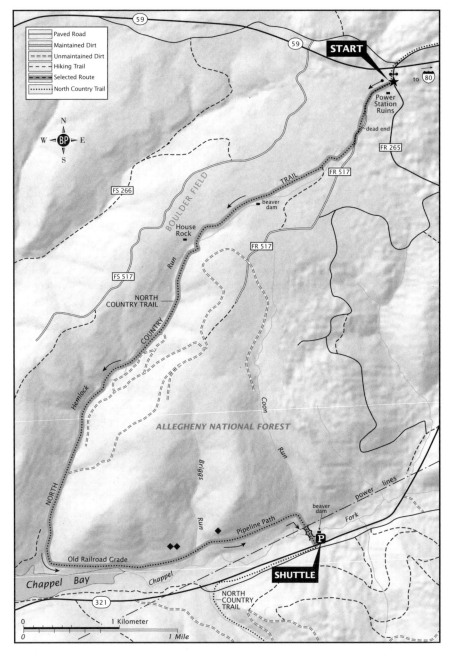

by Titusville and the forests of northwestern Pennsylvania became a virtual oil field, oil companies used these same roads. Today, both the oil and logging industries continue to operate in the forest on a limited scale, but what most hikers encounter are the rusted remains of these once-flourishing industries. Just a half mile into this trail you can see for yourself the ruins of an oil field power station.

The hike in this section is little more than a leisurely stroll through a forest of tall hemlock trees. At intervals, you may emerge from the deep shade of the hemlocks and enter grassy meadows with odd-looking humps of earth. These are old oil wells sites. The humps are piles of dirt that resulted as the area was cleared of trees and flora. Also in the meadows, look for scarlet berries of the teaberry bush, a low-growing evergreen plant also known as wintergreen. Oil from these berries is used to make the popular wintergreen flavoring.

On your way down into the valley floor you come to the first of two beaver dams. The pristine setting of this first, smaller dam makes this a genuine photo opportunity. Also on your way down, you pass through an area of hundreds of sandstone and conglomerate boulders, ranging in size from a Volkswagen to that of a small house. Look for "House Rock," a mid-sized boulder that because of its sloped top and straight sides is said to resemble a house.

FYI

- Pennsylvania has the nation's largest rural population. Seven of its 67 counties are classified by the state as 100 percent rural: Forest, Fulton, Juniata, Pike, Sullivan, Susquehanna, and Wyoming counties.

- Pennsylvania has more small towns (population less than 5,000) than any other state.

At about the four-mile mark, you pick up an abandoned railroad bed that was used to haul logs down this ravine to the Kinzua Mill. The mill, as well as the towns of Kinzua and Corydon, is long gone—submerged forever under the waters of the 27-mile-long, 12,000-acre Allegheny Reservoir, which was created when the Army Corps of Engineers built the Kinzua Dam across the Allegheny River in 1968.

A little farther on, the trail parallels a pipeline path. Before you leave the pipeline, look for a bright blue patch of low-growing bluets. These low-lying plants, also known as Quaker-ladies, have four pale blue or violet flower petals with a yellow eye in the center. Shortly after this, you'll cross a power line swath and make your way to the edge of a giant beaver dam across Chappel Fork. Head over to the wooden footbridge and take a seat. It's said that if you are quiet and very patient on this bridge, you may get to photograph a beaver at work. Good luck.

A pair of Canada Geese float on a giant beaver pond.

Hike Information

☎ Trail Contacts:
Bradford Ranger District, Bradford, PA (814) 362–4613 • **Allegheny National Forest,** Warren, PA (814) 723–5150 or *www.fs.fed.us/r9/allegheny*

◷ Schedule:
Open year round

⑂ Fees/Permits:
No fees or permits required

❓ Local Information:
Northern Alleghenies Vacation Region, Warren, PA (814) 726–1222 or 1–800–624–7802 • **Allegheny National Forest Vacation Bureau,** Custer City, PA (814) 368–9370 or *www.allegheny-vacation.com*

☀ Local Events/Attractions:
Warren County Fair, second week in August, Warren, PA (814) 563–3565 Kinzua Dam/Allegheny Reservoir, Warren, PA (814) 726–0661

⊖ Accommodations:
The Acorn B&B, Warren, PA (814) 723–3632 • **Kiasutha Camping Area,** Allegheny National Forest, Warren, PA

(814) 723–5150 or *www.fs.fed.us/ r9/Allegheny – limited camping after October*

⍟ Restaurants:
The Liberty Street Café, Warren, PA (814) 726–3082

⊛ Organizations:
Allegheny Outdoor Club, Warren, PA (814) 723–2568

⊕ Local Outdoor Retailers:
Jock Shop of Warren, Warren, PA (814) 723–6762

Ⓝ Maps:
USGS maps: Cornplanter Bridge, PA; Westline, PA • **North Country National Scenic Trail map** – *For a trail map and complete details, including elevations, food availability, water, shelters, campsites, lodging, gas stations, ranger stations, and hospitals, write the Allegheny Outdoor Club, c/o Don and Brita Dorn, Star Route, Box 476, Sheffield, PA 16347. Or write Seneca Highlands Association, 10 East Warren Road, Drawer G, Custer City, PA 16725.*

Tom's Run

Hike Specs

Start: From the picnic area at Hearts Content Recreation Area

Length: 4.0-mile loop

Approximate Hiking Time: 1.5–2 hours

Difficulty Rating: Easy, with a short, moderate climb over the ridge and an easy ascent in the last 1.5 miles

Terrain: Pass through sun-filled meadows to a forest of towering hemlocks along a footpath and abandoned railroad grade groomed for cross-country skiing. Hike alongside a stream where outcroppings of giant boulders create gushing narrows and waterfalls.

Elevation Gain: 465 feet

Land Status: National forest

Nearest Town: Sheffield, PA

Other Trail Users: Anglers and cross-country skiers

Canine Compatibility: Leashed dogs permitted

Getting There

From Pittsburgh: Drive north on I-79 to I-80. Drive east on I-80 and take Exit Three at Barkeyville. Drive north on PA 8 to Franklin. Take PA 62 north to Tidioute. Turn right on old PA 337 and drive 10.1 miles. Make a hard right onto Hearts Content-Sheffield Road. Drive 3.7 miles to the trailhead. *DeLorme: Pennsylvania Atlas & Gazetteer:* Page 31 C4

Hearts Content Recreation Area is a hiker's mecca. Aside from having great hikes like Tom's Run, the area provides the launching point for the popular Hickory Creek Wilderness Trail and affords connections with the more epic Tanbark and North Country trails. The recreation area also offers a one-mile interpretive trail, as well as beginner, intermediate, and advanced orienteering courses.

You'll share parking with hikers using the Hickory Creek Trail, but don't worry; there's ample room. The Hickory Creek Trail leads hikers on an 11-mile loop through the 8,663 acres of old-growth forest in the Hickory Creek Wilderness Area. The estimated time for this hike is seven hours, but many hikers prefer to strap on a backpack and turn their hike into a one- or two-day overnight excursion.

Because of the popularity of the wilderness area, the picnic area at Hearts Content is one of the most comfortable trailheads in the state. There is a seasonal water fountain and a modern year-round restroom facility. The

This giant hemlock is estimated to be 300 to 400 years old.

large bulletin board displays a detailed map, brochures, and all the necessary information about the trails and the adjacent area. There is also a Braille pad for the sight-impaired. The picnic area also has a pavilion and, of course, plenty of picnic tables. Check out the pavilion for an informative display on logging in the forest. It explains how early loggers in the area squared off white pine timbers by hand into giant sections that were hauled out on the logging railroad.

Hearts Content Campground is located less than half a mile away. There are 22 campsites with picnic tables, electricity, and fire rings. There are also toilets and water. Some of the sites have camping pads and others have lean-to shelters. The campground operates on an honor system, so make sure you don't forget to pay the daily fee.

The Tom's Run hike departs from the picnic area and begins on a gently sloping trail. At about a quarter mile you cross the first of many small footbridges. At a half mile you connect with the Tanbark Trail and begin a moderate climb across a ridge. Notice the abundance of ferns. They grow unmolested while deer feast on the young saplings, for the simple reason that deer don't like fern. To protect new seedlings from the deer, the forest service has fenced in hundreds of seedlings and shrubbery. Look for these seedlings in an area beside the trailhead.

The trail leads you past hemlock, white pine, and beech trees that are 300 to 400 years old. Take a good look at the beech trees, though. Many of them of them have a disease called beech bark scale, which produces tiny

MilesDirections

0.0 START by walking to the sign "Hearts Content Cross Country Ski Trails" at the east side of the parking lot. Walk 50 feet beyond that sign to the sign, "Tom's Run Skiing Trail." Look for blue blazes. The interpretive trail is a short loop located off the south side of the parking lot.

0.5 Turn left onto the white-blazed Tanbark Trail.

1.1 Turn right onto Tom's Run Trail.

2.2 Pass the Ironwood Trail on your left.

3.1 Cross the handrail footbridge.

3.4 Turn right at the sign "Tom's Run Trail."

3.5 Come to the original point where Tom's Run Trail meets Tanbark Trail. Turn left.

4.0 Arrive back at the trailhead.

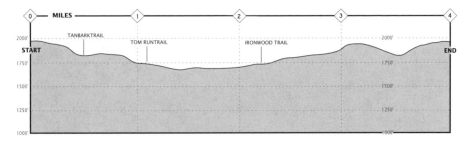

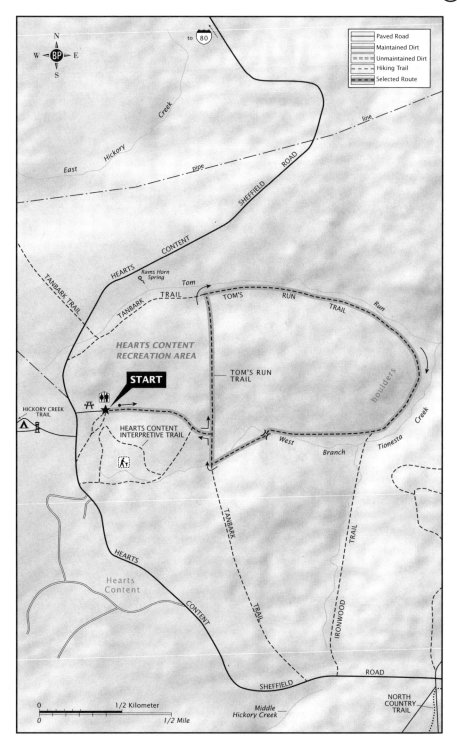

white spots on their bark. It is predicted that within 20 years there will be no more living beech trees in this area.

Not long after reconnecting with the Tom's Run Trail, you'll come to your first meadow. Here, the remains of the logging railroad begin. The corrugated-looking trail is where the railroad tracks used to be. When the tracks were pulled up, the railroad ties (no more than roughly hewn logs) were left in place. As the logs decomposed, they left behind a corrugated landscape. Keep an eye out; most have rotted away, but remnants of some logs remain.

As you approach the stream, you'll hear the sound of the rushing waters of Tom's Run as it surges against, around, and under moss-covered boulders. These boulders look as if they might have slid down the ridge slope to rest precariously along the stream. On your right, up the slope, huge sandstone boulders are scattered about as if some giant of the forest had laid out his own rock garden. Here, overhanging hemlock branches form dark tunnels over the trail. At one point you'll pass through a patch of mountain laurel and cross perhaps a dozen small footbridges spanning the washes that empty into Tom's Run.

You come to a fork in the trail as Tom's Run Trail heads up the slope and the Ironwood Trail starts. You leave Tom's Run behind as the trail aligns itself with the west branch of Tionesta Creek. Shortly you come to the only handrail bridge, and shortly after that you retrace your steps back to the trailhead.

Hike Information

🍂 Trail Contacts:
Sheffield Ranger District, Sheffield, PA (814) 968–3232 • **Allegheny National Forest**, Warren, PA (814) 723–5150 or *www.fs.fed.us/r9/allegheny* • **U.S. Orienteering Federation**, Box 1444, Forest Park, GA 30051

🕐 Schedule:
Open year round

💲 Fees/Permits:
No fees or permits required

❓ Local Information:
Northern Alleghenies Vacation Region, Warren, PA (814) 726–1222 or 1–800–624–7802

📍 Local Events/Attractions:
Warren County Fair, second week in August, Warren, PA (814) 563–3565 • **Pennsylvania State Championship Fishing Tournament**, Inc., last full weekend in September, Tidioute, PA (814) 484–3585 • **Kinzua Dam/Allegheny Reservoir**, Warren, PA (814) 726–0661

🛏 Accommodations:
Horton House B&B, Warren, PA (814) 723–7472 • **Hearts Content Campground**, c/o Allegheny National Forest, Warren, PA (814) 723–5150 or *www.fs.fed.us/r9/allegheny* – *open May 10 to October 10* • **Hickory Creek Wilderness Ranch**, Tidioute, PA (814) 484–7520

🍴 Restaurants:
The Liberty Street Café, Warren, PA (814) 726–3082

👥 Organizations:
Allegheny Outdoor Club, Warren, PA (814) 723–2568

🎒 Local Outdoor Retailers:
Jock Shop of Warren, Warren, PA (814) 723–6762 • **Haller's Sporting Goods**, Tionesta, PA (814) 755–4475 • **Forest County Sports Center**, Tionesta, PA 1–800–458–6093 or *www.troutshop.com*

🅝 Maps:
USGS maps: Cherry Grove, PA; Cobham, PA

Minister Creek

Hike Specs

Start: From the trailhead half a mile from the Minister Creek Campground parking lot on PA 666

Length: 8.0-mile loop

Approximate Hiking Time: Experienced hikers, 3 hours; beginners, 4 hours

Difficulty Rating: Moderate, with strenuous uphill climbing

Terrain: Well-maintained footpaths carry you through sunny meadows alongside a stream; there's also an opportunity to climb among huge boulders.

Elevation Gain: 1,362 feet

Land Status: National forest

Nearest Town: Sheffield, PA

Other Trail Users: Campers, anglers, through-hikers, and backpackers

Canine Compatibility: Leashed dogs permitted

Getting There

From I-80: Take the Dubois Exit and drive north on U.S. 219 to Ridgway. Take PA 948 north out of Ridgway and drive to the intersection of PA 948 and PA 666. Turn left on PA 666 and drive 14.7 miles to the Minister Creek Campground parking area on your left.

DeLorme: Pennsylvania Atlas & Gazetteer: Page 31 C5

The centerpiece of this hike is, of course, Minister Creek—a crystal-clear, three-forked trout stream that converges here and meanders along the valley floor. Along the stream are gently swaying wheat grass and fern, and sturdy hemlocks that provide both shade and a deep sense of serenity.

Of course, for every hiker who says the stream is the best part of this hike, there's another who'll tell you it's the Minister Valley Overlook. The overlook—the flat top of a giant boulder 0.8 miles from the trailhead—is considered the reward hikers get for climbing out of the deep valley. If you sit a while on the overlook, and if you're lucky, you may see bald eagles floating on the thermal uplifts that rise out of the valley.

But the beauty of this hike really begins as soon as you get on Pennsylvania 666, a gently winding road that runs alongside Tionesta Creek. While this stream is often too shallow to canoe, it's a favorite among anglers. The annual Pennsylvania State Championship Fishing Tournament is held on this stream in nearby Tidioute, the last full weekend in September. This catch-and-release tournament has categories for all ages, from the Junior Derby (for ages three to 10) to a $100 prize for oldest angler

to catch a fish. There are also prizes for the largest muskellunge, northern pike, walleye, small mouth bass, and trout.

Testimony to the abundant fishing and hunting in this area, both sides of Pennsylvania 666 are dotted with rustic fishing and hunting cabins. There are villages and year-round houses here and there, but the traveler gets the distinct sense he's leaving the modern world behind and entering a true forest sanctuary. Even the tiny Minister Creek Campground feels rustic; there are no fancy motor homes here. With just one road in and only six family campsites, this place is for serious campers who like to get away from it all, even if they have to rough it. In the campground, just past the second campsite, there is a hand-pumped water supply. Campers use pit toilets. There are no toilet facilities for hikers.

If the established campground isn't your thing, there are flat footpaths that lead to a series of excellent camping sites along Minister Creek. These are ideal during the summer months. Maple, black cherry, beech, basswood,

MilesDirections

0.0 Start from the parking area. Walk across PA 666 to the trail sign.

0.1 Bear right at FS 537. (This road is closed to traffic.)

0.2 New white diamond blazes mark the trail.

0.5 Arrive at trailhead. Turn right and descend to the valley floor.

0.7 [*FYI. Notice on your right how a yellow birch tree has wrapped its roots onto a giant boulder.]*

0.9 Cross Minister Creek on small footbridge.

1.4 Cross Minister Creek again on larger handrail bridge and begin ascent. [*FYI. The new sluices were built on the trail to channel run-off and eliminate muddy sections.]*

1.6 Encounter sign for Deer Lick Camp. [*FYI. From here it's a one-mile round trip to the hike-in overnight campsites along Minister Creek.]*

1.7 Cross a branch of Minister Creek. [*FYI. Notice the large trees uprooted by a tornado.]*

2.5 Cross a second branch of Minister Creek.

2.6 Meet North Country Trail for the first time. Turn left. The trails combine for 0.4 miles.

2.9 Come to Minister Creek Spring.

3.0 Come to Triple Fork Camp and cross two forks of Minister Creek. The North Country Trail (blue blazes) takes off to the right. Continue to follow Minister Creek Trail (look for the white blazes).

3.3 Cross a third bridge over Minister Creek. The trail runs alongside the stream; campers have worn a footpath in this area. Look for a white blaze with a black arrow pointing to the right.

3.4 Follow the trail uphill and away from Minister Creek.

4.4 Take a sharp left and cross another branch of Minister Creek.

4.8 Begin your ascent through giant boulders. [*FYI. Notice the caves.]* Walk through a six-foot-wide, one-hundred-foot-long fissure.

5.0 Reach the top of the ridge.

5.4 Follow the trail to Minister Valley Overlook.

6.7 Reach Minister Valley Overlook.

7.5 Reach the trailhead. Retrace the way you came in.

8.0 Arrive back at the parking lot.

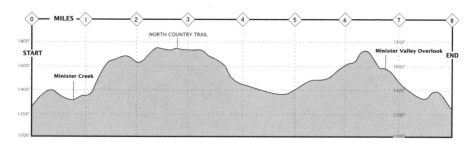

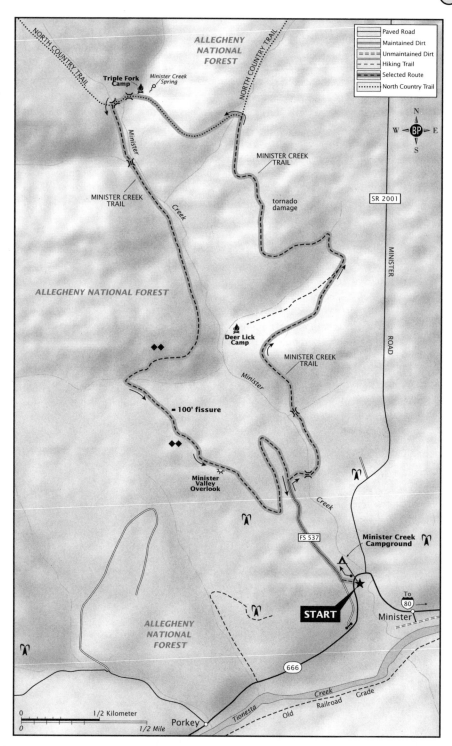

and hemlock trees provide shade so that, aside from the slight dappling sunlight that sprinkles your path, you're protected from the sun from one end of the trail to the other. Also, there is an almost constant breeze to cool you off, which is nice on those hot summer days when the dense growth takes on a jungle-like mugginess.

Out on the trail, one of the first things you're bound to notice is the way in which the trees, ferns, and moss grow on the sandstone boulders. Look around; despite the variety of species, almost all of the trees on the boulders are the same height. A closer examination of the system reveals why. Lichen and moss form on the boulder first, creating a pocket in which to catch rain and other detritus essential for tree growth. But there are limited nutrients and resources here on the sandstone surface. With only so much food to go around, young trees cannot reach their full potential. The trees grow only to a certain height, and there they stop. Don't be fooled; despite their size, these trees can be quite old. This phenomenon, called suppression, is the reason the broad top of a boulder seems to support a garden of trees all the same height.

The species of trees that survive on these boulders are the more adaptable species, such as American beech, Eastern hemlock, and maples. More particular species, like black walnut, ash, and some oaks would not survive on the boulders because they could not compete with their less fussy neighbors.

As you make your final ascent past the silent monolithic boulders, you may get the feeling you've stumbled back in time to another era. Or you may feel you have stumbled forward, into the middle of the next Indiana Jones movie. Either way, enjoy the solitude.

White blazes and boulders mark the trail.

Believe it or not, the best is yet to come. Even after your hike is finished, there is one more treat to look forward to. Jump in your car and continue on Pennsylvania 666 about 17 miles to Pennsylvania 62. Turn left at the intersection and go less than one mile to George's Little Store, which has everything from fishing tackle to cold cuts to ice cream served in their giant, homemade waffle cones (sometimes still warm from the oven). From this point, with your waffle cone in hand, you can either retrace the route you came in on, or, as many sightseers do, you can opt for a leisurely drive on Pennsylvania 62, enjoying the many vistas along the Allegheny River.

Hike Information

● Trail Contacts:

Sheffield Ranger District, Sheffield, PA (814) 968-3232 • **Allegheny National Forest,** Warren, PA (814) 723-5150 or *www.fs.fed.us/r9/allegheny* • **Bradford Ranger District,** Bradford, PA (814) 362-4613 or *www.penn.com/~anf*

● Fees/Permits:

No fees or permits required

● Local Information:

Northern Alleghenies Vacation Region, Warren, PA (814) 726-1222 or 1-800-624-7802

● Local Events/Attractions:

Pennsylvania State Championship Fishing Tournament, last full weekend in September, Tidioute, PA (814) 484-3585 • **Octoberfest,** weekends in September and October, Sheffield, PA (814) 968-5558

● Restaurants:

Flying W Ranch, Kellettville, PA (814) 463-7663 • **Knotty Pine Restaurant,** Tionesta, PA (814) 755-4074

● Local Outdoor Retailers:

George's Little Store, East Hickory, PA (814) 463-7660 – open every day but Christmas, 8 A.M. to 9 P.M.

● Maps:

USGS maps: Mayburg, PA; Cherry Grove, PA

Cook Forest State Park

Hike Specs

Start: From the Log Cabin Inn Visitor Center off Vowinkle Road

Length: 6.6-mile loop

Approximate Hiking Time: 4 hours

Difficulty Rating: Moderate to strenuous

Terrain: Follow abandoned logging roads, rocky footpaths, and cliff edges alongside a river and through 200-foot-tall white pine.

Elevation Gain: 1,528 feet

Land Status: State park

Nearest Town: Cooksburg, PA

Other Trail Users: Equestrians, campers, anglers, and cross-country skiers

Canine Compatibility: Leashed dogs permitted

Getting There

From Brookville: Drive north 13 miles on PA 36 to Cooksburg. At the fork in Cooksburg, go right on Vowinkle Road. Drive north one mile to the Log Cabin Inn Visitor Center parking area. *DeLorme: Pennsylvania Atlas & Gazetteer:* Page 44 B5

Cook Forest State Park is a year-round family camping park with endless attractions. You'll find horseback riding stables alongside bumper car parks, a swimming pool, a theater, and a craft center, as well as 226 campsites and 23 cabins. And, of course, there's fishing, canoeing, and tubing on the Clarion River. In winter there's even sledding, cross-country skiing, and a lighted ice-skating pond.

But don't let all these attractions fool you. Cook Forest has some serious hiking trails. Each year more than 150,000 hikers make their way through the 17 trails that comprise the park's 30 miles of hiking trails. Moreover, the North Country National Scenic Trail passes through Cook Forest via the Baker Trail. The hike featured here, the Cook Forest Trail, was designed to give a sampling of all the best features the park has to offer. Just follow the orange blazes.

When John Cook came to this area in 1826, he found a true forest cathedral. The giant hemlock and white pine were so dense it was said that sunlight never reached the forest floor—which accounts for this part of the Allegheny Plateau being known as Pennsylvania's "Black Forest.") Like any good pioneer, after purchasing 765 acres, Cook set up a sawmill, along Tom's Run. His descendants continued the operation until the 1920s, when the Cook Forest Association was formed to save the last stand of virgin white pine and hemlock. When the association failed to raise enough money to

buy the land, the state of Pennsylvania stepped in and bought 6,055 acres, which has since become Cook Forest State Park.

While the trees are indeed impressive, and a major attribute to the park, there is another major attraction: the *highest highlight* of this hike, the fire tower. If you make it to the top landing of this 80-foot tower, you'll be 1,600 feet above sea level.

On your way to the tower you pass through old-growth forest that looks exactly as it did when the first Europeans settled in this area. There's a real primeval feel to this forest. The trail winds between giant hemlocks and moss-covered boulders along the dark, damp forest floor. Then there's the Clarion River, supposedly named by an early settler who thought the ripples of the river sounded like a clarion (a kind of trumpet with a loud, shrill call). After you've sat for a spell with your ear to the river, it's time to move on. From the river, it's a healthy climb out of the gorge to the top—a plateau with large, flat boulders forming its edge. It's here, on these boulders, that Fire Tower No. 9 awaits you.

View from the banks of the Clarion River as it makes its way to the Allegheny River.

MilesDirections

0.0 START from the parking area at the Log Cabin Inn Visitor Center. Turn left on the paved road, cross the stream on the traffic bridge. Walk to the sign "Shelter 1". Turn right, cross the road to the Ridge Trail sign. Look for orange blazes. Begin an uphill climb. [**FYI.** *Notice the large oak tree wrapped around boulder.*]

0.7 Reach the summit. The trail levels off.

0.8 Begin a downhill trek.

0.9 Arrive at the Ridge Camp Campgrounds. Turn left onto a paved road. Immediately after passing the gate, turn left.

1.0 Arrive at PA 36. Cross the road and veer right to the exit sign. Enter the one-way exit road. Come to the gate and turn right, heading back toward PA 36.

1.1 Turn left onto the Mohawk Trail.

1.2 The trail passes through a pair of giant hemlocks.

1.8 Come to a trail junction. Turn right on Tower Road.

2.2 Turn right on the River Trail. Begin descent.

2.3 Come to a gate with a sign "Road Closed to Vehicles."

2.4 [**FYI.** *Look for a large rhododendron and mountain laurel patch.*]

2.7 Come to a gate that bars motorized vehicles.

2.8 Turn left on the River Trail.

3.0 Cross a meadow. Trail starts uphill away from the river.

3.2 Encounter two switchbacks.

3.4 Turn left at the sign "Baker Trail and River Trail." Head into the rock outcropping. Come to the flat boulders and the fire tower. Climb the fire tower (if you like). Afterwards, turn right onto the exit road, walk a short distance and turn left to the Seneca Point Overlook sign.

3.5 Reach the Seneca Point Overlook. Retrace your steps back to the junction of Seneca Trail and Baker Trail. Take the Seneca Trail downhill into the forest.

3.7 [**FYI.** *Log cabin bathrooms are on your left.*]

3.8 Pass through a rhododendron patch. The trail becomes rocky.

4.0 Pass between two boulders. Enter a boulder outcropping area.

4.2 Come to a sign "Deer Park Trail and Baker Trail." Stay on Seneca Trail. Follow the orange blazes.

4.5 Arrive at a cliff overlooking Clarion River; the trail parallels the river.

4.8 Cross PA 36. The Park office will be on your left.

4.9 Turn left onto the paved road beside the park office.

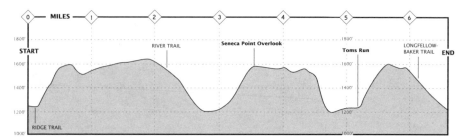

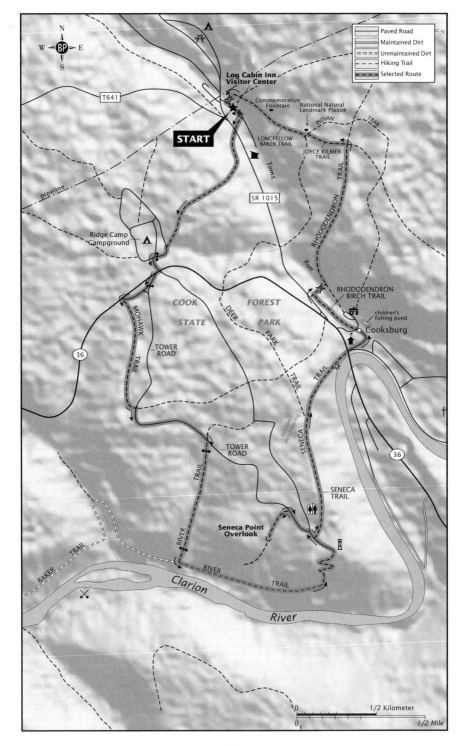

5.0 The children's fishing pond will be on your right. Take the paved road uphill toward PA 36.

5.1 Turn right onto the Rhododendron-Birch Trail.

5.3 Turn right onto a cable bridge. Cross Tom's Run. Turn right into the forest.

5.5 Turn left onto the Rhododendron Trail. *[**Note.** There is no sign.]* Enter the Forest Cathedral area.

6.1 Turn left onto Joyce Kilmer Trail. Begin descent.

6.3 Turn left on the Indian Trail. Go downhill. *[**FYI.** Notice the national landmark plaque attached to a giant white pine tree.]* Turn right onto the Longfellow-Baker Trail.

6.4 Turn left on the Longfellow-Baker Trail.

6.5 Trail becomes the Longfellow Trail.

6.6 Arrive back at the Log Cabin Inn Visitor Center.

Widest at the base and narrower as it goes up, the tower resembles heavy, fenced-in scaffolding. A powerful, almost constant wind makes you thankful for the handrails. When workers tried to dig holes to install the tower legs, they encountered solid rock. Rather than abandoning the project, they drilled four-foot deep holes into the rock and anchored the tower that way. It certainly worked. The tower was built in 1929, retired from fire protection service in 1966, and has been climbed by thousands of tourists and hikers since.

Once on the top platform of the tower, you have an unobstructed view of the surrounding mountains and valleys. The tower was built high enough so watchers could see over the treetops. If there were a forest fire, you would certainly see it from this perch. (These days, the forest service watches for forest fires from small airplanes.)

After the tower, the fun continues. As you make your way back toward the river, you'll have to walk for a short distance on a cliff edge about 50 feet above the river. Where the trail is most precarious, there are safety rails, wooden steps, and platforms. Just the same, if you drop anything, don't expect to ever see it again.

Shingle maker.

In terms of sheer grandeur, the end of this hike is far and away the most dramatic. There's an opportunity to cross Tom's Run on a cable bridge, which will put you at the base of the Forest Cathedral. In this section, some of the white pine and hemlock trees are over 300 years old and over 200 feet high. Just think: with only four of these trees, you could build a six-room house.

In 1969, Cook Forest was designated a National Natural Landmark. The trail in this section leads you past this plaque and also past a commemorative memorial fountain dedicated to the volunteers who worked to establish Cook Forest. End your hike with a visit to the rustic Log Cabin Inn Visitor Center where you can learn all about the early logging industry in this part of the state.

Hike Information

● Trail Contacts:
Cook Forest State Park, Cooksburg, PA (814) 744–8407 or *www.state.pa.us* or *www.dcnr.state.pa.us* or *www.cook forest.com*

● Schedule:
Open year round

● Fees/Permits:
No fees or permits required

● Local Information:
Cook Forest Vacation Bureau, P.O. Box 50, Cooksburg, PA 16217 or *www.penn.com/cforest*

● Local Events/Attractions:
Cook Forest State Park has continuous programs: **June 2:** 3.0-mile guided hike to celebrate National Trails Day; 4.0-mile interpretive canoeing program **June 4:** Annual Children's Fishing Rodeo **June 17:** Learn the art and intricacies of tracking. *Contact the park for complete schedule* • **All-Wood Festival at the Sawmill Center,** July 8–9, Cooksburg, PA • **Summerfest and Quilt Show at the Sawmill Center,** August 18–20, Cooksburg, PA

• **Sawmill Art Center and Theater,** Cooksburg, PA (814) 744–9670 or *www.sawmill.org* • **Double Diamond Deer Ranch,** Cooksburg, PA (814) 752–6334 or *users.penn.com/~dddr*

● Accommodations:
Cook Forest State Park Camping, Cooksburg, PA (814) 744–8407 or *www.state.pa.us* or *www.dcnr. state.pa.us* • **Hominy Ridge Lodge and Cabins,** Cooksburg, PA 1–800–851–6377 or (814) 752–2277 or *www.cookforest.com*

● Restaurants:
Gateway Lodge, Cooksburg, PA (814) 744–8017 or 1–800–843–6862 or *www.gatewaylodge.com*

● Organizations:
Allegheny Outdoor Club, c/o Mr. Bill Massa, Warren, PA (814) 723–2568

● Local Outdoor Retailers:
Cook Forest Motel and Sports Center, Clarington, PA (814) 752–2327 or 1–800–897–9211 or *www.cook forest.com*

● Maps:
USGS maps: Cooksburg, PA

46 Oil Creek State Park

Hike Specs

Start: From the Jersey Bridge parking area at the northern end of Oil Creek State Park

Length: 5.9-mile loop

Approximate Hiking Time: 2.5–3 hours

Difficulty Rating: Moderate, due to steep climbs

Terrain: Follow dirt roads, rocky forest footpath, grassy meadow, and wetlands boardwalk through hemlock ravines, mixed hardwood forest of giant oaks and maples, and cattail wetlands.

Elevation Gain: 1,042 feet

Land Status: State park

Nearest Town: Titusville, PA

Other Trail Users: Hikers only

Canine Compatibility: Leashed dogs permitted

Getting There

From Youngstown, OH: Drive east on I-80 to Exit 3 at Barkeyville. Drive north on PA 8 through Franklin and Oil City; continue on PA 8 to Titusville. Look for the Drake Well Museum sign on your right. Turn right at the stoplight on Bloss Street and drive one mile to the parking area at Jersey Bridge. *DeLorme: Pennsylvania Atlas & Gazetteer:* Page 31 C1

There are over 73 miles of hiking and interpretive trails in Oil Creek State Park, the most impressive of which, the Gerard Hiking Trail, is a 36-mile loop that encompasses the entire park. Since this may be a bit ambitious for the average day hiker, there are a number of shorter connecting hikes that allow visitors to map out their own routes. This hike is one of those hikes.

As soon as you hit the parking lot, you realize there is so much to do and see in this 7,000-acre park that the tough part is not the climb out of the gorge, but choosing an activity for after your hike. This hike, which is set in the northern end of the park, gives you an opportunity to go canoeing, try a little trout fishing, visit the Drake Well Museum, cross the expansive Oil Creek on a cable bridge, explore the world's first oil field, or take a 26-mile roundtrip ride on the Oil Creek & Titusville Railroad.

The park stretches 13 miles on both sides of Oil Creek, through Oil Creek Gorge. A paved 8.5-foot-wide bicycle path runs from the Jersey Bridge parking area in the north end of the park to Petroleum Centre in the southern end—a distance of 9.5 miles. To get to your hike, you'll have to walk a short stretch of this path—one of the nicest bike paths in the state. The bike trail is built on an old railroad grade that parallels the creek and

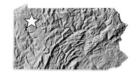

passes through a broadleaf forest whose canopy provides deep shade from early morning until the sun goes down. The bicycle path is a well-maintained and popular trail. On any given day, you're likely to encounter serious runners, mothers pushing jogging strollers, road cyclists, or the casual retirees just ambling along.

Once you begin this hike, however, you leave all this behind. It's a serious climb out of the gorge to the top. When you reach the top, glance down

This paved multi-use trail is over nine miles long.

305

at the Drake Well Museum grounds below. You'll notice an original oil pump still pumping away. The well is located more or less at the midpoint of this trail, so the rhythmic clank-clank-clank will keep you company for a good bit of the hike, swelling and fading as you approach and then pass it. While it may be an annoyance to your tranquility, the steady clamoring of an oil rig has always signaled prosperity to folks in this area.

The trail across the ridge top is rocky. After a while you get used to the fact that just about all the ridge tops in the state are rocky. (When these mountains were formed, the earth was folded upward and pushed the rocks out of the top.) Your descent is easier, but no picnic. It consists of a series of knee-jolting switchbacks down an old oilfield road.

Back on level ground, cross the small footbridge to the Oil Creek & Titusville Railroad tracks. Unlike most of the sights in the park, the railroad is still very much operational. There is no fencing and no sign to warn you about the train, which clips right along, so be careful. (If you happen to be at this spot when the train comes by, you can see that it's critical to stay a good distance away from the tracks.) Cross the train tracks and enter the creekside wetlands. Here you can see wild violets, red trilliums, spring beauties, and bedstraw, as well as the ever-present skunk cabbage—which got its name because it smells like decaying meat. While unpleasant to us, its odor is important to the wetland ecosystem because it attracts pollinating insects.

Although there is nothing left to see of it, the trail takes you through Boughton, one of the many settlements that sprung up during the oil boom years. Residents of Boughton worked across Oil Creek at the Boughton Acid Works (now the Boughton Ruins). Cross over the tracks and make your way to the cable bridge. Although this isn't the same bridge, it's in the same spot where a cable bridge was built so workers who lived in Boughton could cross the creek to their jobs at the acid works. Across this bridge, shortly after crossing the bicycle trail, you'll find the ruins. Here, workers used sulfuric acid to refine oil from the wells. The trail passes a flat, open area that looks like it was the scene of a fire. Sulfuric acid from the old refineries leached into the soil, leaving the area barren. Nothing has grown here since.

Wildcatting

Back in the 1860s, soon after Colonel Edwin Drake drilled the world's first successful oil well, would-be oil barons descended on the area. In no time drilling rigs popped up, seemingly, on every square foot of land. Those entrepreneurs who got to the area first got the prime drilling locations; those who came later were forced farther out into the inhospitable hills. The most unfortunate were forced to drill in the barren Wildcat Hollow, a deep hillside indentation along the banks of Oil Creek.

Ever since then, when an oilman drills for oil in an untested area, he is said to be wildcatting. The oil boom surrounding Drake Well lasted less than 20 years, but the term that began here has survived to become a lasting part of our language.

From your vantage point on the bridge, take in the view of the clear waters of the wide creek. Oil Creek is the largest trout stream in Pennsylvania. You're chances of seeing a bass or brook trout are pretty good. If you get the urge to try your luck, you can purchase tackle and bait at the bicycle concession at the south end of the park.

During the second climb out of the gorge, keep an eye out for a grouping of boulders. You'll notice that some of the oak trees in this area are just plain huge—a few over three feet in diameter. A magnificently manicured park, with picnic tables, awaits outside the Drake Well Museum and grounds. Here you'll also find a fully restored, working oilfield. The grounds and museum are fenced off, however, and there is an admission fee. But rest assured, the museum is top-rate and well worth visiting. There are over 70 exhibits on the origin of oil, the first oil companies, and well drilling. A movie tells about Colonel Drake and the first oil well. One of the most fascinating aspects of the museum is the enlarged photographs and newspaper clippings of the disastrous fires and floods that befell the area as thousands rushed here to strike it rich. Don't miss it.

Hike Information

● Trail Contacts:
Oil Creek State Park, Oil City, PA (814) 676–5915

● Schedule:
Open year round

● Fees/Permits:
No fees or permits required

● Local Information:
Oil Heritage Region, Inc., Oil City, PA (814) 677–3152 or 1–800–483–6264 • **Crawford County Convention and Visitors Bureau,** 1–800–332–2338 or www.visitcrawford.org • **Titusville Area Chamber of Commerce,** Titusville, PA (814) 827–2941

● Local Events/Attractions:
Drake Well Museum, Titusville, PA (814) 827–2797 or www.drakewell.org • **Oil Creek & Titusville Railroad,** Perry Street Station, Titusville, PA (814) 676–1733

● Accommodations:
Oil Creek Camp Resort, Titusville, PA (814) 827–1023 – Open May 1 to October 15 • **Valley View Turkey Farm Campgrounds,** Titusville, PA (814) 827–7893

● Restaurants:
Papa Carone's Inn, Titusville, PA (814) 827–7555

● Local Outdoor Retailers:
Hopkins Sporting Goods, Titusville, PA (814) 827–1299 • **Wilderness Connection,** Titusville, PA (814) 827–6533

● Maps:
USGS map: Titusville South, PA

MilesDirections

0.0 START from the parking area at Jersey Bridge. Walk to the road and cross Jersey Bridge. Walk within the painted-white bike trail to where the guardrail ends. Cross the road at the end of the guardrails and turn left onto an access road. Turn right onto the access road and cross over the railroad tracks.

0.2 Find a trail sign on your right. Look for yellow blazes. *[FYI. Notice the skunk cabbage.]*

0.3 Turn right onto the wooden steps. *[Note. Sign in at the trail register.]*

0.4 Notice a crooked tree with yellow blaze on the trail.

0.8 Arrive at a power line swath.

1.6 Begin a downhill trek.

1.7 Come to a second power line swath. Arrive at a fork in the trail. Turn right onto the Westside Trail and follow the white blazes.

1.8 Encounter a large downed tree across the trail. Turn right onto the steps just before the tree.

2.3 Cross Oil Creek & Titusville Railroad tracks a second time. Cross Oil Creek on a swinging bridge. Turn left and come to sign that reads Westside Trail. Stay on the Westside Trail.

2.9 The trail turns right at double white blazes.

3.0 Cross the paved bicycle path.

3.3 Pass through Boughton ruins.

3.5 Arrive at a fork in the trail and a sign that reads: "Drake Well Museum: 2 miles." Veer right and continue uphill on the Westside Trail. Follow the yellow blazes.

3.6 Begin a series of switchbacks.

4.1 Cross a two-log footbridge. Enter a boulder field.

4.5 Cross over a gully on a footbridge.

4.6 Come to a pipeline swath.

4.9 Cross over a washout on a plank footbridge.

5.4 Arrive at a trail register.

5.6 Pass under the green arches. Cross the paved bicycle path to the wooden steps. Follow the Gerard Hiking Trail sign onto a boardwalk.

5.7 Turn left on an access road.

5.9 Arrive back at the Jersey Bridge parking lot.

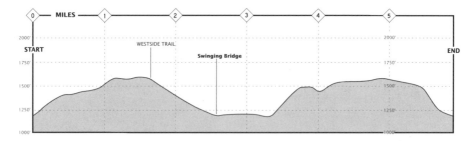

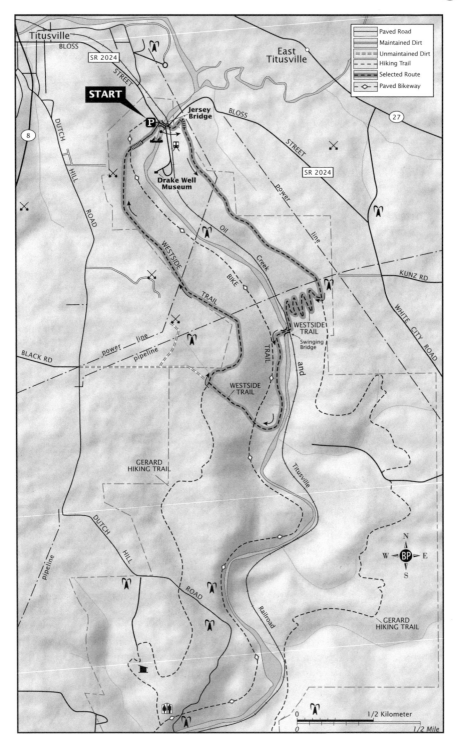

47

Allegheny Gorge

Hike Specs

Start: From the state game land parking area at the end of Dewoody Road
Length: 8.0-mile loop
Approximate Hiking Time: 4 hours
Difficulty Rating: Difficult, due to steep climbs out of two gorges
Terrain: Abandoned roads groomed for cross-country skiing, forest footpaths, and rocky washouts lead you through a mixed hardwood forest on a high plateau to the edge of a river gorge.
Elevation Gain: 1,214 feet
Land Status: State game land and state forest
Nearest Town: Franklin, PA
Other Trail Users: Equestrians, cross-country skiers, and hunters (in season)
Canine Compatibility: Leashed dogs permitted

Getting There

From Youngstown, OH: Drive east on I-80 and take Exit 3 at Barkeyville. Drive north on PA 8. Take the PA 308 exit, turn left and go under the thruway. Turn right on Old PA 8 and drive 0.4 mile and turn right on Dennison Run Road. Drive 1.7 miles and turn right on Dewoody Road to the state game land parking area. *DeLorme: Pennsylvania Atlas & Gazetteer:* Page 43 B7

For the most part, the forest in this area is like any other in the region. There are the ubiquitous hemlock trees, as well as your typical oaks and maples. However, there's one discernable difference. When you're this high above deep gorges, you can feel the height. At this elevation the wind blows all the time. There are so many downed trees in the area that it's a bit disconcerting. Every time the wind blows and the trees rub against each other—making that worrisome creaking, moaning sound—you may catch yourself looking up, just to make sure that none of these trees are on their way down.

The hike begins easily enough on two relatively level state game land access roads, but in less than half an hour you're headed down a steep gorge on a washed-out road alongside Bullion Run—to the Bullion Run Iron Ore Furnace. That's right, this road was once considered the best and easiest way to ship materials. Workers, back in the 1800s, used this route to transport dense iron ore and massive logs to the Bullion Run Furnace. Remember this road the next time you feel like complaining about your job.

The smelting process required enormous amounts of wood to make charcoal, which was used to fire the furnace. Limestone was added to the iron ore, heated, and the result was iron, which could be poured into a cast. The

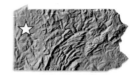

cast iron finished products were then loaded onto rafts on the Allegheny River and floated downstream to Pittsburgh.

When you begin your climb back up the canyon from the furnace, turn right onto the South Trail. You may be thinking: This is better than retracing my steps all the way back up to the top of the gorge. It is. But it's still uphill all the way to the forest plateau. At this point on the plateau, the steep-and-deep Bullion Run Canyon is on your right and the steeper-and-deeper Allegheny Gorge is straight ahead.

Make your way to the Kennerdell Trail, an old road that has been groomed for cross-country skiing. The first portion of this trail follows the edge of the Allegheny Gorge. You can hear faint sounds of traffic from the

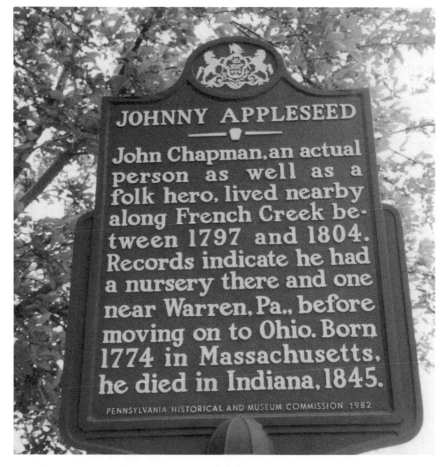

MilesDirections

0.0 START from the State Game Lands parking area south gate. Look for the white blazes.

0.3 Turn left onto an access road. Look for the red blazes.

0.9 Come to the fenced-in deer exclosure. Go through the gate.

1.1 Come to a T-intersection and a sign that reads "Bullion Run Iron Furnace." Turn right and cross an access road. *[FYI. Notice the maple tree bent into an arch.]*

1.3 Arrive at the fence at the south end of the exclosure. Go through the gate.

1.4 Cross the headwaters of Bullion Run on a footbridge. Enter a hemlock stand.

1.5 Come to the second sign for Bullion Run Iron Furnace. Steep descent.

1.7 Come to the third sign for Bullion Run Iron Furnace.

1.8 Come to the fourth sign for Bullion Run Iron Furnace. Turn left. Arrive at the furnace. Retrace your steps back up the hill.

2.0 Arrive back at the third Bullion Run Furnace sign and turn right.

2.2 Turn right again onto the South Trail.

2.3 Bear right at the trail junction. Reach the plateau.

2.6 Cross a series of washouts on four footbridges. *[FYI. Notice how a tree across the trail is notched for hikers.]*

3.1 Come to a fork in the trail. Turn left at the "Cross Country Ski Trail" sign. Walk a short distance through a rough clearing and turn left onto the ski trail, which is the Kennerdell Trail.

4.1 Pass a sign that directs you to turn right for the overlook.

4.6 Turn right at the sign "Dennison Point Overlook." Arrive at the overlook. Retrace your steps to the sign "Dennison Run." Turn right.

4.7 Pass the sign "No Horses Beyond This Point."

5.0 Arrive at an intersection. Turn left onto an access road; follow the red blazes.

5.1 Come to a steep, rugged washout and follow it downhill. *[**Note.** There are no blazes in this washout.]*

5.4 Turn left at footpath beside Dennison Run.

5.5 Make hairpin turn to the right. Come to the "Dennison Run Trail" sign. Turn left onto the trail and cross the first suspension bridge over Dennison Run.

5.7 Cross the second suspension bridge.

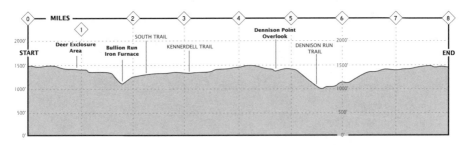

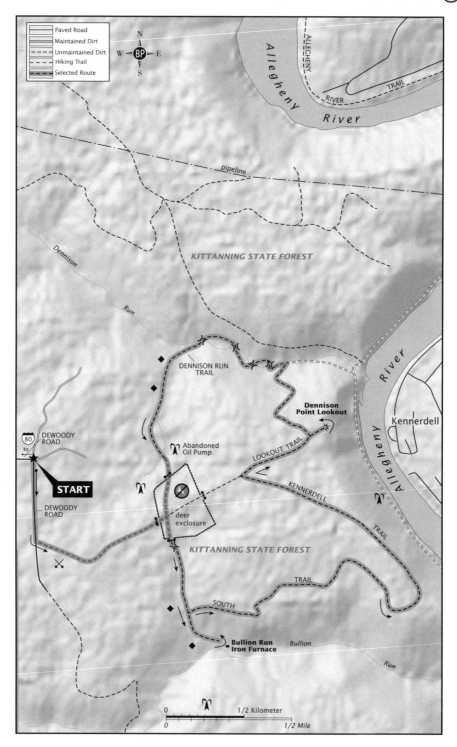

5.8 Cross the third suspension bridge.

6.0 Arrive at the sign "Bullion Run Iron Furnace." Turn left and cross a fourth suspension bridge.

6.1 Turn right onto a bridge over an intermittent tributary stream. Turn left and begin an uphill climb.

6.4 Cross a small footbridge. *[FYI. Notice the circular tree.]*

6.5 Turn left onto a small bridge over the stream.

6.7 Pass the "No Horses Beyond This Point." *[FYI. Notice the abandoned oil well pump on your left.]* Pass through a bog.

6.9 Turn right onto an old road. *[FYI. Notice the odd boulders.]*

7.0 Arrive at the north end of the deer exclosure. Go through the gate.

7.1 Arrive at a major trail intersection. Turn right. Exit the exclosure and retrace your steps toward the parking area.

7.7 Turn right onto an access road.

8.0 Arrive back at the parking area.

This view of the Allegheny River is from a platform 480 feet above the water.

village of Kennerdell sweeping up the gorge from across the river. This stretch is an easy walk that leads to the Dennison Point Overlook. The overlook is a railed-in, wooden platform perched on the edge of the gorge, 480 feet above the Allegheny River. It provides a breathtaking view. This is an excellent place to eat your lunch, take photos, and rest up for the rougher half of this hike.

Down the steep canyon you'll find Dennison Run, and four cable bridges stretched at intervals across the stream. All is well until you come to the beginning of your climb out of the canyon and face some of the steepest climbing around. But all things, good and bad, must end and eventually you make it to higher ground, where it's relatively flat and the wind cools you down. From here it's less than a mile to the parking area and your vehicle.

Hike Information

● Trail Contacts:
Department of Conservation and Natural Resources, Bureau of Forestry, Clarion, PA (814) 226–1901 or *www.dcnr.state.pa.us*

● Schedule:
Open year round

● Fees/Permits:
No fees or permits required

● Local Information:
Oil Heritage Region Tourist Promotion Agency, National Transit Building, Oil City, PA (814) 677–3152, ext. 18 or 1–800–483–6264, ext. 18 or *www.usachoice.net/oilregiontourist*

● Local Events/Attractions:
American Folkways Festival, fourth weekend in June and Labor Day weekend, Clintonville, PA (814) 385–6040 or *www.usachoice.net/americanfolkways*

● Accommodations:
Quo Vadis Bed & Breakfast, Franklin, PA (814) 432–4208 • **Kozy Rest Kampground,** Harrisville, PA (724) 735–2417

● Restaurants:
Kings Family Restaurant, Franklin, PA (814) 437–6997 • **Inn at the Franklin Hotel,** Franklin, PA (814) 437–3031 or *www.innatfranklin.com*

● Local Outdoor Retailers:
Maurer's Trading Post, Franklin, PA (814) 437–9570 • **Sports World,** Franklin, PA (814) 437–7623

● Maps:
USGS maps: Kennerdell, PA

Schollard's Wetlands

Hike Specs

Start: From the state game land parking lot off Nelson Road

Length: 5.8-mile out-and-back

Approximate Hiking Time: 2.5 hours

Difficulty Rating: Easy, due to the extremely flat trail

Terrain: Follow an old railroad bed past huge cattail marshes and bogs, as well as pristine ponds edged by clusters of pines.

Elevation Gain: 406 feet

Land Status: State game land

Nearest Town: Grove City, PA

Other Trail Users: Waterfowl enthusiasts and hunters (in season)

Canine Compatibility: Dogs permitted (Because of the waterfowl population and muddy bogs, dogs should be kept on leash.)

Getting There

From I-80: Take I-79 South to Exit 31 (PA 208). Drive west on PA 208 for 3.7 miles to U.S. 19. Turn left on U.S. 19, and drive 0.7 miles to a fork at Pennsy Road. Bear left on Pennsy Road and drive 1.5 miles to Nelson Road. Turn left onto Nelson Road and continue 0.3 miles to the state game land parking lot. *DeLorme: Pennsylvania Atlas & Gazetteer:* Page 42 C4

This out-and-back hike and can be divided into two distinct sections. The first 2.5 miles, from the beginning to Pennsylvania 208, is the quietest and most picturesque. It's in this section where you see the diversity of the plants and trees that provide the seeds, wild grapes, and berries that foster the impressive array of wildlife. Notice the variety of trees: shingle oak, chestnut oak, white oak, red oak, dogwood, and cucumber, as well as hemlock and other varieties of pine. You can also observe breeding nests for the wood duck and the Canada goose. The wood ducks' nests are the silver tubular devices with a circular entry hole, resembling something from an old science fiction movie. The nests for the Canada geese are open and resemble huge funnels stuffed with straw. They're attached to a pole that's implanted over the water. In either case, the nests are built to keep hungry predators away from the eggs. If you're lucky enough to see a Canada goose roosting, you'll notice its mate circling the pole, functioning as an early warning system and first line of defense.

This longest section of this hike is extremely well kept. The State Game Commission uses this abandoned railroad grade as an access road, so it's high, wide, and dry, and all the underbrush is trimmed away. Although out

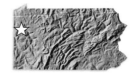

of sight much of the time, Schollard's Run meanders alongside the trail from bog to bog, heading for Springfield Falls.

When you reach Pennsylvania 208, you leave the idyllic life behind and enter back into civilization. From here to the falls the trail is not as well kept, and to make matters worse, a grade bridge is out. Supposedly, you can take this path to get to the falls, but it's tough going—I checked it out. Finding the trail in the marshy field isn't easy, and it doesn't get any better. Because the bridge is out, I had to leave the trail and walk along the stream through thick underbrush. The high stream made it difficult to find a decent spot to cross. For a while there were white markers on a few trees, but those ran out and I was left to simply follow the stream until I reached Falls Road. I do not recommend this route. Instead, I recommend that when you reach Pennsylvania 208 you turn left, stay on the shoulder, and merely walk the quarter mile or so to

Hike Information

● Trail Contacts:
Pennsylvania Game Commission, Harrisburg, PA (717) 783–7507 or *www.state.pa.us/pa-exec/pgc*

● Schedule:
Open year round

● Fees/Permits:
No fees or permits required

● Local Information:
Lawrence County Tourist Promotion Agency, New Castle, PA 1–888–284–7599 or *www.lawrence county.com/tourism*

● Local Events/Attractions:
Prime Outlets Mall, Grove City, PA 1–888–545–7221 or *www.prime outlets.com – over 140 manufacturers' outlet stores • **Harlansburg Station,** Museum of Transportation, New Castle, PA (412) 652–9002 – at the intersection of U.S. 19 and PA 108

● Accommodations:
Candleford Inn B&B, Volant, PA (724) 533–4497 • **Junction 19-80 Campground,** Mercer, PA (724) 748–4174

● Restaurants:
Rachel's Road House, Mercer, PA (724) 748–3193 or www.spring-fields.com

● Local Outdoor Retailers:
Ski & Sport Den Inc., New Castle, PA (724) 652–1105

● Maps:
USGS maps: Mercer, PA; Harlansburg, PA

Springfield Falls. There is very little traffic on Pennsylvania 208 at this point. See the Miles/Directions for more route specifics.

At the stop sign at the intersection of State Route 2002 and the Falls Road, turn right into the field and walk past the back of the antique shop. You come to a large wooden bulletin board with a sign that reads "Springfield Falls Nature Trail." If there is a "No Trespassing" sign stapled to the marker, disregard it. (The owners of the antique shop place it there so that their customers' children don't wander off into the trail and possibly get hurt.)

MilesDirections

0.0 START at the State Game Commission parking lot on Nelson Road. Turn right on Nelson Road.

0.1 Arrive at the railroad grade. Turn left.

1.0 Power line veers off to the left.

2.3 Reach PA 208. Turn left.

2.4 Turn right on SR 2002.

2.7 Reach a stop sign on Falls Road. Walk into the field toward the antique shop.

2.8 Reach Springfield Falls Nature Trail sign. Follow the trail.

2.9 Arrive at Springfield Falls. Retrace your steps.

5.8 Arrive back at Nelson Road parking lot.

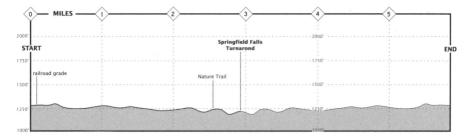

If you have children with you, the nature trail is safe and an interesting diversion, but as you make your way toward the falls, be wary of the steep drop-offs. The 60-foot falls have created some serious gorges.

Eat your lunch below the falls. Take off your boots and stick your feet in the clear, icy water of Schollard's Run. Rest and then simply retrace your steps back to your vehicle.

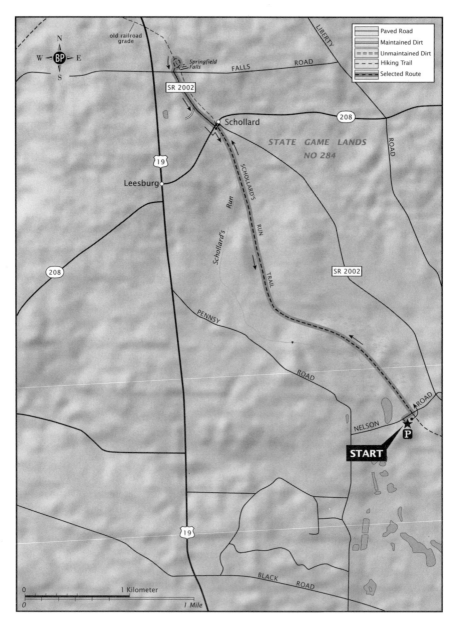

McConnell's Mill State Park

Hike Specs

Start: From the Alpha Pass Trail trailhead parking lot

Length: 3.3-mile loop

Approximate Hiking Time: 2 hours

Difficulty Rating: Moderate, with strenuous climbs out of the gorge

Terrain: Follow a typical rocky footpath down a deep gorge and walk alongside a whitewater creek, occasionally along wet and slippery rocks.

Elevation Gain: 346 feet

Land Status: State park

Nearest Town: New Castle, PA

Other Trail Users: Canoeists, rafters, and tourists

Canine Compatibility: Leashed dogs permitted

Getting There

From Pittsburgh: Drive north on I-79 to Exit 29. Drive west on U.S. 422 for 1.7 miles. Turn left and drive south on McConnell's Mill Road for 0.6 miles to the Alpha Pass Trail trailhead parking area on your right. *DeLorme: Pennsylvania Atlas & Gazetteer:* Page 57 A4

Only 40 miles north of Pittsburgh and surrounded by countless tourist attractions, shopping malls, restaurants, and campgrounds, Slippery Rock Gorge and McConnell's Mill State Park provide an excellent way to spend a day. McConnell's Mill State Park is both a national and a state natural landmark, comprised of 2,529 acres that surround the spectacular Slippery Rock Gorge. The gorge was formed 140,000 years ago when a continental glacier retreated, leaving behind lakes Prouty, Watts, and Edmund. Waters from these lakes drained swiftly into the channel, carving out the gorge. While little else remains of the glacial melt, the waters are still swift and turbulent.

In season, as you hike the trail, you can watch whitewater kayakers and canoeists wend their way downstream between the precariously balanced boulders that litter the stream. Where the creek widens and the water calms, you can watch novice canoeists as they learn the basics of keeping their craft headed in one direction.

The trail passes through the historic section of the park, where you may encounter tourists or school children touring McConnell's Mill and photographing the covered bridge. If it's a hot day, you may see young people from three nearby colleges picnicking or sunbathing on the large, flat boulders

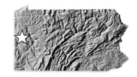

protruding from the stream. But as soon as you're through this area, visitors on the trail are sparse.

It's hard to estimate how long it takes to do this hike. As its name suggests, the gorge offers up plenty of *slippery rocks*, where even the most experienced hiker may fall. So, recognize that this is a challenging hike and don't try to rush through it. Interestingly, Slippery Rock Gorge actually got its name not because of the hundreds of slippery rocks along the way, but rather because of one especially slippery shelf of sandstone rocks. This shelf,

McConnell's Mill operated from 1868 to 1928.

which is located near the mill, was part of a Native American trail. A nearby oil seep deposited oil in the water, which ran over the shelf and made the passage a slippery one. The rock is still there, but, unfortunately, it's off limits to visitors.

Most hikers will want to stop and tour McConnell's Mill, a fully restored gristmill. One of its many interesting features are the turbines. The owners abandoned the typical waterwheel—which froze up in winters—in favor of turbines that were placed into the water race, inside the mill where the waters wouldn't freeze. Water channeled through these underwater turbines, which in turn were connected to gears and rods that distributed the power throughout the mill. Workers made ongoing maintenance checks (underwater, of course), which were always dangerous and sometimes fatal.

MilesDirections

0.0 START at the Alpha Pass Trail trailhead parking area on McConnell's Mill Road. Walk to the trailhead of the North Country National Scenic Trail. Follow Alpha Pass Trail arrows down the gorge. Look for blue blazes. Take the wooden steps.

0.1 Come to the first lifesaver stanchion. Walk to the boulders at the edge of Slippery Rock Creek. Retrace your steps back to the trail

0.2 Pass two small washout streams.

0.3 Come to a trail intersection. Continue straight.

0.4 Pass a runoff stream. Come to an intersection with a second trail. Continue straight.

0.6 Come to McConnell's Mill. Walk through the parking lot to the paved Kildoo Trail

0.9 Cross Kildoo Creek on a small footbridge. The pavement ends.

1.6 Cross two washout streams and a small waterfall. The trail becomes rocky.

1.7 Arrive at Eckert Bridge. Turn right and cross over the creek. Turn at the sign "Old Mill" and head upstream. This section of the Kildoo Trail is part of the North Country National Scenic Trail.

1.9 Pass through a large washout area.

2.0 *[FYI. Notice the runoff water creating a waterfall over the sandstone boulder.]*

2.7 Arrive at the covered bridge. Cross the stream to McConnell's Mill. Walk across the parking lot and continue walking uphill on the road.

3.2 Turn left onto McConnell's Mill Road.

3.3 Arrive back at the Alpha Pass Trail trailhead parking area on your left.

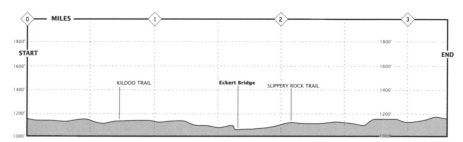

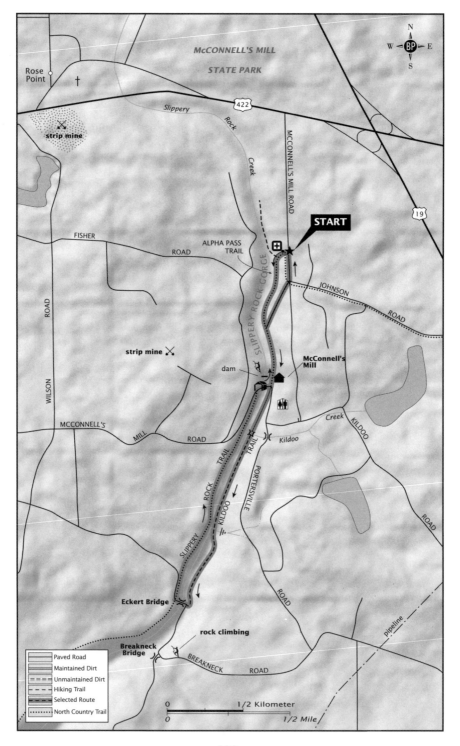

McCONNELL'S MILL
STATE PARK

Rose
Point

strip mine

Slippery

Rock

Creek

422

McCONNELL'S MILL ROAD

19

FISHER

ROAD

ALPHA PASS
TRAIL

START

SLIPPERY ROCK GORGE

JOHNSON

ROAD

ROAD

strip mine

dam

**McConnell's
Mill**

WILSON

MCCONNELL'S

MILL

ROAD

SLIPPERY ROCK TRAIL

KILDOO TRAIL

Kildoo

Creek

KILDOO

Kildoo

PORTERSVILLE

ROAD

SLIPPERY ROCK

KILDOO

Eckert Bridge

**Breakneck
Bridge**

rock climbing

BREAKNECK

ROAD

pipeline

	Paved Road
	Maintained Dirt
	Unmaintained Dirt
	Hiking Trail
	Selected Route
	North Country Trail

0   1/2 Kilometer

0   1/2 Mile

In fact, it was in mills like this where the expression "put you through the mill" (to give someone a hard time) originated.

The Slippery Rock Creek rapids, too, are dangerous. There's no swimming allowed. Stanchions hold white lifesaver devices attached to ropes stationed at intervals along the hiking trails, should there be any need. If you are insistent about living on the edge, there are two places along the trail where rock climbing and rappelling are permitted. The beginner area, the Rim Road Climbing Area, is across the stream from the mill. The advanced area is, appropriately, near Breakneck Bridge.

Hike Information

Trail Contacts:
McConnell's Mill State Park, Portersville, PA (724) 368–8091

Schedule:
Open spring through fall. McConnell's Mill hours are 10:30 A.M. to 5:30 P.M.; closed Tuesdays

Fees/Permits:
No fees or permits required

Local Information:
Lawrence County Tourist Promotion Agency, New Castle, PA (724) 654–8408 or 1–888–284–7599 or www.lawrencecounty.com/tourism

Local Events/Attractions:
Fireworks Festival, week of July Fourth, New Castle, PA (724) 654–5593 – children's activities, entertainment • Volant Main Street, Volant Merchants Association, Volant, PA (724) 533–2591 or www.volantshops.com – Shop old-fashioned Main Street (crafts and gift shops, Amish furniture); tour the restored grist mill and railcar depot.

Accommodations:
Snow Goose Inn, Grove City, PA (724) 458–4644 or www.bbonline.com/pa/snowgoose • Moraine State Park, Portersville, PA (724) 368–8811 – cabins and cottages open year round • Cooper's Lake Campground, Slippery Rock, PA (724) 368–8710 – open second week in April through the end of October

Restaurants:
The Olde Carriage Inn, New Castle, PA (724) 654–6533

Other Resources:
Western Pennsylvania Conservancy, Pittsburgh, PA (412) 288–2777

Local Outdoor Retailers:
Ski & Sport Den Inc., New Castle, PA (724) 652–1105

Maps:
USGS maps: Portersville, PA

Moraine State Park

Hike Specs

Start: From the North Country National Scenic Trail parking area on the west side of PA 528

Length: 10.5-mile circuit

Approximate Hiking Time: 6 hours

Difficulty Rating: Difficult, due to a series of climbs in and out of deep ravines

Terrain: Follow a typical forest footpath and dirt roads. You'll climb and descend a series of deep gorges as you weave your way along lake coves.

Elevation Gain: 1,619 feet

Land Status: State park

Nearest Town: Butler, PA

Other Trail Users: Anglers and hunters (in season)

Canine Compatibility: Leashed dogs permitted

Getting There

From Pittsburgh: Drive north on I-79. Take Exit 29 and drive east on U.S. 422 for 5.8 miles. Turn left onto PA 528 into Moraine State Park and drive north for 4.5 miles to the North Country National Scenic Trail parking lot on your left. *DeLorme: Pennsylvania Atlas & Gazetteer:* Page 57 A5

I f you've ever wondered if you're ready for a major hike or backpacking trip, this hike could be the test. In fact, most of this hike is part of the ambitious North Country National Scenic Trail, which, when completed, will span 4,600 miles from the central plains of North Dakota to the Adirondacks in New York. The 25-mile section that runs through McConnell's Mill and Moraine State Parks is a challenging hike. There are a seemingly endless number of climbs and descents along the ridges of this trail.

This route through Moraine State Park covers four major ridges, which means you go up and down each of them on the way out, and up and down again on the way back. While walking uphill is challenging, going down steep grades can be murder on the knees. And unless you can go six hours without eating, you'll also have the added burden of carrying food on this hike. Luckily, as far as water is concerned, there is an outdoor drinking fountain at the Davis Hollow Marina restrooms. There's even a down spigot so you can take off your shoes and give your feet a squirt or two.

Continental glaciers, as the name suggests, once stretched from the Atlantic to the Pacific. Where they ended they formed a moraine—a geo-

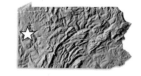

Trout Cove.

logic term for an accumulation of stones, boulders, and other debris carried and deposited by a glacier. Four of these glaciers ended at the area around Moraine State Park (again, demystifying the name). The debris they left behind blocked the natural flow of water, creating a number of glacial lakes and the rugged ridges and valleys that surround them. The largest of these glacial lakes stretched for over six miles. When it receded, it left behind a smaller lake with a series of waterways, creeks, and coves that stretched into valleys like so many crooked fingers.

View from Davis Hollow Marina looking south across Lake Arthur.

These odd land formations intrigued the English botanist and geologist Frank W. Preston. Beginning in the 1920s, he studied the area (which was then called Muddy Creek Valley) for decades. With support from his friends, Preston formed the Western Pennsylvania Conservancy, which purchased the land and set about to preserve it in all its uniqueness. State agencies later joined forces with the Conservancy, and in 1970 Moraine State Park was opened.

One of the centerpieces of the park is the popular 3,222-acre Lake Arthur, built in 1968 by damming Muddy Creek, and named after prominent Pittsburgh attorney and naturalist Edmund Watts Arthur. Today, dozens of sailboats line the marina and fishermen troll the coves for northern pike, muskellunge, walleye, and other warm-water fish.

Hike Information

🔗 Trail Contacts:
Moraine State Park, Portersville, PA (724) 368–8811 • **Bob Tait,** (Pennsylvania) State Coordinator, North Country Trail Association (724) 287–3382

🕐 Schedule:
Open spring through fall. McConnell's Mill hours are 10:30 A.M. to 5:30 P.M.; closed Tuesdays

💲 Fees/Permits:
No fees or permits required

❓ Local Information:
Butler County Tourist Promotion Agency, Butler, PA 1–888–741–6772 or *www.butlercountychamber.com*

📍 Local Events/Attractions:
National Trail Day Celebration, first week in June, Davis Hollow Outdoor Center at Moraine State Park – *hikes, bicycle rides, demonstrations, outdoor gear flea market* • **Annual Butler (Runners) Road** Race, third week in June, Butler, PA 1–888–741–6772 – *5K and 2 mile*

🛏 Accommodations:
As Thyme Goes By, Harrisville, PA (724) 735–4003 or 1–877–278–4963 or *www.asthymegoesby.com* • **Moraine State Park,** Portersville, PA (724) 368–8811 – *cabins and cottages open year round* • **Bear Run Campground and Cabins,** Portersville, PA (724) 368–3564 – *open mid-April through the end of October, some sites available in winter season. Call to confirm.*

🍴 Restaurants:
Iron Bridge Inn, Mercer, PA (724) 748–3626

🏢 Organizations:
Butler Outdoor Club, P.O. Box 243, Butler, PA 16001

🔄 Other Resources:
Western Pennsylvania Conservancy, Pittsburgh, PA (412) 288–2777

🎒 Local Outdoor Retailers:
Kirkpatrick's Sporting Goods, Butler, PA (724) 285–8600

🅝 Maps:
USGS maps: Prospect, PA

MilesDirections

0.0 START at the North Country National Scenic Trail parking area on PA 528. Walk to the bulletin board and trail marker. Follow the blue blazes. Begin a severe uphill climb.

0.8 Come to an intersection with the yellow-blazed "528 Bridge Trail." Continue straight to the Glacier Ridge Trail.

1.5 Cross a deep washout. Come to small footbridge.

1.6 Come to a second small footbridge.

1.7 Begin a serious uphill climb.

1.9 The trail levels off and veers to the left. Cross a meadow.

2.2 Cross a dirt road and re-enter the woods. *[FYI. Notice the signpost for NCNST and the sign on your right for snowmobile and mountain bike trails. Note traffic access gate also.]* Begin descent.

2.5 Cross a large washout.

2.6 Begin an uphill climb.

2.8 Reach the ridge top. Begin your descent.

3.3 Come to a junction with the mountain bike trail. Turn right and continue on the Glacier Ridge Trail.

3.5 Cross a small washout. Begin a gradual ascent.

3.8 Encounter a switchback.

4.2 Turn left on the yellow-blazed Marina Trail toward Davis Hollow Marina.

4.4 Cross small, deep washout.

4.7 Begin your ascent.

4.8 Cross a power line swath. Get on an old road and walk parallel to the lake to Davis Hollow Marina.

4.9 Arrive at the marina. Walk east across the parking lot to the walkway at northern tip of the inlet. Walk on the road around the inlet.

5.1 Turn left and begin climbing an on old road. Follow the pink blazes.

5.5 Reach the crest of the hill and begin your descent.

5.7 Pass a marsh on your right. *[FYI. Notice the cattails, wild grape, and milkweed.]*

6.1 The road turns left, away from lake. Follow the pink blazes and the black blazes.

6.4 Reach the crest of a hill and begin your descent.

6.6 Pass stone ruins.

6.7 Begin an uphill climb.

6.8 Note the mountain bike trail junction on your right.

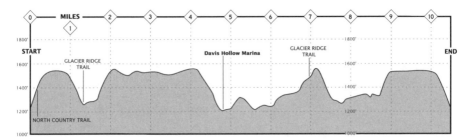

6.9 Turn right onto Glacier Ridge Trail. Follow the blue blazes.

7.2 Begin your descent.

7.5 Cross a small stream on wooden footbridge.

7.6 Cross second small stream on a wooden footbridge. Turn left. Begin an uphill climb.

7.9 Arrive at a trail intersection and sign that reads "528 Bridge." Take the yellow-blazed Lakeshore Trail.

8.0 Cross a marshy area on a wooden footbridge. Turn left and begin a climb.

8.1 Cross a second wooden bridge.

8.3 Cross a small washout.

8.6 Turn left and begin climb.

8.9 Turn right and follow the yellow blazes.

9.7 Turn right onto Glacier Ridge Trail and cross under power line.

10.2 Begin descent to parking area.

10.5 Arrive back at the parking area.

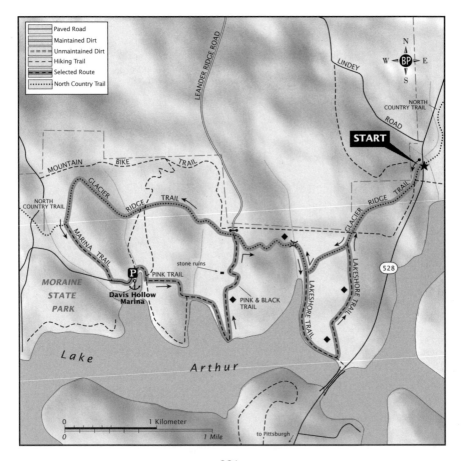

Northwest Pennsylvania

Compiled here is an index of great hikes in the Northwest region that didn't make the A-list this time around but deserve recognition. Check them out and let us know what you think. You may decide that one or more of these hikes deserves higher status in future editions or, perhaps, you may have a hike of your own that merits some attention.

(S) The Erie National Wildlife Refuge

The refuge is 35 miles south of Erie in Crawford County. There are two separate sections: the 5,025-acre Sugar Lake Division and the 3,545-acre Seneca Division. You'll find three short hikes in Sugar Lake and one in Seneca. The refuge, named after the Erie Indians who once inhabited the area, is a bird lover's paradise: over 230 species of birds have been reported here. The hikes, which total about seven miles, are easy but can be wet in the springtime.

To get there from Meadville, drive east on PA 27 and SR 2032 about 12 miles to Guys Mills. Take PA 198 in Guys Mills and drive east for 0.8 miles and turn right for the headquarters. For more information, call the Erie National Wildlife Refuge at (814) 789–3585. *DeLorme: Pennsylvania Atlas & Gazetteer:* Page 29 C6

(T) Chapman State Park

Located in Warren County, Chapman State Park is surrounded by the Allegheny National Forest. There's a network of seven hiking trails within its 805 acres. There's also the 68-acre Chapman Dam and an 83-site campground, as well as a group camping area. The trails, which are mostly old logging roads and railroad beds, make excellent short hikes. If you did all the hikes, the total would be around 11 miles. This is a great little park to visit and relax and get away from it all.

To get there from Warren, drive south on U.S. 6 for about seven miles to the (only) stoplight in Clarendon. Turn right at the stoplight onto Chapman Dam Road and drive about five miles to the park. For more information, call Chapman State Park at (814) 723-5030. *DeLorme: Pennsylvania Atlas & Gazetteer:* Page 31 B5

The Art of Hiking

The Art of Hiking

When standing nose to snout with a grizzly, you're probably not too concerned with the issue of ethical behavior in the wild. No doubt you're just wetting yourself. But let's be honest. How often are you nose to snout with a grizzly? For most of us, a hike into the "wild" means loading up the 4-Runner with everything North Face® and driving to a toileted trailhead. Sure, you can mourn how civilized we've become—how GPS units have replaced natural instinct and Gore-Tex®, true-grit—but the silly gadgets of civilization aside, we have plenty of reason to take pride in how we've matured. With survival now on the back-burner, we've begun to reason—and it's about time—that we have a responsibility to protect, no longer just conquer, our wild places; that *they*, not *we*, are at risk. So please, do what you can. Now, in keeping with our chronic tendency to reduce everything to a list, here are some rules to remember.

Zero impact. Always leave an area just like you found it—if not better than you found it. Avoid camping in fragile, alpine meadows and along the banks of streams and lakes. Use a camp stove versus building a wood fire. Pack up all of your trash and extra food. Bury human waste at least 100 feet from water sources under six to eight inches of topsoil. Don't bathe with soap in a lake or stream—use prepackaged moistened towels to wipe off sweat and dirt or bathe in the water without soap.

Stay on the trail. It's true, a path anywhere leads nowhere new, but purists will just have to get over it. Paths serve an important purpose; they limit our impact on natural areas. Straying from a designated trail may seem innocent but it can cause damage to sensitive areas—damage that may take years to recover, if it can recover at all. Even simple shortcuts can be destructive. So, please, stay on the trail.

Keep your dog under control. You can buy a flexi-lead that allows your dog to go exploring along the trail, while allowing you the ability to reel him in should another hiker approach or should he decide to chase a rabbit. Always obey leash laws and be sure to bury your dog's waste or pack it in resealable plastic bags.

Yield to horses. When you approach these animals on the trail, always step quietly off the trail and let them pass. If you are wearing a large backpack, it's a good idea to sit down. From a horse's perspective, a hiker wearing a large backpack is a scary trail monster and these sensitive animals can be spooked easily.

GETTING INTO SHAPE

Unless you want to be sore—and possibly have to shorten your trip or vacation—be sure to get in shape before a big hike. If you're terribly out of shape, start a walking program early, preferably eight weeks in advance. Start with a 15-minute walk during your lunch hour or after work and gradually increase your walking time to an hour. You should also increase your elevation gain. Walking briskly up hills really strengthens your leg muscles and gets your heart rate up. If you work in a storied office building, take the stairs instead of the elevator. If you prefer going to a gym, walk the treadmill or use a stair-master. You can further increase your strength and endurance by walking with a loaded backpack. Stationary exercises you might consider are squats, leg lifts, sit-ups, and push-ups. Other good ways to get in shape include biking, running, aerobics, and, of course, short hikes.

PREPAREDNESS

It's been said that failing to plan means planning to fail. So do take the necessary time to plan your trip. Whether going on a short day hike or an extended backpack trip, always prepare for the worst. Simply remembering to pack a copy of the *U.S. Army Survival Manual* is not preparedness. Although it's not a bad idea if you plan on entering truly wild places, it's merely the tourniquet answer to a problem. You need to do your best to prevent the problem from arising in the first place. These days the word "survival" is often replaced with the pathetically feeble term "comfort." In order to remain comfortable (and to survive if you really want to push it), you need to concern yourself with the basics: water, food, and shelter. Don't go on a hike without having these bases covered. And don't go on a hike expecting to find these items in the woods.

Water. Even in frigid conditions, you need at least two quarts of water a day to function efficiently. Add heat and taxing terrain and you can bump that figure up to one gallon. That's simply a base to work from—your metabolism and your level of conditioning can raise or lower that amount. Unless you know your level, assume that you need one gallon of water a day. Now, where do you plan on getting the water?

Preferably not from natural water sources. These sources can be loaded with intestinal disturbers, such as bacteria, viruses, and fertilizers. *Giardia lamblia*, the most common of these disturbers, is a protozoan parasite that lives part of its lifecycle as a cyst in water sources. The parasite spreads when mammals defecate in water sources. Once ingested, Giardia can induce cramping, diarrhea, vomiting, and fatigue within two days to two weeks after ingestion. Giarda is treatable with the prescription drug Flagyl. If you believe you've contracted Giardia, see a doctor immediately.

Treating Water. The best and easiest solution to avoid polluted water is to carry your water with you. Yet, depending on the nature of your hike and the duration, this may not be an option—seeing as one gallon of water weighs 8.5 pounds. In that case, you'll need to look into treating water.

Regardless of which method you choose, you should always carry *some* water with you, in case of an emergency. Save this reserve until you absolutely need it.

There are three methods of treating water: boiling, chemical treatment, and filtering. If you boil water, it's recommended that you do so for 10 to 15 minutes. This is often impractical because you're forced to exhaust a great deal of your fuel supply. You can opt for chemical treatment (e.g. Potable Aqua) which will kill Giardia but will not take care of other chemical pollutants. Another drawback to chemical treatments is the unpleasant taste of the water after it's treated. You can remedy this by adding powdered drink mix to the water. Filters are the preferred method for treating water. Filters remove Giardia, organic and inorganic contaminants, and don't leave an aftertaste. Water filters are far from perfect as they can easily become clogged or leak if a gasket wears out. It's always a good idea to carry a back-up supply of chemical treatment tablets in case your filter decides to quit on you.

Food. If we're talking about "survival," you can go days without food, as long as you have water. But we're talking about "comfort" here. Try to avoid foods that are high in sugar and fat like candy bars and potato chips. These food types are harder to digest and are low in nutritional value. Instead, bring along foods that are easy to pack, nutritious, and high in energy (e.g. bagels, nutrition bars, dehydrated fruit, gorp, and jerky). If you are on an overnight trip, easy-to-fix dinners include rice mixes with dehydrated potatoes, corn pasta with cheese sauce, and soup mixes. For a tasty breakfast, you can fix hot oatmeal with brown sugar and reconstituted milk powder topped off with banana chips. If you like a hot drink in the morning, bring along herbal tea bags or hot chocolate. If you are a coffee junkie, you can purchase coffee that is packaged like tea bags. You can pre-package all of your meals in heavy-duty resealable plastic bags to keep food from spilling in your pack. These bags can be reused to pack out trash.

Shelter. The type of shelter you choose depends less on the conditions than on your tolerance for discomfort. Shelter comes in many forms—tent, tarp, lean to, bivy sack, cabin, cave, etc. If you're camping in the desert, a bivy sack may suffice, but if you're above the treeline and a storm is approaching, a better choice is a three or four season tent. Tents are the logical and most popular choice for most backpackers as they're lightweight and packable—and you can rest assured that you always have shelter from the elements. *[See Equipment: Tents on page 337]* Before you leave on your trip, anticipate what the weather and terrain will be like and plan for the type of shelter that will work best for your comfort level.

Finding a campsite. If there are established campsites, stick to those. If not, start looking for a campsite early—like around 3:30 or 4:00 PM. Stop at the first decent site you see. Depending on the area, it could be a long time before you find another suitable location. Pitch your camp in an area that's

level. Make sure the area is at least 200 feet from fragile areas like lakeshores, meadows, and stream banks. And try to avoid areas thick in underbrush, as they can harbor insects and provide cover for approaching animals.

If you are camping in stormy, rainy weather, look for a rock outcrop or a shelter in the trees to keep the wind from blowing your tent all night. Be sure that you don't camp under trees with dead limbs that might break off on top of you. Also, try to find an area that has an absorbent surface, such as sandy soil or forest duff. This, in addition to camping on a surface with a slight angle, will provide better drainage. By all means, don't dig trenches to provide drainage around your tent—remember you're practicing minimum-impact camping.

If you're in bear country, steer clear of creekbeds or animal paths. If you see any signs of a bear's presence (i.e. scat, footprints), relocate. You'll need to find a campsite near a tall tree where you can hang your food and other items that may attract bears such as deodorant, toothpaste, or soap. Carry a lightweight nylon rope with which to hang your food. As a rule, you should hang your food at least 20 feet from the ground and five feet away from the tree trunk. You can put food and other items in a waterproof stuff sack and tie one end of the rope to the stuff sack. To get the other end of the rope over the tree branch, tie a good size rock to it and gently toss the rock over the tree branch. Pull the stuff sack up until it reaches the top of the branch and tie it off securely. Don't hang your food near your tent! If possible, hang your food at least 100 feet away from your campsite. Alternatives to hanging your food are bear-proof plastic tubes and metal bear boxes.

Lastly, think of comfort. Lie down on the ground where you intend to sleep and see if it's a good fit. For morning warmth (and a nice view to wake up to), have your tent face east.

FIRST AID

I know you're tough, but get 10 miles into the woods and develop a blister and you'll wish you had carried that first aid kit. Face it, it's just plain good sense. Many companies produce light-weight, compact first-aid kits, just make sure yours contains at least the following:

First Aid

- band aids
- mole skin
- various sterile gauze and dressings
- white surgical tape
- an ace bandage
- an antihistamine
- aspirin
- Betadine® solution
- a first-aid book
- Tums®
- tweezers
- scissors
- anti-bacterial wipes
- triple-antibiotic ointment
- plastic gloves
- sterile cotton tip applicators
- syrup of ipecac (to induce vomiting)
- a thermometer
- a wire splint

Here are a few tips to dealing with and hopefully preventing certain ailments.

Sunburn. To avoid sunburn, wear sunscreen (SPF 15 or higher), protective clothing, and a wide-brimmed hat when you are hiking in sunny weather. If you do get sunburn, treat the area with aloe vera gel and protect the area from further sun exposure.

Blisters. Be prepared to take care of these hike-spoilers by carrying moleskin (a lightly padded adhesive), gauze and tape, or Band-Aids. An effective way to apply moleskin is to cut out a circle of moleskin and remove the center—like a donut—and place it over the blistered area. Cutting the center out will reduce the pressure applied to the sensitive skin. Other products that can help you combat blisters are Bodyglide® and Second Skin®. Bodyglide® (1–888–263–9454) is applied to suspicious hot spots before a blister forms to help decrease friction to that area. Second Skin® (made by Spenco) is applied to the blister after it has popped and acts as a "second skin" to help prevent further irritation.

Insect bites and stings. You can treat most insect bites and stings by applying hydrocortisone 1% cream topically and taking a pain medication such as ibuprofen or acetaminophen to reduce swelling. If you forgot to pack these items, a cold compress or a paste of mud and ashes can sometimes assuage the itching and discomfort. Remove any stingers by using tweezers or scraping the area with your fingernail or a knife blade. Don't pinch the area as you'll only spread the venom.

Some hikers are highly sensitive to bites and stings and may have a serious allergic reaction that can be life threatening. Symptoms of a serious allergic reaction can include wheezing, an asthmatic attack, and shock. The treatment for this severe type of reaction is epinephrine (Adrenaline). If you know that you are sensitive to bites and stings, carry a pre-packaged kit of epinephrine (e.g., Anakit®), which can be obtained only by prescription from your doctor.

Ticks. As you well know, ticks can carry disease, such as Rocky Mountain Spotted Fever and Lyme disease. The best defense is, of course, prevention. If you know you're going to be hiking through an area littered with ticks, wear long pants and a long sleeved shirt. You can apply a permethrin repellent to your clothing and a DEET repellent to exposed skin. At the end of your hike, do a spot check for ticks (and insects in general). If you do find a tick, coat the insect with Vaseline® or tree sap to cut off its air supply. The tick should release its hold, but if it doesn't, grab the head of the tick firmly—with a pair of tweezers if you have them—and gently pull it away from the skin with a twisting motion. Sometimes the mouthparts linger, embedded in your skin. If this happens, try to remove them with a disinfected needle. Clean the affected area with an anti-bacterial cleanser and then apply triple antibiotic ointment. Monitor the area for a few days. If irritation persists or a white spot develops, see a doctor for possible infection.

Poison ivy, oak, and sumac. These skin irritants can be found most anywhere in North America and come in the form of a bush or a vine, having leaflets in groups of three, five, seven, or nine. Learn how to spot the plants. The oil they secrete can cause an allergic reaction in the form of blisters, usually

poison ivy

about 12 hours after exposure. The itchy rash can last from ten days to several weeks. The best defense against these irritants is to wear protective clothing and to apply a non-prescription product called IvyBlock® to exposed skin. This lotion is meant to guard against the effects of poison ivy/oak/sumac and can be washed off with soap and water. Taking a hot shower after you return home from your hike will also help to

poison oak

remove any lingering oil from your skin. Should you contract a rash from any of these plants, use Benadryl® or a similar product to reduce the itching. If the rash is localized, create a light Clorox®/water wash to dry up the area. If the rash has spread, either tough it out or see your doctor about getting a dose of Cortisone® (available both orally and by injection).

poison sumac

Snakebites. First off, snakebites are rare in North America. Unless startled or provoked, the majority of snakes will not bite. If you are wise to their habitats and keep a careful eye on the trail, you should be just fine. Though your chances of being struck are slim, it's wise to know what to do in the event you are.

If a *non-poisonous* snake bites you, allow the wound to bleed a small amount and then cleanse the wounded area with a Betadine® solution (10% povidone iodine). Rinse the wound with clean water (preferably) or fresh urine (it might sound ugly, but it's sterile). Once the area is clean, cover it with triple antibiotic ointment and a clean bandage. Remember, most residual damage from snakebites, poisonous or otherwise, comes from infection, not the snake's venom. Keep the area as clean as possible and get medical attention immediately.

If you are bitten by a *poisonous* snake, remove the toxin with a suctioning device, found in a snakebite kit. If you do not have such a device, squeeze the wound—do NOT use your mouth for suction as the venom will enter your bloodstream through the vessels under the tongue and head straight for your heart. Then, clean the wound just as you would a non-poisonous bite. Tie a clean band of cloth snuggly around the afflicted appendage, about an inch or so above the bite (or the rim of the swelling). This is NOT a tourniquet—you want to simply slow the blood flow, not cut it off. Loosen the band if numbness ensues. Remove the band for a minute and re-apply a little higher every ten minutes

If it is your friend who's been bitten, treat him or her for shock—make him comfortable, have him lie down, elevate the legs, and keep him warm. Avoid applying anything cold to the bite wound. Immobilize the affected area and remove any constricting items such as rings, watches, or restrictive clothing—swelling may occur. Once your friend is stable and relatively calm, hike out to get help. The victim should get treatment within 12 hours, ideally, which usually consists of a tetanus shot, antivenin, and antibiotics.

Now, if you are alone and struck by a poisonous snake, stay calm. Hysteria will only quicken the venom's spread. Follow the procedure above and do your best to reach help. When hiking out, don't run—you'll only increase the flow of blood throughout your system. Instead, walk calmly.

In terms of poisonous snakes, the three found in Pennsylvania belong to the pit viper group: the copperhead, timber rattlesnake, and Eastern massasauga rattlesnake. While these snakes vary in color and marking, they can all be identified by a small "pit" found between the eye and nostril. Be especially careful of where you put your hands and feet with rattlers around, since they enjoy sunning themselves on rock ledges and outcroppings.

The copperhead gets its name from its coloring; you'll most likely recognize its dull orange with dark brown, hourglass bands. The large head is triangular, unmarked, and a coppery red. The adult male has a thick body and is generally three feet in length.

The timber rattlesnake adult male is usually four feet in length and has a large, triangular, unmarked head. It has two color phases: In its dark phase, the head is black and the body is gray; in its light phase, it is yellowish brown with a black tail. Naturally, this snake has a silvery rattle on its tail it vibrates as a warning; you may be more likely to hear a timber rattler before seeing it. If you really threaten it, the timber rattlesnake will coil just before striking. Consider yourself warned.

The massasauga, also known as the "swamp rattler," is a small multi-colored rattlesnake found only in the northwestern section of the state. It's becoming increasingly rare in Pennsylvania (and much of North America), so its highly unlikely that you'll come across one in the wilderness.

The copperhead likes wooded hillsides, and can be found in the southern part of the state. The timber rattler lives in the mountains of the central part of the state. Due to a number of factors, such as loss of habitat, hunters, and the encroachment of civilization, the snake population in Pennsylvania is dwindling. In fact, most hikers will never see a poisonous snake in Pennsylvania.

Dehydration. Have you ever hiked in hot weather and had a roaring headache and felt fatigued after only a few miles? More than likely you were dehydrated. Symptoms of dehydration include fatigue, headache, and decreased coordination and judgment. When you are hiking, your body's rate of fluid loss depends on the outside temperature, humidity, altitude, and your activity level. On average, a hiker walking in warm weather will lose four liters of fluid a day. That fluid loss is easily replaced by normal consumption of liquids and food. However, if a hiker is walking briskly in hot, dry weather and hauling a heavy pack, he can lose one to three liters of water an hour. It's important to always carry plenty of water and to stop often and drink fluids regularly, even if you aren't thirsty.

Heat exhaustion is the result of a loss of large amounts of electrolytes and often occurs if a hiker is dehydrated and has been under heavy exertion. Common symptoms of heat exhaustion include cramping, exhaustion, fatigue, lightheadedness, and nausea. You can treat heat exhaustion by getting out of the sun and drinking an electrolyte solution made up of one teaspoon of salt and one tablespoon of sugar dissolved in a liter of water. Drink this solution slowly over a period of one hour. Drinking plenty of fluids (preferably an electrolyte solution like Gatorade®) can prevent heat exhaustion. Avoid hiking during the hottest parts of the day and wear breathable clothing, a wide brimmed hat, and sunglasses.

Hypothermia is one of the biggest dangers in the backcountry—especially for day hikers in the summertime. That may sound strange, but imagine starting out on a hike in mid-summer when it's sunny and 80 degrees out. You're clad in nylon shorts and a cotton T-shirt. About halfway through your hike, the sky begins to cloud up and in the next hour a light drizzle begins to fall and the wind starts to pick up. Before you know it, you are soaking wet and shivering—the perfect recipe for hypothermia. More advanced signs include decreased coordination, slurred speech, and blurred vision. When a victim's temperature falls below 92 degrees Fahrenheit, the blood pressure and pulse plummet, possibly leading to coma and death.

To avoid hypothermia, always bring a windproof/rainproof shell, a fleece jacket, Capilene® tights, gloves, and hat when you are hiking in the mountains. Learn to adjust your clothing layers based on the temperature. If you are climbing uphill at a moderate pace you will stay warm, but when you stop for a break you'll become cold quickly, unless you add more layers of clothing.

If a hiker is showing advanced signs of hypothermia, dress him in dry clothes and make sure he is wearing a hat and gloves. Place him in a sleeping bag in a tent or shelter that will protect him from the wind and other elements. Give him warm fluids to drink and keep him awake.

Frostbite. When the mercury dips below 32 degrees Fahrenheit, your extremities begin to chill. If a persistent chill attacks a localized area, say your hands or your toes, the circulatory system reacts by cutting off blood flow to the affected area—the idea being to protect and preserve the body's overall temperature. And so it's death by attrition for the affected area. Ice crystals start to form from the water in the cells of the neglected tissue. Deprived of heat, nourishment, and now water, the tissue literally starves. This is frostbite.

Prevention is your best defense against this situation. Most prone to frostbite are your face, hands, and feet—so protect these areas well. Wool is the material of choice because it provides ample air space for insulation and draws moisture away from the skin. However, synthetic fabrics have recently made great strides in the cold weather clothing market. Do your research. A pair of light silk liners under your regular gloves is a good trick to keeping warm. They afford some additional warmth, but more importantly they'll allow you to remove your mitts for tedious work without exposing the skin.

Now, if your feet or hands start to feel cold or numb due to the elements, warm them as quickly as possible. Place cold hands under your armpits or bury them in your crotch. If your feet are cold, change your socks. If there's plenty of room in your boots, add another pair of socks. Do remember though that constricting your feet in tight boots can restrict blood flow and actually make your feet colder more quickly. Your socks need to have breathing room if they're going to be effective. Dead air provides insulation. If your face is cold, place your warm hands over your face or simply wear a head stocking (called a balaclava).

Should your skin go numb and start to appear white and waxy, chances are you've got or are developing frostbite. Don't try to thaw the area unless you can maintain the warmth. In other words, don't stop to warm up your frostbitten feet only to head back on the trail. You'll do more damage than good. Tests have shown that hikers who walked on thawed feet did more harm, and endured more pain, than hikers who left the affected areas alone. Do your best to get out of the cold entirely and seek medical attention—which usually consists of performing a rapid rewarming in water for 20 to 30 minutes.

The overall objective in preventing both hypothermia and frostbite is to keep the body's core warm. Protect key areas where heat escapes, like the top of the head, and maintain the proper nutrition level. Foods that are high in calories aid the body in producing heat. Never smoke or drink when you're in situations where the cold is threatening. By affecting blood flow, these activities ultimately cool the body's core temperature.

NAVIGATION

Whether you are going on a short hike in a familiar area or planning a weeklong backpack trip, you should always be equipped with the proper

navigational equipment—at the very least a detailed map and a sturdy compass.

Maps. There are many different types of maps available to help you find your way on the trail. Easiest to find are Forest Service maps and BLM (Bureau of Land Management) maps. These maps tend to cover large areas, so be sure they are detailed enough for your particular trip. You can also obtain National Park maps as well as high quality maps from private companies and trail groups. These maps can be obtained either from outdoor stores or ranger stations.

U.S. Geological Survey topographic maps are particularly popular with hikers—especially serious backcountry hikers. These maps contain the standard map symbols such as roads, lakes, and rivers, as well as contour lines that show the details of the trail terrain like ridges, valleys, passes, and mountain peaks. The 7.5-minute series (1 inch on the map equals approximately two-fifths of a mile on the ground) provides the closest inspection available. USGS maps are available by mail (U.S. Geological Survey, Map Distribution Branch, PO Box 25286, Denver, Colorado 80225) or you can visit them online at *http://mapping.usgs.gov/esic/to_order.html.*

If you want to check out the high tech world of maps, you can purchase topographic maps on CD-ROM. These software-mapping programs let you select a route on your computer, print it out, and then take it with you on the trail. Some software mapping programs let you insert symbols and labels, download waypoints from a GPS unit, and export the maps to other software programs. Mapping software programs such as DeLorme's TopoUSA™ (*www.delorme.com*) and MAPTECH's Terrain Navigator™ (*www.maptech.com*) let you do all of these things and more.

The art of map reading is a skill that you can develop by first practicing in an area you are familiar with. To begin, orient the map so the map is lined up in the correct direction (i.e. north on the map is lined up with true north). Next, familiarize yourself with the map symbols and try and match them up with terrain features around you such as a high ridge, mountain peak, river, or lake. If you are practicing with an USGS map notice the contour lines. On gentler terrain these contour lines are spaced further apart, and on steeper terrain they are closer together. Pick a short loop trail and stop frequently to check your position on the map. As you practice map reading, you'll learn how to anticipate a steep section on the trail or a good place to take a rest break, etc.

The Compass. First off, the sun is not a substitute for a compass. So, what kind of compass should you have? Here are some characteristics you should look for: a rectangular base with detailed scales, a liquid-filled housing, protective housing, a sighting line on the mirror, luminous alignment and back-bearing arrows, a luminous north-seeking arrow, and a well-defined bezel ring.

You can learn compass basics by reading the detailed instructions included with your compass. If you want to fine-tune your compass skills, sign up for an orienteering class or purchase a book on compass reading. Once you've learned the basic skills on using a compass, remember to practice these skills before you head into the backcountry.

If you are a klutz at using a compass, you may be interested in checking out the technical wizardry of the **GPS (Global Positioning System)** device. The GPS was developed by the Pentagon and works off 24 NAVSTAR satellites, which were designed to guide missiles to their targets. A GPS device is a handheld unit that calculates your latitude and longitude with the easy press of a button. Although the Pentagon used to scramble the satellite signals a bit, that security feature of GPS ended in 2000, and the system now provides nearly pinpoint accuracy.

Magellan GPS unit.

There are many different types of GPS units available and they range in price from $100 to $400. In general, all GPS units have a display screen and keypad where you input information. In addition to acting as a compass, the unit allows you to plot your route, easily retrace your path, track your travelling speed, find the mileage between waypoints, and calculate the total mileage of your route.

Before you purchase a GPS unit, keep in mind that these devices don't pick up signals indoors, in heavily wooded areas, on mountain peaks, or in deep valleys.

A **pedometer** is a handy device that can track your mileage as you hike. This device is a small, clip-on unit with a digital display that calculates your hiking distance in miles or kilometers based on your walking stride. Some units also calculate the calories you burn and your total hiking time. Pedometers are available at most large outdoor stores and range in price from $20 to $40.

TRIP PLANNING

Planning your hiking adventure begins with letting a friend or relative know your trip itinerary so they can call for help if you don't return at your scheduled time. Your next task is to make sure you are outfitted to experience the risks and rewards of the trail. This section highlights gear and clothing you may want to take with you to get the most out of your hike.

Day Hikes

- camera/film
- compass/GPS unit
- pedometer
- daypack
- First Aid kit
- food
- guidebook
- headlamp/flashlight with extra batteries and bulbs
- hat
- insect repellant
- knife/multi-purpose tool
- map
- matches in waterproof container and fire starter
- polar fleece jacket
- raingear
- space blanket
- sunglasses
- sunscreen
- swim suit
- watch
- water
- water bottles/water hydration system

EQUIPMENT

With the outdoor market currently flooded with products, many of which are pure gimmickry, it seems impossible to both differentiate and choose. Do I really need a tropical-fish-lined collapsible shower? (No, you don't.) The only defense against the maddening quantity of items thrust in your face is to think practically—and to do so *before* you go shopping. The worst buys are impulsive buys. Since most of your name brands will differ only slightly in quality, it's best to know what you're looking for in terms of function. Buy only what you need. You will, don't forget, be carrying what you've bought on your back. Here are some things to keep in mind before you go shopping.

Clothes. Clothing is your armor against Mother Nature's little surprises. Pennsylvania's winters, especially in the northern half of the state, can be brutal; buying clothing that can be worn in layers is always a good strategy. In the winter months the first layer you'll want to wear is a "wicking" layer of long underwear that keeps perspiration away from your skin. Wearing long underwear made from synthetic fibers such as Capilene®, CoolMax®, or Thermax is an excellent choice. These fabrics wick moisture away from the skin and draw it toward the next layer of clothing where it then evaporates. Avoid wearing long underwear made of cotton as it is slow to dry and keeps moisture next to your skin.

The second layer you'll wear is the "insulating" layer. Aside from keeping you warm, this layer needs to "breathe" so you stay dry while hiking. A fabric that provides insulation and dries quickly is fleece. It's interesting to note that this one-of-a-kind fabric is made out of recycled plastic. Purchasing a zip-up jacket made of this material is highly recommended.

The last line of layering defense is the "shell" layer. You'll need some type of waterproof, windproof, breathable jacket that'll fit over all of your other layers. It should have a large hood that fits over a hat. You'll also need a good pair of rain pants made from a similar waterproof, breathable fabric. A fabric that easily fits the bill is Gore-Tex®. However, while a quality Gore-Tex jacket can range in price from $100 to $450, you should know that there are more affordable fabrics out there that work just as well.

Now that you've learned the basics of layering, you can't forget to protect your hands and face. In cold, windy, or rainy weather you'll need a hat made of wool or fleece and insulated, waterproof gloves that will keep your hands warm and toasty. As mentioned earlier, buying an additional pair of light silk liners to wear under your regular gloves is a good idea. They'll allow you to remove your outer-gloves for tedious work without exposing the skin.

Overnight Trips

- backpack and waterproof rain cover
- backpacker's trowel
- bandanna
- bear repellant spray
- bear bell
- biodegradable soap
- pot scrubber
- collapsible water container (2-3 gallon capacity)
- clothing—extra wool socks, shirt and shorts
- cook set/utensils
- ditty bags to store gear
- extra plastic resealable bags
- gaiters
- garbage bag
- ground cloth
- journal/pen
- nylon rope to hang food
- long underwear
- permit (if required)
- rain jacket and pants
- sandals to wear around camp and to ford streams
- sleeping bag
- waterproof stuff sack
- sleeping pad
- small bath towel
- stove and fuel
- tent
- toiletry items
- water filter
- whistle

Footwear. If you have any extra money to spend on your trip, put that money into boots or trail shoes. Poor shoes will bring a hike to a halt faster than anything else. To avoid this annoyance, buy shoes that provide support and are lightweight and flexible. A lightweight hiking boot is better than a heavy, leather mountaineering boot for most day hikes and backpacking. Trail running shoes provide a little extra cushion and are made in a high-top style that many people wear for hiking. These running shoes are lighter,

The Art of Hiking

more flexible, and more breathable than hiking boots. If you know you'll be hiking in wet weather often, purchase boots or shoes with a Gore-Tex® liner, which will help keep your feet dry.

When buying your boots, be sure to wear the same type of socks you'll be wearing on the trail. If the boots you're buying are for cold weather hiking, try the boots on while wearing two pairs of socks. Speaking of socks, a good cold weather sock combination is to wear a thinner sock made of wool or polypropylene covered by a heavier outer sock made of wool. The inner sock protects the foot from the rubbing effects of the outer sock and prevents blisters.

Once you've purchased your footwear, be sure to break them in before you hit the trail. New footwear is often stiff and needs to be stretched and molded to your foot.

Backpacks. No matter what type of hiking you do you'll need a pack of some sort to carry the basic trail essentials. There are a variety of backpacks on the market, but let's first discuss what you intend to use it for. Day hikes or overnight trips?

If you plan on doing a day hike, a daypack should have some of the following characteristics: a padded hip belt that's at least two inches in diameter (avoid packs with only a small nylon piece of webbing for a hip belt); a chest strap (the chest strap helps stabilize the pack against your body); external pockets to carry water and other items that you want easy access to; an internal pocket to hold keys, a knife, a wallet, and other miscellaneous items; an external lashing system to hold a jacket; and a hydration pocket for carrying

courtesy Johnson Coleman

a hydration system (which consists of a water bladder with an attachable drinking hose).

For short hikes, some hikers like to use a fanny pack to store just a camera, food, a compass, a map, and other trail essentials. Most fanny packs have pockets for two water bottles and a padded hip belt.

If you intend to do an extended, overnight trip, there are multiple considerations. First off, you need to decide what kind of framed pack you want. There are two backpack types for backpacking: the internal frame and the external frame. An internal frame pack rests closer to your body, making it more stable and easier to balance when hiking over rough terrain. An external frame pack is just that, an aluminum frame attached to the exterior of the pack. An external frame pack is better for long backpack trips because it distributes the pack weight better and you can carry heavier loads. It's easier to pack, and your gear is more accessible. It also offers better back ventilation in hot weather.

The most critical measurement for fitting a pack is torso length. The pack needs to rest evenly on your hips without sagging. A good pack will come in two or three sizes and have straps and hip belts that are adjustable according to your body size and characteristics.

When you purchase a backpack, go to an outdoor store with salespeople who are knowledgeable in how to properly fit a pack. Once the pack is fitted for you, load the pack with the amount of weight you plan on taking on the trail. The weight of the pack should be distributed evenly and you should be able to swing your arms and walk briskly without feeling out of balance. Another good technique for evaluating a pack is to walk up and down stairs and make quick turns to the right and to the left to be sure the pack doesn't feel out of balance.

Other features that are nice to have on a backpack include a removable day pack or fanny pack, external pockets for extra water, and extra lash points to attach a jacket or other items.

Sleeping bags and pads. Sleeping bags are rated by temperature. You can purchase a bag made of synthetic fiber such as Polarguard® HV or DuPont Hollofil® II, or you can buy a goose down bag. Goose down bags are more expensive, but they have a higher insulating capacity by weight and will keep their loft longer. You'll want to purchase a bag with a temperature rating that fits the time of year and conditions you are most likely to camp in. One caveat: the techno-standard for temperature ratings is far from perfect. Ratings vary from manufacturer to manufacturer, so to protect yourself you should purchase a bag rated 10 to 15 degrees below the temperature you expect to be camping in. Synthetic bags are more resistant to water than down bags, but many down bags are now made with a Gore-Tex® shell that helps to repel water. Down bags are also more compressible than synthetic bags and take up less room in your pack, which is an important consideration if you are planning a multi-day backpack trip. Features to look for in a sleeping bag include: a mummy style bag, a hood you can cinch down around your head in cold weather, and draft tubes along the zippers that help keep heat in and drafts out.

You'll also want a sleeping pad to provide insulation and padding from the cold ground. There are different types of sleeping pads available, from the more expensive self-inflating air mattresses to the less expensive closed-cell foam pads (e.g., Ridge Rest®). Self-inflating air mattresses are usually heavier than closed-cell foam mattresses and are prone to punctures.

courtesy Eureka

Tents. The tent is your home away from home while on the trail. It provides protection from wind, snow, rain, and insects. A three-season tent is a good choice for backpacking and can range in price from $100 to $500. These lightweight and versatile tents provide protection in all types of weather, except heavy snowstorms or high winds, and range in weight from four to eight pounds. Look for a tent that's easy to set up and will easily fit two people with gear. Dome type tents usually offer more headroom and places to store gear. Other tent designs include a vestibule where you can store wet boots and backpacks. Some nice-to-have items in a tent include interior pockets to store small items and lashing points to hang a clothesline. Most three-season tents also come with stakes so you can secure the tent in high winds. Before you purchase a tent, set it up and take it down a few times to be sure it is easy to handle. Also, sit inside the tent and make sure it has enough room for you and your gear.

HIKING WITH CHILDREN

Hiking with children isn't a matter of how many miles you can cover or how much elevation gain you make in a day, it's about seeing and experiencing nature through their eyes.

Kids like to explore and have fun. They like to stop and point out bugs and plants, look under rocks, jump in puddles, and throw sticks. If you're taking a toddler or young child on a hike, start with a trail that you're familiar with. Trails that have interesting things for kids, like piles of leaves to play in or a small stream to wade through during the summer, will make the hike much more enjoyable for them and will keep them from getting bored.

You can keep your child's attention if you have a strategy before starting on the trail. Using games is not only an effective way to keep a child's atten-

courtesy Johnson Outdoors

tion, it's also a great way to teach him or her about nature. Play hide and seek, where your child is the mouse and you are the hawk. Quiz children on the names of plants and animals. If your children are old enough, let them carry their own daypack filled with snacks and water. So that you are sure to go at their pace and not yours, let them lead the way. Playing follow the leader works particularly well when you have a group of children. Have each child take a turn at being the leader.

With children, a lot of clothing is key. The only thing predictable about weather is that it will change. In Pennsylvania the weather can sometimes be unpredictable, so you always want to bring extra clothing for your children no matter what the season. In the winter, have your children wear wool socks, and warm layers such as long underwear, a polar fleece jacket and hat, wool mittens, and good rain gear. It's not a bad idea to have these along in late fall and early spring as well. Good footwear is also important. A sturdy pair of high top tennis shoes or lightweight hiking boots are the best bet for little ones. If you're hiking in the summer near a lake or stream, bring along a pair of old sneakers that your child can put on when he wants to go exploring in the water. Remember when you're near any type of water, always watch your child at all times. Also, keep a close eye on teething toddlers who may decide a rock or leaf of poison oak is an interesting item to put in their mouth.

From spring through fall, you'll want your kids to wear a wide brimmed hat to keep their face, head, and ears protected from the hot sun. Also, make sure your children wear sunscreen at all times. Choose a brand without Paba—children have sensitive skin and may have an allergic reaction to sunscreen that contains Paba. If you are hiking with a child younger than six months, don't use sunscreen or insect repellant. Instead, be sure that their head, face, neck, and ears are protected from the sun with a wide brimmed hat, and that all other skin exposed to the sun is protected with the appropriate clothing.

Remember that food is fun. Kids like snacks so it's important to bring a lot of munchies for the trail. Stopping often for snack breaks is a fun way to keep the trail interesting. Raisins, apples, granola bars, crackers and cheese, Cheerios, and trail mix all make great snacks. If your child is old enough to carry his/her own backpack, fill it with treats before you leave. If your kids don't like drinking water, you can bring boxes of fruit juice.

Avoid poorly designed child-carrying packs—you don't want to break your back carrying your child. Most child-carrying backpacks designed to hold a 40-pound child will contain a large carrying pocket to hold diapers and other items. Some have an optional rain/sun hood. Tough Traveler® (1–800–GO–TOUGH or *www.toughtraveler.com*) is a company that specializes in making backpacks for carrying children and other outdoor gear for children. •

HIKING WITH YOUR DOG

Bringing your furry friend with you is always more fun than leaving him behind. Our canine pals make great trail buddies because they never complain and always make good company. Hiking with your dog can be a rewarding experience, especially if you plan ahead.

Getting your dog in shape. Before you plan outdoor adventures with your dog, make sure he's in shape for the trail. Getting your dog into shape takes the same discipline as getting yourself into shape, but luckily, your dog can get in shape with you. Take your dog with you on your daily runs or walks. If there is a park near your house, hit a tennis ball or play Frisbee with your dog.

Swimming is also an excellent way to get your dog into shape. If there is a lake or river near where you live and your dog likes the water, have him retrieve a tennis ball or stick. Gradually build your dog's stamina up over a two to three month period. A good rule of thumb is to assume that your dog will travel twice as far as you will on the trail. If you plan on doing a five-mile hike, be sure your dog is in shape for a ten-mile hike.

Training your dog for the trail. Before you go on your first hiking adventure with your dog, be sure he has a firm grasp on the basics of canine etiquette and behavior. Make sure he can sit, lay down, stay, and come. One of the most important commands you can teach your canine pal is to "come" under any situation. It's easy for your friend's nose to lead him astray or possibly get lost. Another helpful command is the "get behind" command. When you're on a hiking trail that's narrow, you can have your dog follow behind you when other trail users approach. Nothing is more bothersome than an enthusiastic dog that runs back and forth on the trail and disrupts the peace of the trail for others. When you see other trail users approaching you on the trail, give them the right of way by quietly stepping off the trail and making your dog lie down and stay until they pass.

Equipment. The most critical pieces of equipment you can invest in for your dog are proper identification and a sturdy leash. Flexi-leads work well for hiking because they give your dog more freedom to explore but still leave you in control. Make sure your dog has identification that includes your name and address and a number for your veterinarian. Other forms of identification for your dog include a tattoo or a microchip. You should consult your veterinarian for more information on these last two options.

The next piece of equipment you'll want to consider is a pack for your dog. By no means should you hold all of your dog's essentials in your pack—let him carry his own gear! Dogs that are in good shape can carry up to 30 percent to 40 percent of their own weight.

Companies that make good quality packs include RuffWear™ (1–888–RUFF–WEAR; *www.ruffwear.com*) and Wolf Packs® (1–541–482–7669; *www.wolfpacks.com*). Most packs are fitted by a dog's weight and girth measurement. Companies that make dog packs generally include guidelines to help you pick out the size that's right for your dog. Some charac-

teristics to look for when purchasing a pack for your dog include: a harness that contains two padded girth straps, a padded chest strap, leash attachments, removable saddle bags, internal water bladders, and external gear cords.

You can introduce your dog to the pack by first placing the empty pack on his back and letting him wear it around the yard. Keep an eye on him during this first introduction. He may decide to chew through the straps if you aren't watching him closely. Once he learns to treat the pack as an object of fun and not a foreign enemy, fill the pack evenly on both sides with a few ounces of dog food in resealable plastic bags. Have your dog wear his pack on your daily walks for a period of two to three weeks. Each week add a little more weight to the pack until your dog will accept carrying the maximum amount of weight he can carry.

You can also purchase collapsible water and dog food bowls for your dog. These bowls are lightweight and can easily be stashed into your pack or your dog's. If you are hiking on rocky terrain or in the snow, you can purchase footwear for your dog that will protect his feet from cuts and bruises. All of these products can be purchased from RuffWear™ (1–888–RUFF–WEAR; *www.ruffwear.com*).

The following is a checklist of items to bring when you take your dog hiking: collapsible water bowls, a comb, a collar and a leash, dog food, a dog pack, flea/tick powder, paw protection, water, and a First Aid kit that contains eye ointment, tweezers, scissors, stretchy foot wrap, gauze, antibacterial wash, sterile cotton tip applicators, antibiotic ointment, and cotton wrap.

First aid for your dog. Your dog is just as prone—if not more prone—to getting in trouble on the trail as you are, so be prepared. Here's a run down of the more likely misfortunes that might befall your little friend.

Bees and wasps. If a bee or wasp stings your dog, remove the stinger with a pair of tweezers and place a mudpack or a cloth dipped in cold water over the affected area.

Heat stroke. Avoid hiking with your dog in really hot weather. Dogs with heat stroke will pant excessively, lie down and refuse to get up, and become lethargic and disoriented. If your dog shows any of these signs on the trail, have him lie down in the shade. If you are near a stream, pour cool water over your dog's entire body to help bring his body temperature back to normal.

Heartworm. Dogs get heartworms from mosquitoes which carry the disease in the prime mosquito months of July and August. Giving your dog a monthly pill prescribed by your veterinarian easily prevents this condition.

Plant pitfalls. One of the biggest plant hazards for dogs on the trail are foxtails. Foxtails are pointed grass seed heads that bury themselves in your friend's fur, between his toes, and even get in his ear canal. If left unattended, these nasty seeds can work their way under the skin and cause abscesses and other problems. If you have a longhaired dog, consider trimming the hair between his toes and giving him a summer haircut to help prevent foxtails from attaching to his fur. After every hike, always look over your dog for these seeds—especially between his toes and his ears.

Other plant hazards include burrs, thorns, thistles, and poison oak. If you find any burrs or thistles on your dog, remove them as soon as possible before they become an unmanageable mat. Thorns can pierce a dog's foot and cause a great deal of pain. If you see that your dog is lame, stop and check his feet for thorns. Dogs are immune to poison oak but they can pick up the sticky, oily substance from the plant and transfer it to you.

Protect those paws. Be sure to keep your dog's nails trimmed so he avoids getting soft tissue or joint injuries. If your dog slows and refuses to go on, check to see that his paws aren't torn or worn. You can protect your dog's paws from trail hazards such as sharp gravel, foxtails, lava scree, and thorns by purchasing dog boots.

Sunburn. If your dog has light skin he is an easy target for sunburn on his nose and other exposed skin areas. You can apply a non-toxic sunscreen to exposed skin areas that will help protect him from over-exposure to the sun.

Ticks and fleas. Ticks can easily give your dog Lyme disease, as well as other diseases. Before you hit the trail, treat your dog with a flea and tick spray or powder. You can also ask your veterinarian about a once-a-month pour-on treatment that repels fleas and ticks.

When you are finally ready to hit the trail with your dog, keep in mind that National Parks and many wilderness areas do not allow dogs on trails. Your best bet is to hike in National forests, BLM lands, and state parks. Always call ahead to see what the restrictions are.

Clubs & Organizations

Keystone Trails Association

The Keystone Trails Association (KTA) is the coordinating agency in an alliance of statewide (and surrounding states) hiking groups. The KTA, which began in 1956, monitors government actions and publishes a quarterly newsletter for members. P.O. Box 251, Cogan Station, PA 17728 • *www.pennaweb.com/kta/clubs.htm*

NORTHEASTERN PENNSYLVANIA

Allentown Hiking Club

P.O. Box 1542, Allentown, PA 18105-1542 (610) 432–5652, email: *dch@enter.net* • *www.allentownhikingclub.org*

Appalachian Mountain Club: Delaware Valley Chapter

Delaware Valley Chapter, c/o Bill Steinmetz, 1180 Greenleaf Drive, Bethlehem, PA 18017-9319 (610) 694–8677 • *www.amcdv.org*

Pocono Outdoor Club

c/o John Motz, RR 8, Box 8142A, Stroudsburg, PA 18360 (570) 620–2492, email: *pocoutclub@entermail.net*

Susquehanna Trailers Hiking Club

c/o Joe Healey, 93 Cedarwood Drive, Laflin, PA 18702 (570) 655–4979

NORTHCENTRAL PENNSYLVANIA

Alpine Club of Williamsport

P.O. Box 501, Williamsport, PA 17701 • *www.angelfire.com/pa2/alpineclub/*

Mid State Trail Association

P.O. Box 167, Boalsburg, PA 16827 (814) 237–7703

Ridge and Valley Outings Co-op

Rich Scanlon, 336 Hillsdale Avenue, Lewistown, PA 17044 (717) 242–1644 • *www.centreconnect.org/rec_arts/outdoor/rvoc.htm*

Susquehannock Trail Club

P.O. Box 643, Coudersport, PA 16915

NORTHWESTERN PENNSYLVANIA

Allegheny Outdoor Club

c/o Bill Massa, 109A East Wayne Street, Warren, PA 16365 (814) 726–3837 • *http://users.penn.com/~massa/about.html*

Butler Outdoor Club

c/o Dave Adams, P.O. Box 243, Butler, PA 16003-0243 (724) 789–7031 • *www.butler-outdoorclub.com/*

Erie Outing Club

P.O. Box 1163, Erie, PA 16512 (814) 838–6301

Cleveland Hiking Club

c/o Emily Gregor, 6502 Olde York Road, Cleveland, OH 44130 (440) 884–0281

SOUTHEASTERN PENNSYLVANIA

Allentown Hiking Club
P.O. Box 1542, Allentown, PA 18105-1542 (610) 432–5652, email: *dch@enter.net* • *www.allentownhikingclub.org*

Appalachian Mountain Club: Delaware Valley Chapter
Delaware Valley Chapter, c/o Bill Steinmetz, 1180 Greenleaf Drive, Bethlehem, PA 18017-9319 (610) 694–8677

Batona Hiking Club
c/o Sara Dean, 504 Acorn Street, Philadelphia, PA 19128 (215) 482–4397 • *www.members.aol.com/Batona/*

Berks Community Hiking Club
c/o William Coleman, 67 Sabrina Street, Wernersville, PA 19565

Blue Mountain Eagle Climbing Club
P.O. Box 14982, Reading, PA 19612 • *www.bmecc.org*

Brandywine Valley Outing Club
P.O. Box 134, Rockland, DE 19732

Chester County Trail Club
c/o Doug Logan, P.O. Box 636, Kimberton, PA 19442-0636

Friends of the Wissahickon
8798 Germantown Avenue, Philadelphia, PA 19118 (215) 247–0417

Horseshoe Trail Club
c/o Robert Chalfant, P.O. Box 183, Birchrunville, PA 19421 (215) 887–5150 • *www.n99.com/hst/*

Philadelphia Trail Club
741 Golf Road, Warrington, PA 18976 • *http://m.zanger.tripod.com*

Lancaster Hiking Club
c/o Jeanne Schopf, P.O. Box 7922, Lancaster, PA 17604; Joan Drake, Secretary: (717) 397–6546; Frank Geiger, Treasurer: (717) 871–9296; email: *jschopf@lnpnews.com or jeff@admin.fandm.edu*

Lebanon Valley Hiking Club
c/o Sharon L. Southall, 504 Margin Road, Lebanon, PA 17042 (717) 274–5509

Mason-Dixon Trail System
Jim Hooper, President, 309 Bank Hill Road, Wrightsville, PA 17368 • *www.angelfire.com/pa2/yorkhikingclub/mdts.html*

Schuylkill River Greenway Association
960 Old Mill Road, Wyomissing, PA 19610 • *www.schuylkillriver.org*

Springfield Trail Club
Michael Cosgrove, President • *http://pages.prodigy.net/javelin/*

Wilmington Trail Club
P.O. Box 1184, Wilmington, DE 19899 • *www.wilmingtontrailclub.org/*

Wildlands Conservancy
601 Orchid Place, Emmaus, PA 18049

SOUTHCENTRAL PENNSYLVANIA

Cumberland Valley Appalachian Trail Management Association
P.O. Box 395, Boiling Springs, PA 17007-0395

Keystone State Volkssport Association
c/o Frances Humelsine, Secretary, 257 King Street, Chambersburg, PA 17201-8633
(717) 263–8633

Mountain Club of Maryland
c/o Dorothy Guy, President, 1507 Barrett Road, Baltimore, MD 21207

Pennsylvania Women Outdoors
c/o Lynne H. Shelton, 507 Cherry Street, Wrightsville, PA 17368-1124 (717)
292–6655

Potomac Appalachian Trail Club
118 Park Street SW, Vienna, VA 22180 • www.patc.net/index.htm

Susquehanna Appalachian Trail Club
P.O. Box 61001, Harrisburg, PA 17106-1001 • www.libertynet.org/susqatc/

York Hiking Club
9123 East Springfield Road, Seven Valleys, PA 17360 •
www.angelfire.com/pa2/yorkhikingclub/

SOUTHWESTERN PENNSYLVANIA

Hostelling International: Pittsburgh Council
Hostelling International Pittsburgh, 830 East Warrington Avenue, Pittsburgh, PA 15210
(412) 431–4910 • http://trfn.clpgh.org/ayh/

Butler Outdoor Club
c/o Dave Adams, P.O. Box 243, Butler, PA 16003-0243 (724) 789–7031 • www.butler
outdoorclub.com/

Johnstown Inclined Plane, Inc.
(814) 536–1816 • www.inclinedplane.com

North Country Trail Association
49 Monroe Center NW, Suite 200B, Grand Rapids, MI 49503 (616) 454–5506 •
www.northcountrytrail.org/

Shenango Outing Club
Riverside Park Nature Center, P.O. Box 244, Greenville, PA 16125

Sierra Club: Allegheny Group
c/o Peter Wray, 110 Royal Oak Avenue, Pittsburgh, PA 15235, email: pjwray@tele
rama.com • www.enviroweb.org/error.html

Warrior Trail Association, Inc.
P.O. Box 103, Waynesburg, PA 15370-0103

Western Pennsylvania Conservancy
209 Fourth Avenue, Pittsburgh, PA 15222 (412) 288–2771 • www.paconserve.org/

Index

A

Adams Falls, 69
Agricultural College of Pennsylvania (Penn State), 199
Allegheny Front, 68, 136, 213
Allegheny Gorge, 311–315
Allegheny High Plateau, 104–106
Allegheny Mountain, 104–106
Allegheny National Forest, 282–284, 333
Allegheny Outdoor Club, 280
Allegheny Reservoir, 284
Allegheny River, 297
Altoona, PA, 186
American Whitewater, 256
American Youth Hostel, 164–165
Andorra Nature Center, 17
Appalachian Trail (AT), 26, 32, 52–57, 159–171, 212
Appalachian Trail Conference, 162–164
Arkansas River, 256
Army Corps of Engineers, 182–184
Arthur, Edmund Watts (naturalist), 329
Atlantic Flyway, 13
Audobon Society of Western PA, 235, 266–267

B

bacillus thuringiensis (Btk), 182
Balanced Rock, 184
bald eagle, 292
Baltimore & Ohio Railroad, 251
Barbara's buttons, 253
Barton, Clara (founder, Red Cross), 220–221
bats, 187
Battle of Gettysburg, 152–154
Bear Creek, 109
Bear Run Nature Reserve, 236

Bedford County, 213
beech bark scale, 288–290
Beechwood Farms Nature Reserve, 267
Big Pocono State Park, 91
Big Run Valley, 111
Big Spring Reservoir, 221
black bear, 50–51
Black Forest, 121
Black Moshannon Lake, 136
Black Moshannon State Park, 136–139
Blackwell, PA, 112, 116
Blair Limestone Company Kilns, 186–187
"Bloody Run," 154
Blue Ball Tavern, 174
Blue Knob State Park, 213
Blue Mountain, 168
Blue Rocks, 26
bluebird rescue program, 177–178, 262
Boston Tea Party, 22
Boughton Acid Works, 306
Boughton Ruins, 306
Boughton, PA, 306
box huckleberry, 173
Bradford County, PA, 89
Breakneck Bridge, 324
Broad Mountain, 208–210
Brush Ridge Ore Banks, 192
Buffalo Ridge, 174
Bullion Run, 310
Bullion Run Canyon, 311
Bullion Run Iron Ore Furnace, 310–311
Bureau of Forestry, 199, 210
Burr, Theodore , 175–176
Butler County, 266
Butler, PA, 326

C

Caledonia State Park, 212–213
Cambrian Period, 166
Camelback Mountain, 91
Camp Michaux, 158–159
Camptown, PA, 87
Canada geese, 316
Canoe Lake, 186
Carbon County, 90
Carlisle Army Post, 159
Carlisle, PA, 168

Carnegie Mellon University, 226
Carnegie Museum of Natural History, 266
Carolina tassle-rue, 253
Cemetery Ridge, 153–154
Chambersburg, PA, 212
Chapman Dam, 333
Chapman State Park, 333
Chesapeake Bay, 23
Chestnut Hill, PA, 16
Civil War, 68, 152–154
  "Bloody Run", 154
  Battle of Gettysburg, 152–154
  Cemetery Ridge, 153–154
  Devil's Den, 154
  Lee, General Robert E., 152–154
  Little Round Top, 153–154
  Pickett, General George E., 153–154
  Sickles, General Daniel, 153
Civilian Conservation Corps (CCC), 158–159
Clarion River, 298
Clay's Covered Bridge, 175–176
Clearfield County, 143
Clearfield, PA, 130
Colonel Denning State Park, 168
Colton Point State Park, 114
common reed, 278–279
Confluence, PA, 257
Continental Army, 22
Continental Congress, 22
Cook Forest Association, 298–299
Cook, John (Cook Forest namesake), 298–299
Cooksburg, PA, 298
Corydon, PA, 284
Coudersport, PA, 124
Cucumber Meadow, 18
Cumberland Valley, 171–172
Curtiss-Wright Corporation, 130–134

D

Davis Hollow Marina, 326

358

Meet the Author

John Young has a degree in journalism and is a former newspaper reporter. He was born and raised in Altoona. His love affair with the woods and mountains of Pennsylvania began at age 12 when he started deer hunting with his father and brother at their camp on Tussey Mountain in Huntington County. Even before then, he remembers swimming in the icy waters of Spruce Creek and one catastrophic attempt at a family overnighter at their hunting camp. They had just finished dinner when his mother stepped outside to shake the tablecloth and came face to face with her first—and last—black bear. A few hours later they were back in Altoona.

John has hiked the Oak Creek Canyon area of Sedona, Arizona, searching for the fabled vortexes, and the Presidential Range of the White Mountains in New Hampshire. He has also hiked the streets of Toronto and San Francisco, including the world's 'crookedest' street.

Avid cross-country skiers, John and his wife Debra have toured the trails on Presque Isle, in Cooks Forest, and Letchworth State Park in New York. His indoor interests are racquetball and reading the works of selected 20th Century American authors—in chronological order.

John lives with his wife in a small farming community in Warren County, just north of the Allegheny National Forest. His outdoor articles have appeared in *Pennsylvania Magazine* and *Farm & Ranch Living*. He is a member of the Allegheny Outdoor Club, the Keystone Trails Association, and Pennwriters.